THE
MAJOR MYSTERIES

Samael Aun Weor

GLORIAN

The Major Mysteries
A Glorian Book / 2021

Originally published as "Los Misterios Mayores," 1956.

This Edition © 2021 Glorian Publishing

Print ISBN 978-1-943358-17-5
Ebook ISBN 978-1-934206-93-5

Glorian Publishing is a non-profit organization delivering to
humanity the teachings of Samael Aun Weor. All proceeds go to
further the distribution of these books. For more information,
visit glorian.org.

The Major Mysteries

CHRISTUS AND MARIA MAGDALENA BY LUCAS CRANACH (CA 1508)

"Next to the great enlightened men of the past a woman was never missing. The most wonderful Mary Magdalene shines next to Jesus, as Yasodhara, the wife-disciple of Gautama the Buddha Shakyamuni tremendously shines. Great women have always been next to great men. Women have animated them. Women have given them life. Women have incited them to fight. Women have raised them upon the pedestal. Women have guided them to make gigantic works... Woman, as I said, is the most beautiful thought of the Creator made flesh, blood, and life." —Samael Aun Weor

Contents

Illustrations

Editor's Introduction

To aid your study of this profound book, we have included a short glossary of terms at the end. You can find a much more detailed glossary at glorian.org.

Mantra Pronunciation

In this book the author provides mantras for our benefit. Chanting or repetition of sacred sounds is universal in all religions. In Sanskrit, these sounds are called mantras, and their repetition is called japa.

Generally speaking, the sounds in mantras are pronounced using the ancient roots (Latin, Greek, Hebrew, Sanskrit, etc):

> I: as the ee in "tree"
>
> E: as the eh in "they"
>
> O: as the oh in "holy"
>
> U: as the u in "true"
>
> A: as the ah in "father"
>
> M: extended as if humming, "mmmmm"
>
> S: extended like a hiss, "sssss"
>
> CH: if the word is Latin, pronounced as k. If the word is Hebrew, pronounced as a scrape in the back of the throat, as in "Bach"
>
> G: In most mantras, G is pronounced as in "give"

Should Mantras be Spoken Aloud or Silent?

> "...the verb is of triple pronunciation and that it endows three norms: verbal, mental, and conscious. One can articulate with the creative larynx, one can vocalize with his thought, and one can vocalize with the superlative consciousness of the Being." –Samael Aun Weor, *Esoteric Medicine and Practical Magic*

"There are three ways that one learns to use a mantra, to repeat prayers or sounds. They are quite simple: aloud, quietly, or silently.

Vaikhari Japa: verbal, loud

Upamshu Japa: whispered or hummed

Manasika Japa: mental, silent, without moving."
–the lecture Yoga of Devotion

"The fruits of whispered japa are a thousand times more powerful than the verbal japa, and the fruits of the silent, mental japa are hundreds of thousands of times more powerful than the verbal japa. Mental japa can even be kept up while at work." –Swami Sivananda

Introduction

The Esoteric Path

Pay utmost attention, since, obviously, the time has arrived for the esoteric path to be truly comprehended.

First of all, it is not irrelevant to state that, indeed, what we Gnostics are looking for is nothing other than to be transformed into true, Self-realized, perfect beings. What we are asseverating here might seem a little exaggerated, but indeed, I do not see any other basic objective for these Gnostic teachings than to study the Major Mysteries of the esoteric path. Indeed, the path is what is fundamental, the path that distinct messengers came to explain in their messages[1] to this humanity.

The Expulsion from Eden

Life was different in the past, in ancient times, when humanity had not yet developed the abominable Kundabuffer organ within their inner nature, since the Essence[2] was not bottled up within the ego.[3] In other words, the ego did not exist.

The different centers[4] of the organic machine[5] looked like true resounding boxes where the harmonies of the universe vibrated.

This was the Golden Age, when there was neither "this is mine" nor "this is yours," because everything belonged to everybody. Yes, anybody could eat from the orchard of the neighbor without any fear. At that time, those who knew how to play the lyre[6] were shaking nature with its melodies.

---

1 The teachings and scriptures remembered by religions.
2 Unmodified consciousness. See "essence" in the glossary.
3 Psychological defects like envy, lust, pride, etc.
4 Processors of intellectual, emotional, motor, instinctual, and sexual functions.
5 The physical body.
6 "The mission of every human being is to educate themselves on how to play the lyre of Orpheus... the creative larynx..." —Samael Aun Weor, *The Divine Science*

In that ancient age that some call Arcadia, the children of the dawn, the children of the aurora of the mahamanvantara,[7] were worshiped. At that time, the lyre of Orpheus had not yet fallen upon the floor of the temple and broken into pieces.

All of nature was an organism that served as a vehicle for the gods. Yes, this was the Edenic humanity,[8] where the fire of volcanoes, the boisterous ocean that throws its waves on the beaches, the chanting of the rivers in their beds of rocks, and the flight of gigantic birds that existed in those times of yore were felt within the depths of the Being in the most insightful manner. The entire Earth looked like a living organism. Although it is in fact a living organism, in those times this was more of a living reality for all human beings.

The golden language was the only language spoken. The many, many present-day languages of the Tower of Babel[9] had not yet appeared.

Therefore, in the name of truth, I tell you that it is worthwhile for us to try to return to that innocent, primeval state, because at that time the Essence — the soul, the consciousness — was not yet bottled up within the ego. The Essence became bottled up within the ego when the abominable Kundabuffer organ emerged within the human anatomy.

Therefore, in that Lemurian epoch the Earth was trembling incessantly. The geological crust of the world was not yet truly stable. This is why the leaders of humanity had to take serious action. Being acquainted with the fact that the human organism is a machine that receives determined types of energies and automatically transmits them to the interior layers of the planetary organism, they implanted an alteration within the physical organism. Their purpose: to modify those forces in a certain way so that they would eventually permit the stabilization of the geologic crust. Thus, this is how, by means of certain stimuli, they allowed or gave freedom for the origination of the abominable Kundabuffer organ.

---

7   Sanskrit, "cosmic day."
8   The Lemurian root race, symbolized in Bereshit / Genesis by Moses as Adam and Eve.
9   Bereshit / Genesis 11:1-9

THE STORY OF ADAM AND EVE SYMBOLIZES THE LEMURIAN HUMANITY.

Unquestionably, if not for the abuse of sex (symbolized in the myth of Adam and Eve in the terrestrial paradise), the development of the abominable Kundabuffer organ would have been something more than impossible. Yes, abuse of sex allowed the development of that organ.

Now then, in the name of the truth and speaking judiciously before all of those who are dedicated to these esoteric studies, I have to be boldly honest with you in order to courageously tell you what I verified, what I lived, what I have experienced. Listen, I had a physical body in that epoch. I was a Lemurian, another inhabitant of "Mu," as were many others. I still clearly remember the distinct tribes that lived in what we can call in this day and age "farmhouses." However, they had the form of enormous huts whose roofs descended until touching the ground, and which scarcely had a door through which the members of the whole tribe entered. There were also fortified cities in Lemuria, built with the lava of volcanoes. Cultured people lived in those cities, yet in the country, as usual, lived people who were not dedicated to the culture.

THE TEMPTATION OF BLACK TANTRA

Life was very different in Lemuria. There occurred then the case of the existence of a rank of individuals who were priests and warriors at the same time. Among these individuals I knew Javhe,[10] the evil genie, a fallen angel, as stated by Saturninus of Antioch.[11]

Javhe had a physical body in Lemuria. He was a master from ancient mahamanvantaras. He officiated as a priest, and many people venerated him. As a warrior, he was magnificent.

---

10 (Hebrew יהוה) Often spelled Yahweh or Yahwe, and intentionally confused with Jehovah since they are both spelled the same way in Hebrew: יהוה. While Jehovah is a very positive and potent name of God, Yahve (Jahve) is the name of a fallen angel who has been misleading humanity for ages. You can read his story in *The Revolution of Beelzebub*.

11 Gnostic 100–120 AD

He always wore a sword of gold, and what is more, his shield, helmet, mesh, and his entire military garb in general were made of pure gold. Everybody knew that he was an angel, thus everyone venerated him. Nevertheless, he was among the first who betrayed the sanctuary of Vulcan.[12] The traitors of the sanctuary of Vulcan taught him Black Tantra[13]—in other words, sexual rites within which the initiate committed the crime of spilling the cup of Hermes Trismesgistus.[14] I am speaking here in a very special, esoteric language, and I hope that you understand, since I am not supportive of using vulgar language for these matters related with sex, due to the fact that sex is sacred.

Thus, indubitably, Javhe became an enthusiast of Black Tantra. He tried to convince his wife that the Black Tantric system (sexual magic with the ejaculation of the ens seminis[15]) was the most significant one for liberation, yet his wife did not accept it. His wife was also an incarnated Elohim,[16] who preferred to divorce him than to accept Black Tantra.

Well then, as a consequence, Javhe developed the abominable Kundabuffer organ. His wife did not fall, and still has not fallen. She is a primordial Elohim from the aurora of the mahamanvantara.

I disclose the case of Javhe in order to illustrate the sexual aspect of the abominable Kundabuffer organ. Obviously, fornication is what originated the treason to the mysteries of Vulcan and the fall in that ancient age.

Previous to the fall and after the division into opposite sexes, the tribes, in order to procreate, were united in special temples and under the guidance of the Kumaras.[17] At that time, the sexual act was a sacrament, and no one dared to per-

---

12 Vulcan is the Latin or Roman name for the Greek god Ἥφαιστος Hephaestus, known by the Egyptians as Ptah. A god of fire with a deep and ancient mythology, commonly remembered as the blacksmith who forges weapons for gods and heroes. Thus, this sanctuary is not a literal place, but a epithet for the sacred teachings of chastity.

13 Impure methods of using sexual energy, which result in creating demons.

14 See glossary.

15 Latin, "entity of semen," the seed in men and women.

16 See glossary.

17 Divine beings, masters, angels.

form the chemical copulation outside of the temple. The king and queen of any Lemurian country performed that sacred act before the sacred altar.

I lived on the continent of Mu, and I was witness to all of these events. When I lived on the Lemurian continent, I was a member of a tribe and I lived in a great hut with all the members of my clan. Close to us there was what in this day and age we would call a military base: people, soldiers, dedicated to affairs of war. The cities were further away. We attended the temples always, as something normal, sometimes for rites, sometimes in order to receive esoteric instruction from the hierophants. However, from moment to moment the environment was becoming charged with the luciferic power, from which everything was to come: this impelled all of us to perform the chemical copulation outside of the temple.

Before that fatal moment, reproduction was performed by means of Kriya Shakti, in other words, by means of the power of yoga and willpower. At that time, no one committed the crime of spilling the cup of Hermes Trismesgistus. Any zoosperm can easily escape the sexual endocrine glands and fecundate the womb. However, couples from the tribes started to break the law. I still remember one morning, after having fornicated, all of us presented ourselves in the temple. Yet, from the profundities of the sanctuary, a hierophant with his unsheathed sword cast all of us out while uttering: "Get out, you unworthy ones!" Thus all of us left, fleeing.

So, the same event occurred in all of the corners of that gigantic continent named Lemuria, which was a continent that occupied almost the entire Pacific Ocean. Obviously, that anthropological event belongs rightly to anthropogenesis, since it is symbolically described in different religious scriptures of the world. This is the departure of Adam and Eve from the terrestrial paradise (Hebraic myth). Understand that we were cast out because of having eaten of the forbidden fruit, of which we were warned: "You must not eat of it." Thus, due to this anomaly, the abominable Kundabuffer organ developed.

Since we were accustomed to perform the sexual act during the religious rites of the temple, in other words, to perform

THE KUNDABUFFER IS THE "TAIL" OF SATAN, INVERTED, FALLEN KUNDALINI.

the sexual act according with the Sacraments of the Church of Romae (Amore) during reproduction, when we fornicated the outcome was the development (in our subtle anatomy) of the abominable Kundabuffer organ. Thus, the igneous serpent of our magical powers (the Kundalini),[18] that was previously lifted up victoriously throughout the spinal medulla, descended, and became entwined three and a half times within the Muladhara chakra (such as it is perfectly described by Kundalini yoga). The abominable Kundabuffer organ, the descending serpent, the horrible Python with seven heads that the irritated Apollo hurt with his darts, was projected from the coccyx downwards, towards the atomic infernos of the human being, and became the famous "tail" of the Biblical Satan.

Thus, this is how the leaders of humanity attained the stabilization of the geological crust of the Earth. It is not, therefore, an exaggeration to emphatically affirm that in that ancient age, human beings had a tail similar to that of the apes.

---

18 The serpent of bronze raised by Moses in the book of Numbers.

When passing through the human organisms, the cosmic, planetary energies permutated and became lunar,[19] thus stabilizing the geological layers of the world. When this happened, then the leaders of humanity resolved to eliminate the abominable Kundabuffer organ from the human species, and they achieved it. Notwithstanding, they had errors when performing their mathematical calculations. As an outcome of such errors, they delayed more than they should have, and the experiment ended up being detrimental, since, unfortunately, the evil consequences of the abominable Kundabuffer organ remained within the five cylinders (intellect, emotion, movement, instinct, and sex) of the organic human machine. In other words, the pluralized "I," the ego, the myself, the self-willed, remained. If not for the mistake of those sacred individuals, this humanity would not have ego at this time. Obviously, those who committed such a mistake have a terrible cosmic karma, which they unfortunately will have to pay in the future mahamanvantara.

Of course, much later in time, different messengers or avatars came from the superior worlds, and all of them pronounced themselves against the abominable Kundabuffer organ and against its evil consequences, yet everything was to no avail. The very saintly Ashiata Shiemash worked intensely in the continent of Asia, yet it was useless. Buddha Gautama Shakyamuni brought the teachings to India and, as a fact, pronounced himself against the abominable Kundabuffer organ; unfortunately, throughout the centuries, the original Buddhist teaching has been lost. In this day and age, very little remains of the authentic teachings of our Lord the Buddha Gautama Shakyamuni. Regarding Jeshua ben Pandira, Jesus of Nazareth, the Christ, in fact, he pronounced himself against the abominable Kundabuffer organ. Of course, his teachings have appeared in the texts of alchemy and other texts, and those who comprehend them can indeed perform the entire Great Work.

---

19 See glossary.

Buddha and Christ

Unquestionably, the two greatest leaders of all time are the Buddha Gautama Shakyamuni and Jesus Christ. On a certain occasion, I had to present myself in a Buddhist monastery in Japan. I had the occasion of speaking on behalf of Christ. Since it was a Buddhist and not a Christian temple, and due to my approach, a certain scandal arose amongst the Buddhist brothers and sisters, and therefore a complaint was presented to the master, who approached me and interrogated me as follows, "Why did you speak on behalf of Christ, knowing that this is a Buddhist monastery?"

"With the most profound respect to this sacred institution, I have to emphatically affirm that Buddha and Christ complement each other."

I was expecting a response from the master's point of view, yet with great amazement, I witnessed his agreement. He said, "Indeed, Buddha and Christ complement each other. This is how it is…"

Then, he asked for a thread or cord, and when they brought it to him, he told me, "Show me your right hand."

When I showed him my right hand, he tied the thread on my thumb. Thereafter, he tied the same thread on the thumb on my left hand, and ended by saying in a Zen way, "Buddha and Christ complement each other…"

Then, I left that monastery, having perfectly understood the Koan.[20] In the name of the truth, we have to recognize that this is a very wise Koan: Buddha and Christ are joined within us, because the right thumb represents the Christ and the left represents the Buddha: the two of them are two factors within us.

Our Inner Buddha

Buddha Siddhartha Gautama Shakyamuni brought the doctrine of the inner Buddha[21] to the world. Who is our Inner

---

20 An enigmatic phrase designed to confound the intellect and provoke intuitive understanding.

21 The word buddha means "awakened." It is not a personal name.

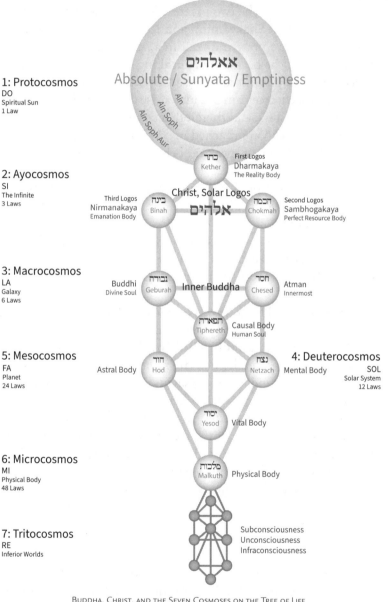

1: Protocosmos
DO
Spiritual Sun
1 Law

2: Ayocosmos
SI
The Infinite
3 Laws

3: Macrocosmos
LA
Galaxy
6 Laws

5: Mesocosmos
FA
Planet
24 Laws

6: Microcosmos
MI
Physical Body
48 Laws

7: Tritocosmos
RE
Inferior Worlds

אאלהים
Absolute / Sunyata / Emptiness

Ain
Ain Soph
Ain Soph Aur

כתר
Kether
First Logos
Dharmakaya
The Reality Body

Christ, Solar Logos
אלהים

בינה
Binah
Third Logos
Nirmanakaya
Emanation Body

חכמה
Chokmah
Second Logos
Sambhogakaya
Perfect Resource Body

Buddhi
Divine Soul
גבורה
Geburah
Inner Buddha
חסד
Chesed
Atman
Innermost

תפארת
Tiphereth
Causal Body
Human Soul

Astral Body
חור
Hod
נצח
Netzach
Mental Body

4: Deuterocosmos
SOL
Solar System
12 Laws

יסוד
Yesod
Vital Body

מלכות
Malkuth
Physical Body

Subconsciousness
Unconsciousness
Infraconsciousness

BUDDHA, CHRIST, AND THE SEVEN COSMOSES ON THE TREE OF LIFE

Buddha? The Innermost is the Buddha; in a rigorously theosophical, Sanskrit language the Inner Buddha of each one of us is Atman-Buddhi.[22] So, Siddhartha Gautama Shakyamuni brought to us the doctrine of the Innermost. This is why it is written in the *Testament of Learning*:

> *"Before the false dawn came over this earth, those who survived the hurricane and the storm gave praise to the Innermost, and to them appeared the heralds of the dawn."*

So, the Innermost is the Inner Buddha within each one of us. Nonetheless, it is true that the Innermost is not incarnated within the humanoids, because, certainly, we understand that the Innermost dwells in the Milky Way [the Macrocosmos; see diagram]. Yet, to each one of us is related an inner Buddha, who dwells up there in the galaxy.

In regards to Christ,[23] this is a different matter.

The Cosmic Christ

Jesus of Nazareth, the great Kabir, the great Gnostic initiate, one of the most exalted members of the Essenian Order, who lived among them at the shores of the Dead Sea many centuries ago, brought to us the doctrine of the inner Christ.

Notwithstanding, the great mistake of modern people consists in believing that Christ was exclusively the great Master Jeshua ben Pandira (this is his birth name; it is only a local name).

Understand that Christ is a cosmic force, the Second Logos,[24] a perfect multiple unity. As electricity is energy, Christ

---

22 Atman ("self") and buddhi ("comprehension") correspond to Chesed and Geburah on the Tree of Life.

23 Derived from the Greek Christos, "the Anointed One," and Krestos, whose esoteric meaning is "fire." The word Christ is a title, not a personal name. See glossary.

24 Greek λόγος, from λέγω lego "I say," means Verb or Word. The unifying principle. The Logos is the manifested deity of every nation and people; the outward expression or the effect of the cause which is ever concealed. (Speech is the "logos" of thought). The Logos has three aspects, known universally as the Trinity, Trikaya, or Trimurti. These are related to the three primary forces behind all forms of creation.

is also energy. As universal gravity is a force, Christ is also a force, a force as the force of fire, or as the force of water, or as the force of air, etc. Christ is a force, and can express itself through any man or woman (since women have the same rights of men) who is duly prepared, and that is all.

If it is true that Christ expressed itself and continues expressing itself through the great Kabir Jesus, it is also true that Christ also expressed itself through our Lord Quetzalcoatl.[25] Therefore it is worthwhile to read the life, passion, death, and resurrection of the blessed Quetzalcoatl.

Moreover, if it is true that Christ resplendently shone in Quetzalcoatl, it is also true that Christ shone resplendently on Mount Nebo upon the face of Moses, and it is also true that Christ sang the sacred "Song of God" (Bhagavad-Gita) in India when incarnated within the avatar named Krishna.

Comprehend that the Cosmic Christ expresses itself wherever there is a human being (a Buddha) who is duly prepared.

Christ is not an individual. Christ is not a person. Christ is not an "I." Christ is a cosmic force that is latent within every atom of the universe. Christ is the universal fire of life, and this is very important to understand, because Christ is fire.

I witnessed the aurora of the Mahamanvantara (cosmic day). Yes, I was a witness of the dawning of life, when the Army of the Word started to make the chaotic matter fecund so that life could emerge. I saw the great Cosmic Christ. I saw his human shape. I saw him enter into the temple and how he signed a pact. I saw him crucify himself on his cross in order to save humans and gods.

The Sacred Fire

Christ is therefore the universal fire of life. Much can be said about Christ, and I will tell you the following: Christ is defined with the four letters that are written on the top of the cross of the martyr of Calvary, namely INRI (Ignis Natura Renovatur Integra): "the fire renews nature incessantly."

---

25 The Christ of ancient Mexico. Read *Aztec Christic Magic.*

Listen, the fire is crucified here in the Earth. Proof? Well, see how the fire leaps when we strike a rock against another? Where is the deposit it jumped from? It is hidden within the very rock: it is the petrous fire. Within water, we find liquid fire; within air, gaseous fire. Therefore, fire is within everything that is, has been, and will be. The fire has neither a beginning nor an end.

If we strike a match, we will see with astonishment how the flame sprouts from it. You will state that the flame that sprouted from the match is the outcome of chemical combustion, yet such a concept is false. We Gnostics asseverate that combustion exists due to the fire, and that without the fire, there could be no combustion. The fire is enclosed there within that thin piece of wood or cardboard tipped with phosphorus, thus when we strike it what we have accomplished is the liberation of the flame so that the match can be completely ignited. Notwithstanding, the fire is what makes the hand move in order to strike the match. Yes, without fire, without life, the hand does not move. So, fire is latent within wood, cardboard, or phosphorus, otherwise the fire would not appear, because fire cannot emerge from something that does not contain it.

Through its processes, fire preserves all of the existing organisms, namely all the human species, all the animal species, and everything that is, has been, and will be.

Fire in itself is sacred. Who is the one who knows the nature of fire? No one, is it not the truth? Life exists because of fire: even the Essence [consciousness] is living fire. When that Essence, which is fire, comes into existence, then the creature is formed and is born; then, when that fire (the Essence) abandons the physical body, the body dies. Therefore, we come into the world thanks to fire, and we leave the world when the fire abandons us.

Now then, what we the Gnostics are interested in is not merely physical fire, but the fire of the fire, the flame of the flame—that is, the astral signature of the fire, which in itself is the inner Christ. Only this inner fire from within ourselves can save us, by performing the final annihilation of the undesirable elements that we carry in our interior.

Now you understand how Christ and Buddha complement each other within us. Yet, there are some students that believe that Gautama the Buddha Shakyamuni is more elevated than Jesus of Nazareth, the Christ, and others think that Christ is superior to Buddha. Well, everybody is free to think whatever they please; however, I place the occultists and esotericists within the living field of these esoteric studies.

We know very well that Atman-Buddhi is the inner Buddha, the Buddha, the Innermost; this is how it is written in the Sanskrit books. Now then, we know that Christ is the Second Logos [Chokmah]. The First Logos is Brahma, the Second is Vishnu (the Son), and Shiva is the Third Logos (the Holy Spirit). Therefore, the inner Christ, evidently and within the levels of the Being, or better said, within the levels of our superlative and transcendental Being, is beyond our inner Buddha, yet they complement each other.

The Incarnation of Christ

When the Solar Logos want to incarnate within the body of any human being, obviously it has to descend from its elevated sphere and penetrate within the maternal womb of our Divine Mother Kundalini (the igneous serpent of our magical powers) who is the Virgin of the Sea (Stella Maris), the astral signature of the sperm as it is said in Alchemy. She is a virgin before and after delivering, and from her the Logos is born and becomes humanized.

Behold for yourselves such a miracle: how the abstract fire emerges from her and becomes humanized, and how it finally enters within the initiate by means of the Initiation of Tiphereth,[26] which is the Venustic Initiation.[27]

Afterwards, Christ grows and develops within us. Christ is born amongst the animals of desire,[28] because the initiate

---

26 Read *The Three Mountains.*
27 See glossary.
28 The so-called "manger" of Christianity.

still has not completely reached the elimination of his "I's." Therefore, Christ has to develop itself within the initiate. In the beginning, the initiate does not feel any change, yet, over time, he feels the change. The inner Christ is born weak, small, yet he has to grow; he has to become a grown man. It is by means of the elimination of the undesirable elements that we carry within our interior that he grows up.

Lo and behold, how Christ, not being a sinner, is transformed into something like a sinner, since without being a sinner, as a fact, he becomes responsible for all of our mental, sexual, emotional, volitional, etc., activities. Then, he lives as a human amongst humans, even when people do not recognize him. Thus, Christ, having conquered, has to conquer again. Christ has to live the entire cosmic drama within the heart of the human being, such as it is written in the four gospels.

So, the three traitors[29] condemn him to death, since the multitudes of "I's" that we carry with our interior are the ones who scream, "Crucifixia! Crucifixia! Crucifixia!" Yes, Judas, the demon of desire is the one who exchanges the Inner Christ for all the pleasures of the world (represented by the famous thirty silver coins). Pilate, the demon of the mind, who at any time washes his hands (as if saying with such an attitude, "I am not guilty of anything"), in other words, he betrays the Christ by always find evasiveness and justifications, and thus commands the whipping of Christ before the council, and the placement of a crown of thorns on his temples, and the flagellation of the Lord five thousand and more times. Moreover, Caiaphas, the demon of evil will who sells the sacraments, who prostitutes the altar, who fornicates with the devotees, etc., also betrays the inner Christ. The whole of this is fulfilled within the internal worlds of any human being that is duly prepared.

Finally, in the causal world, the world of natural causes, the Lord has to climb the Golgotha of supreme sacrifice.

---

29 An ancient esoteric symbol of our inner psychology. They are present in the Christian Gospel (Judas, Pilate, Caiaphas), in the Masonic legend of Hiram Abiff, and are the three Egyptian demons who killed Osiris. These three traitors are related to our three brains and the three protoplasmatic lunar bodies.

Thereafter, he descends to the sepulcher, and with his death he kills death.

As he resurrects within us, we also resurrect within him, and he make us immortal. As a fact, Christ convert us into glorified masters. Christ converts us into masters of the degree of Morya or Kout Humi or Serapis or Hermes Trismesgistus, or Jesus Christ.

Therefore, the crude reality of the facts is that just as Buddha lives within us, likewise the Lord Christ lives within, yet beyond, within the profound interior of each one of us.

Thus, just as Gautama brought the message of Buddha, the inner Buddha, likewise the great Kabir Jesus brought the message of the Cosmic Christ, and both complement each other, as was recognized in that Buddhist monastery of Japan.

Therefore, it is worthwhi le that we reflect upon these matters. We must be insightful, by delving into all of these issues.

The Experience of Reality

There are two types of Buddhas. Yes, we know this. There are transitory Buddhas and permanent Buddhas.

A transitory Buddha is a Buddha who still has not achieved the incarnation of the inner Christ.

A permanent Buddha or Buddha of Contemplation is a Buddha who has already Christified, a Buddha that has already received the inner Christ within. This type of Buddha is a Buddha Maitreya,[30] since it is a Buddha who incarnated the inner Christ (this is how the term "Maitreya" should be understood). So, Buddha Maitreya is not a person: Buddha Maitreya is a title, a degree, which indicates any given Buddha who already achieved Christification.

A long time ago—a very long time ago—I lived in China. This was during the second subrace of this great Aryan root race.[31] At that time, my name was Chou Li, and as Chou Li I entered into the "Order of the Yellow Dragon." While within

---

30 Sanskrit मैत्रेय, "benevolent, friendly, love."
31 The word Aryan is not a term only for "white people" or an ancient, dead civilization, but instead refers to to the vast majority of the population. All modern races are "Aryan."

this order, I learned their "Seven Unutterable Secrets." Yes, I knew "The Seven Jewels of the Yellow Dragon."

In the Order of the Yellow Dragon, we dedicated ourselves especially to in-depth meditation. A Chinese brother played a marvelous musical instrument: he made it vibrate in order to resonate the forty-nine notes. The synthesis of such a strange instrument was the Nirioonossian sound of the universe. When the first note vibrated, we tried to have our mind quiet and in silence. Then, when the second note resounded, we entered into the second level of the subconsciousness. We also confronted our "I's" with the purpose of recriminating them and to force them to keep silence. However, if our mind did not achieve quietude, we would then recriminate our ego even more... When the third note resounded, we would then delve a little bit deeper: we directed ourselves into the third subconscious zone in order to fight against the "I's," in order to force them to keep silence. Thus, with each note of that mysterious instrument (the Alla-attapan), we submerged ourselves successively within each of the forty-nine levels of our subconsciousness, thereby fighting against the diverse psychic aggregates that we carried within our interior. Conclusion: the one who achieved working with the forty-ninth note and had correctly worked with all of the previous ones, achieved the absolute quietude of the mind within all of the forty-nine levels of the subconsciousness, and here was when the Essence, the Buddhadhatu, momentarily escaped from the ego in order to precipitate itself into the Illuminating Void,[32] thus experiencing, in this way, the truth, reality.

During that time, my friend Li Chang excelled in the profound science of meditation. My friend Li Chang does not live upon the face of the Earth anymore. He lives on one of the planets of Christ; this is a planet from a distant universe of this galaxy. There, he lives (from moment to moment) within ecstasy; there, he is happy, due to the fact that Li Chang successfully attained the Tao. But, what is the Tao? The Tao is the Being, the Tao is INRI, the Tao is the inner Christ, and so, Li Chang received the Tao.

---

32 Shunyata, voidness, emptiness, the absolute.

Within Zen Buddhist esotericism, the dialectics of mere reasoning are not in use, but instead the dialectics of the consciousness, which are different.

> *"A monk asked Master Chao Chou, 'What is the meaning of Bodhidharma's coming from the West?'*
>
> *'The cypress tree in the courtyard."*
>
> —G.C.C.Chang, The Practice of Zen (1959)

We might say, "Well, the answer does not coincide with the question," since we are accustomed to the dialectics of reasoning, or formal dialectics. However, that answer actually corresponds wisely to the dialectics of the consciousness. Listen: it does not matter where Bodhidharma came from; the truth is that Bodhidharma is everywhere.

On another occasion, the abbot, the master of a monastery, said to his disciples, "Ask whatever you want to ask."

Thus one disciple said, "I want to ask something."

Then, unexpectedly, before the student could utter his question, the master, with his reed, struck the disciple on the mouth. It is not pleasant to receive a strike on the mouth, right? Yet, this is how they act in Zen and Ch'an Buddhism. Listen: the question the disciple was going to ask was not correct.

One day a master arrived and presented himself in the chamber of meditation. The disciples bowed before him, and rendered unto him a lot of worship and honor. Then the master addressed them and said, "Why did you delay in doing all of this?"

Then the disciples, without foundation, answered him with all kinds of foolishness, thus the master disqualified all of them and said, "Foolish, stubborn, get out of here, you are worthless!"

Yet, if one addresses "Gnostics" with strong words, the psychological "I" of the younger brothers and sisters reacts terribly. This is discouraging indeed.

All of you need to learn what the cross of esoteric discipline is. In Zen, discipline is a cross, yet the discipline of Zen goes to the depths: it goes to the inner Buddha of each of us.

Here, another example: having the longing to know something about Satori,[33] with the longing to experience Satori, to
attain, at least once, an experience of the Illuminating Void, a
student asked the master inside the temple, "Master, what is
the Illuminating Void?" The answer of the master was nothing
but a very fast and terrible kick to the disciple's abdomen!
Thus, the wretched disciple fell and passed out on the floor—
yet he experienced the Illuminating Void. Thus, when the
disciple returned from that state and got up, instead of losing
his time with reactions, he hugged the master, and filled with
happiness, said to him, "Finally, I experienced the Illuminating
Void!"

Fortunately, the master did not finish his teaching there: he
fulfilled his duty by strongly slapping the face of his disciple.
When a disciple attains the experience of Satori and filled with
joy (still imbibed within that state of ecstasy) presents himself
before the master, then the master has to take him out of that
state with a slap. Indeed, otherwise (as they say) the student
could get "the sickness of Satori," in other words, the disciple
might remain ill for the rest of his life. Thus, in order for this
not to happen, the master returns the disciple to his senses
with a strong slap.

So, behold for yourselves how Zen Buddhism goes directly
to the Essence, to the consciousness, to the inner Buddha of
each one of us, and this is transcendental in its depths.

How can I explain to you this matter about the dialectic of
the consciousness? In which way? Well, let us observe a chick
when it still is within the eggshell. When the chick is ready to
come out of the egg, as usual the hen helps the chick. The hen
assists her chick with her beak: she strikes the eggshell a few
times with her beak, and this is how the hen helps the chick to
come out. Likewise, when the disciple is mature enough for the
experience of Satori, the master helps him (even with a kick, as
we illustrated clearly). This might seem very harsh, yet in Zen
this is a reality. This is how sometimes the master assists the
chick (disciple) that is ready to come out of the eggshell.

---

33 Japanese, a Buddhist term for the experience of reality, the voidness or
emptiness (shunyata). Comparable to the Sanskrit word samadhi.

Anyhow, this is the unique Zen and Ch'an language that goes directly to the consciousness and this is what is transcendental; that is their dialectic. It is not formal dialectics; no, it is not that type of dialectic, but rather, the dialectics of the consciousness. This is very clear.

We must learn how to see within ourselves. We need to learn to see inside our interior nature. Thus when we achieve it, we will become Buddhas.

How are we going to learn to see into our interior nature, in what way? Well, first of all, by developing the capacity of psychological observation. As one is psychologically observing himself, one is seeing his own "I's," his inhuman psychological aggregates. Thereafter, one can eliminate, disintegrate, and pulverize them with the help of our Devi Kundalini Shakti, because without the igneous serpent of our magical powers, it is impossible to disintegrate our "I's."

Therefore, it is necessary to learn how to see into our interior nature in order to become Buddhas. This is obvious when we talk about something important and transcendental.

Now then, on another occasion, a Zen master was invited to give a sermon at the Buddhist pagoda; thus, all the monks were waiting. Finally, the master arrived. He looked at all of them, turned his back to them, and withdrew to his cell. Then, the monks who were the most interested in listening to his sermon and who invited the whole brotherhood to attend went to him to complain. The master's answer was, "An expert on shastras can teach you shastras, and an expert on any other religious scripture can perhaps teach you. Yet, I am a Zen master."

That was his unique answer, in which he said everything. Yet, you do not understand this type of language, because you are accustomed to formal logic or dialectical logic, and Zen is a different language.

What did this Zen master tell them? What did he say? Listen, he said, "Gentlemen, you must learn to listen to yourselves. Search for your Innermost. Search within yourselves, since everything is within you." This is what the Zen master meant.

Here, I am giving you these explanations because you are accustomed to formal logic. Yet, if I was in Japan, any given Zen master would strongly yank my ear and I would endure a small reprimand with the yanking of my ear; why? Because it would be said that I am "castrating the teachings." Yes, this is what they call "the castration of the teachings," since it is necessary to capture or apprehend the meaning with the dialectics of the consciousness.

Therefore, continuing ahead with this subject, we see that it is impossible to reach the degree of Buddha if one has not eliminated the undesirable elements from within one's self. Thus, the transitory Buddha is still fighting, because he or she has not yet dissolved the ego. This one is a Buddha with egotistical residues, while the permanent Buddha is the one who already christified his Self.

Hence, Buddha and Christ are intimately related: these are two factors within us.

In the future, I will have to go to Asia in order to accomplish a great mission. At that time, I will have to teach to humanity the necessity to fuse the Buddhist and Christic teachings, because the future religious facet of humanity will be a mixture of the best of Buddhist esotericism with the best of Christic esotericism. After all, Gnosis is Christic and Buddhist esotericism integrated. This is why the Gnostic movement it is called to perform a crucial revolution.

Alchemy

Of course, what we need is to liberate ourselves, to terminate the evil consequences of the abominable Kundabuffer organ.

Likewise, it is obvious that a Buddha cannot exist without having previously created the existential superior bodies[34] of the Being, and in order to create them, we need to be alchemists. A Buddha who does not possess the existential superior

---

34 Our Innermost becomes a buddha after the creation of the solar astral and mental bodies.

bodies of the Being is inconceivable. Just to consider it is an absurdity.

But, how do we create those bodies? First of all, it is convenient that you put due attention to this doctrine, because this teaching is precious.

We need, therefore, to know the mysteries of the Great Work: we need to know how to elaborate the Mercury of the secret philosophy. Yes, this is something imperative.

What is Mercury? Do you know? Why is it said that the initiate has to wear the boots of Mercury? To clarify this, I tell you that Mercury is the metallic soul of the sperm,[35] and that Mercury in itself is very sacred. But, how is Mercury elaborated? Well, this is the unutterable secret that all of the medieval alchemists kept silent.

Is it urgent to elaborate it? Yes, it is, and here I am going to give to you the clue: obviously, the clue is precisely the Arcanum A.Z.F. Here is where the clue is hidden; within those three letters is the clue of the Great Arcanum, namely, the "A" (aqua, water) refers to that metallic water, to that "metallic radical number" or Exioëhary—in other words, the glandular sexual secretions, the sacred sperm. The "F" is fire, Fohat, because without fire, the "A," the pure waters of life, the Mercury of the Great Work, cannot be elaborated.

The water in itself is the mercury, the "metallic radical number" that we need to learn to sublimate. Yet, first of all, it is necessary to know the secret of how the existential superior bodies of the Being are created. Unquestionably, the secret is an artifice that is very easy: very simple, yet grandiose.

The living secret for the preparation of the Mercury is called, when speaking in Latin language, "secreta secretorum." Here, I will not use vulgar terminology for this theme; now I will justly say that the connection of the lingam-yoni[36] within the perfect matrimony is necessary, and the cup of Hermes Trismesgistus (the three times great god ibis of Thoth) must never in life be spilled. To be exact, so that you can understand

---

35 Latin "seed" in both males and females.
36 Male and female sexual organs.

me, the Mercury is elaborated by avoiding the physiological orgasm.

Three Types of Mercury

The Mercury is the metallic soul of the sperm; understand, it is the metallic soul. Allow me to illustrate this better: there are three types of Mercury. The first Mercury is called the Brute Azoth or the sperm. The second Mercury is called the metallic soul of the sperm, and the third Mercury is called Mercury plus Sulfur (Mercury fecundated by fire). To conclude, the Mercury is the metallic soul of the sperm, and the Sulfur is the sacred fire.

However, something is missing. In organic physiology, we find that salt also exists, and that this must also be sublimated by means of all the Tantric operations within the laboratory. So, it is necessary to carefully study this subject matter.

Unquestionably, when the sacred sperm is transmuted into creative energy, this rises to the brain through a pair of sympathetic cords in our organic anatomy.

Understand that what must rise through these ganglionic cords towards the cerebral mass are the permutated energetic currents, and that this is the Mercury. Moreover, we know that such energetic sexual currents must polarize themselves into positive and negative, into solar and lunar. Thus, when these are already polarized, they make contact in the Triveni, close to the coccyx, and here is where the sacred fire appears, which rises throughout the dorsal spine in the form of Sulfur.

Therefore, the fire united with the solar and lunar currents of the Mercury ascends throughout the dorsal spine, along the Shushumna canal (medullar canal) until reaching the brain. As this fire ascends, it opens within our spine our own particular spiritual centers. Unquestionably, the surplus of this third Mercury is what comes to crystallize as the existential superior bodies of the Being, and this is how the permutation of our selves into Buddhas happens.

Let us now focus our attention on the third Mercury. Sulfur and Salt are within the third Mercury.

What is the nebula within the infinite space? It is a mixture of Salt, Sulfur, and Mercury. If we dissolve any metal of the Earth, it is reduced to Salt, Sulfur, and Mercury. Everything that exists in any creation has it source in the Salt, Sulfur, and Mercury; this is obvious.

Therefore, any nebula has Salt, Sulfur, and Mercury. The nebula is the Archeus of the Greeks. From this Archeus emerge the worlds that afterwards rotate around their gravitational centers. Thus, if in starry space an Archeus is necessary for the universe so that the worlds can sprout into existence, likewise it is the same here below in the microcosmos. Here, within our organism, it is necessary to create an Archeus, a very special nebula with Salt, Sulfur, and Mercury.

Thus, precisely, we extract these substances from our endocrine sexual glands, so that the Archeus from below (within the microcosmic human being) can be formed, so that the existential superior bodies of the Being can be born from it.

Normally, the notes Do, Re, Mi, Fa, Sol, La, and Si vibrate in sex; however, if we pass them to another superior octave, then the Archeus comes to crystallize into the astral body; and in another superior octave the Archeus crystallizes into the mental body; and in another even more superior octave the Archeus crystallizes into the body of conscious will. Again, this is how the permutation of ourselves into Buddhas happens.

Do you have questions?

Question: Master, what consequences can we generate if we fake that we possess virtues?

Answer: To fake virtues? Well, when we fake that we possess virtues, the consequences that we generate are those that you see in the hypocritical Pharisees: those who bless their food when their sit at the table; those who make clean the outside of the cup and of the platter, but within they are full of extortion and excess, those who are like unto whitened sepulchers, which indeed appear beautiful outward, but are within full of dead men's bones, and of all uncleanness; those who feel that they are pure, even when from within they are rotten. They are those who believe they are righteous when indeed they have nothing that can be called virtues; they only possess false jewels, and that is all. The Pharisee "I" is born by means of putting a lot of strength into the simulation of virtues.

Question: When we achieve the perception of an "I," i.e. the "I" of lust, yet we are afraid to confront this lust, what then can we do?

Answer: Then, we have to terminate the "I" of fear. Yes, when one feels fear towards anything, then such a fear, such a fright, must be dissolved, since this is another "I." There are people who are afraid of consciously projecting themselves at will out of their physical bodies. What happens to them? Their "I" of fear does not allow them to do it. What must they do in order for that fear to leave them? Well, they must terminate such an "I" of fear, obviously. So, as we are working upon our self, as we are self-observing determined elements, we are being informed. We perceive the "I's" through the sense of psychological self-observation that is developed in this way; yet if one is afraid, then one has to dissolve the "I" of fear.

Question: Can Gnosis be considered a religion?

Answer: Gnosis is the flame from which all religions sprouted, because in its depth Gnosis is religion. The word "religion" comes from the Latin word "religare," which implies "to link the Soul to God." So, Gnosis is the very pure flame from where all religions sprout, because Gnosis is knowledge, Gnosis is wisdom. This is how Gnosis must be understood.

Question: Master, regarding the ego that each one of us possesses, do we bring this ego at the very moment when we come into the world? I ask this because I have noticed that we like to be egocentrics even since childhood.

Answer: Unquestionably, we bring many "I's" when we come into the world, yet we always create new "I's." Some "I's" die and some "I's" are born. Indeed, within us, new "I's" are always being born while other "I's" are dying. Many times, even a tempest, rain, or strong sunshine can produce enough contrariety in us so that a new "I" can be born, and this is the crude reality of facts. Thus, we have within the depth of ourselves "I's" that we do not even remotely suspect that we have. For example, how could an honest person, who has never stolen even a single cent from anyone, accept that he or she has in their depth many "I's" of thievery? Or how could a person who has never assassinated anyone, who has never hurt anyone, not even with their finger, admit that in their depth have some homicidal "I's"? Or how could a righteous woman, a good spouse, a magnificent citizen, against whom no one can say anything wrong about her conduct, about her rectitude, admit that within her depths she has a crowd of "I's" related with prostitution? Nevertheless, this how it is. It is lamentable to tell you that in the depths of each one of us is profound darkness, which we are living in the most frightful, unconscious state of the universe, thus living like miserable robots.

Question: Master, since we are limited to the ego and the personality, can you give us a clue by means of which we can know for ourselves what is the true path?

Answer: We have already precisely talked about this, we have already indicated it. I told you that we must have an order in our psychological work and that such a precise order or method must be established by our own particular inner profound Being.

First of all, we must begin by observing ourselves. In this way, we discover ourselves, and thus, we comprehend and fight for the dissolution of the "I"s that we are discovering. Thus, as time passes, we become more aware that all of those "I"s that we are discovering are part of a direction that has been established within us by our inner Being. Yes, our Being is the one who directs that order, and from the beginning to the end, it is our inner Being who directs the entire psychological work extraordinarily. When we become aware of all of this, then that which we might call Work Memory is formed within our mind. Therefore, the one who has dissolved his "I"s completely can write a book perfectly (with its chapters very well-structured) related to each of the parts of the psychological work. So, the Work Memory that is formed as we work upon ourselves is very interesting.

Question: How do we nourish our will?

Answer: Which will are you referring to? Because we have many wills. Each "I" has its own will, since each "I" is a complete person with its three brains: namely, intellectual, emotional, and motor-instinctual-sexual brains. Each "I" has its own mind, criterion, ideas, emotions, and will. Therefore, if each "I" has its own will, then these wills clash amongst themselves, originating terrible inner conflicts within us. Thus, in order to acquire an authentic will, here and now, we need to destroy the ego. So, the day in which your Essence becomes liberated, then you will have a liberated consciousness endowed with a sovereign will in order to command the fire, air, waters, and earth. Moses could command the elements of nature because he had eliminated his ego and liberated his will, a sovereign will capable of unleashing plagues over the land of Egypt, and of liberating his people. However, when a person has not yet liberated his own will, he has not yet taken possession of himself. To that end, the authentic will emerges from within only when the ego has died.

Question: Master, in what psychological state must we find a person who longs for the realization of the Self?

Answer: He or she must be found precisely in the state of self-observation, which is the case of a person that has already realized that he or she has a particular psychology; since, normally, people do not acknowledge it. They acknowledge that they have a physical body because they perceive it with their sensual mind, yet they do not acknowledge that they have a particular psychology, and therefore they do not observe themselves. So, when someone acknowledges that he or she has a particular psychology, then as matter of fact, this person begins to self-observe him or herself, and therefore, their state is always that of alert perception, alert novelty, since, if they are not in such a state, they cannot observe themselves.

Question: On the esoteric path, can we receive any other help besides the help that our real Innermost grants to us?

Answer: Yes, of course; the Divine Mother Kundalini will help you to disintegrate errors. Besides the particular, individual Divine Mother, the Father who is in secret will guide you in the work, and many of the other parts of your Being will do something for you, i.e. your own particular Minerva, the individual Minerva, that part of the Being that cultivates sapience, will give you the necessary wisdom that you need, if you persevere.

Question: Master, when Christ was asked "What is the truth?" he turned his back and walked away, yet he also said that he was "the way, the truth, and the life." Is there any contradiction in this?

Answer: First of all, Christ did not turn his back and walk away; he just kept silence before Pilate. The one who turned his back and walked away was the Buddha Shakyamuni.

Undoubtedly, when Jesus Christ said, "I am the way, the truth, and the life," it was not the human person who said it, but the inner Christ [the "I Am"]. Unquestionably, the one who works on himself and advances in that way will, on some day among many, be assisted by the inner Christ. The Christ in itself is the truth and the way, yet Christ is not a human or divine individual. Christ is a force, just as the force of gravity or electric energy or universal cohesion.

Christ emerges from within, not from without. Therefore, those who await the second coming of Christ from without are very mistaken. Christ will come from within, from the Spirit, from the consciousness, from within the depths of our own soul. When we incarnate Christ, he then enters within our temple (which is the physical body) in order to help us in our psychological work. He then takes possession of our mental, volitional, sexual, etc., processes. Christ becomes a human among humans, and fights in order to disintegrate all of the undesirable elements that we carry in our interior. Yes, he fights against our own egos as if they were part of himself. In other words, not being a sinner, he will look like a sinner. Not being an indweller of darkness, he will look as if he is one. He will become a person of bones and flesh in order to liberate us. Then, one day among many, he will have to climb to the Golgotha of supreme sacrifice in order to give his life so that others can live. Finally, within the heart of the one who has him incarnated, Christ must die, because with his death he kills death. Thereafter, Christ resurrects within that human being, and the human being resurrects within him, and glorification arrives.

However, no one can receive the inner Christ if he or she does not work upon themselves, therefore:

> *Uselessly Christ in Bethlehem was born*
> *If within our heart his birth is forlorn.*

> *His crucifixion, death, and resurrection on the third day*
> *from among the dead were in vain,*

> *Unless his crucifixion, death, and resurrection, be set up*
> *within each one of us again.*

Resurrection must be attained, now, in bones and flesh, alive, here and now. Those who think that the resurrection is in a remote future are mistaken. Those who think that the resurrection is for all human beings are very far from the truth, since resurrection is not for everybody, and can only be attained if we truly decide to psychologically die within ourselves here and now. Again, Christ comes to us from within and when we are very much ahead in this very difficult psychological work.

Question: Master, much has been spoken about the coming of the Antichrist, yet indeed, who is the Antichrist?

Answer: The Antichrist is now here living amongst humanity, and is making a gigantic crusade in all of the countries of the world. Namely, the Antichrist speaks through millions of people, invents rockets that even reach the Moon, invents ultrasonic airplanes, drugs that as "medicine" produce portentousness, etc. Understand that the Antichrist is precisely the contrary of the inner Christ. In other words, the Antichrist is the animal ego, which, with its sparkling and terrible mind, victoriously develops. Behold, how the entire world kneels before the Antichrist and says, "There is no one like unto the Antichrist." The Antichrist of false science performs marvels and the entire world reverently kneels before him. Millions of people say, "Who is like the Antichrist? Who is capable of doing what he does?" The scientists of the Antichrist hate the Eternal One.

Question: How can the poor conciliate the two polarities, I mean, to conciliate the economical situation with the matters related with the consciousness?

Answer: Well, this matter about the psychological work is completely different. It is convenient to know how to educate so that the poor can be liberated. If we observe the poor, we will see indubitably that the poor are living in an infrahuman state. Some time ago I was observing a group of "parachutists" (a Mexican term for those who invade private estate properties; "squatters," in other words) who in the capital of Mexico had unexpectedly expropriated some private land. The place they expropriated was close to my home, thus I decided to observe them from the balcony of my home. They had an infrahuman life. They were always inebriated. In the colony where I lived, we very seldom saw a police patrol, yet after those "parachutists" invaded the place, the police patrols started to circulate very often in the neighborhood. Previously, we never witnessed any blood incident, yet with them around, these became frequent. They were always fighting amongst themselves, treating each other very badly instead of sharing, in the midst of their own suffering, as good neighbors, instead of treating each other as brothers and sisters. I thought that if one of these people changed their level of Being, how different this person could become. However, in order for them to make a step ahead in their level of Being, unquestionably, they would have to receive the information from someone who would have the amiability of descending to them to explain the way they could change their level of Being, the way in which they could pass to a higher level of Being.

A person can pass into a higher level of Being if, already aware of this psychological work, he will decide to eliminate his or her inhuman defects, to eliminate his or her psychological errors. Yet, unquestionably, if his or her errors are eliminated, he or she will move out of the level with respect to those who live with them. Yet, by means of the law of affinities, they would become in contact with other types of people with the same level of their Being. They would be in contact with another type of human who would bring new opportunities to them, and then help them to abandon that level of poverty and therefore live better.

Thus, the poor can stop being miserable by changing their level of Being and thus entering into another—better—economical situation. This demands years of psychological work within ourselves. Thus, what we need is to educate those people who live in disgrace.

Question: Besides the economical necessities of those people, there is also ignorance; thus, in order for them to acquire the Gnostic teachings, it is necessary that the one who will instruct them has a great deal of patience, right?

Answer: Yes, a great deal of patience is necessary, and indeed, I would like you to have such patience and to instruct those poor people, so that they can start working upon themselves psychologically and thus pass to a higher level of Being.

Understand that the level of Being of each one of us brings the type of life that we have. I.e. we find a cow in a stable, since its level of Being brings her to that life as a cow. Yet, if we take that cow and bring her to a luxurious apartment and we perfume her, and dress her with satin, even in that luxurious apartment that animal will continue to be a cow, because the level of Being of every creature brings its own particular type of life. We can take a person of an inferior inhuman level of Being, who lives in disgrace, and we dress this person as best we can and afterwards we take them to Buckingham Palace, so that they can live next to Queen Elizabeth, yet unquestionably, according to his or her level of Being, this person will bring their own type of life into Buckingham Palace, and we can be absolutely sure that in very few days this person will be in conflict, having problems with the butlers, etc.

Therefore, the level of Being of each person brings his or her own type of life. So, if we pass to another higher level of Being, we will bring to our life different circumstances, new ways of life, and therefore we will have a most edifying and essentially dignifying life; this is obvious.

Question: Master, what part of the Being are we?

Answer: Are you asking me, what part of the Being are we? Well, this is a crucial question, because as we presently are, we are not any part of the Being, we are nothing but miserable robots, programmed for this or that type of job, according with what we have studied from kindergarten, in school, etc., which have developed a false personality and a false consciousness. Thus, the true superlative consciousness of our Being has been displaced; the wretched has been cornered there, within the depths, in oblivion.

Therefore, we are robots, machines, which are controlled by unknown forces, by the "I's," and our inner, profound Being, with all of its sublime parts, are beyond, very much beyond the unconscious machine, much, much beyond the miserable robot. What can a robot know about its Being? What can the sensual mind know about the diverse parts of the Being and its functionalisms? Nothing!

Therefore, let us begin to explore ourselves in order to evidence by ourselves the crude reality of what we are. Thus, only like this, indeed, can we reach the most pure parts of the Being.

FIRST PART

THE EXPULSION FROM EDEN

"Therefore אלהים יהוה Jehovah Elohim sent him forth
from the garden of Eden, to till the ground from
whence he was taken. So he drove out אדם Adam;
and he placed at the east of the garden of עדן Eden
Cherubim, and a flaming sword which turned every
way, to keep the way of the tree of life."
—Bereshit / Genesis 3:23-24

Chapter 1
Eden

Eden[1] is the ethereal world.[2] Eden is sex itself.
The ethereal world is the abode of the sexual forces. The ethereal world is Eden.

We were driven out of Eden through the doors of sex, thus we can return to Eden only through the doors of sex.

We cannot enter into Eden through false doors; we must enter into Eden through the doors out of which we were driven.

The governor of Eden is the Lord Jehovah.[3] The Lord Jehovah dwells in Eden. The Lord Jehovah dwells in the ethereal world, because Eden is the ethereal world. The ethereal world is paradise.

Ether is the fifth element[4] of nature. The blue color that we see in the distant mountains is the ether of Eden. In future times, the ethereal world will become visible and tangible in the air. In those future times, the elemental gods of fire, air, water, and earth will become visible and tangible in the air for us.

Everything comes from the ether, everything returns into the ether. The ether is the orchard of Eden.

---

1   The symbolic paradise described by Moses where humanity was created and lived happily before falling into temptation. The Hebrew word עֵדֶן Eden literally means "pleasure, bliss." Read Bereshit / Genesis 1-4.

2   The fourth dimension, also called the vital world.

3   Hebrew יהוה, poorly translated in the Bible as "God."

4   The five elements of alchemy and tantra are earth, water, fire, air, and ether (space).

JESUS AT THE WELL

Jesus said to the woman, "If thou knewest the gift of God, and who it is that saith to thee, Give me to drink; thou wouldest have asked of him, and he would have given thee living water. ...whosoever drinketh of the water that I shall give him shall never thirst; but the water that I shall give him shall be in him a well of water springing up into everlasting life." The woman saith unto him, "Sir, give me this water, that I thirst not, neither come hither to draw." Jesus saith unto her, "Go, call thy husband, and come hither." —John 4

Chapter 2

The Labarum of the Temple

Christonic semen[5] is the raw matter of the Great Work. Semen is pure, living water. Semen is the spring water of everything that exists. Semen is the water of Genesis. A plant without water dries and dies. The water is vegetable semen within plants; this vegetable semen is transformed into leaves, flowers, and fruits. The combinations of this infinite substance are marvelous.

The sea is the semen of the planet Earth. Everything comes from the sea and returns to the sea. The continents emerged from the sea and will return into the sea.

We have the sea within our sexual glands, thus the mystery of life is hidden within our seminal waters. We emerged from the spermatic semen in that initial moment.

All animal species carry in their seminal waters the secret of their existence. People can only see the gross physical matter particles that form the material cortex of the pure, living waters, yet in Eden we know the waters of the sea of life; yes, in Eden we see the waters of Genesis glittering with glory. All created things emerge from this raw matter of the Great Work. The combinations of this infinite substance are marvelous.

A sacred cup filled with pure, living water was never missing in the sacred shrines of the temples; this is the labarum of the temple. Whosoever drinks of this water of everlasting life

---

5   Latin "seed" whether in males or females.

LABARUM

A labarum is a military standard used by Roman Emperor Constantine that displayed the symbol of Christ, which is formed by Chi (χ) and Rho (ρ), the first two Greek letters of the word Krestos ΧΡΙΣΤΟΣ or Χριστός. This is a glyph of a labrys, the double-headed ax of the Earth-goddess taken from Hippolyta by Heracles, and carried by the kings of ancient times. The labrys is a vital symbol of the ancient mystery schools of Greece.

LABRYS

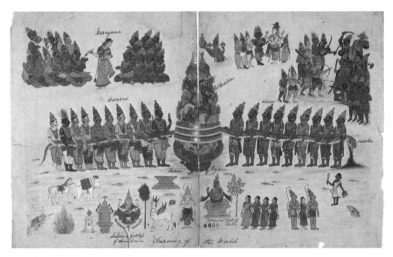

SAMUDRA MANTHANA, THE CHURNING OF THE OCEAN OF "MILK." AMRITA GIVES THE GODS THEIR POWER. MOHINI (TOP LEFT), AN INCARNATION OF VISHNU (CHOKMAH / CHRIST) PROVIDES IT.

shall never thirst, and out of his belly shall flow rivers of living water.

These are the waters of Amrita,[6] which is the Mulaprakriti[7] of the Orientals. When the great night[8] arrives, the entire universe will fade to dusk and be reduced to its semen (Mulaprakriti). The universe emerged from this water and will return to it.

The pure living water is the labarum of the temple. The waters of Genesis are governed by the rays of the Moon and by the elemental gods of the waters.

---

6   Sanskrit, a symbolic beverage that provides immortality.
7   The "root or origin of nature; primary cause or originant; original root or germ out of which matter or all apparent forms are evolved." The abstract deific feminine principle. Undifferentiated substance.
8   Mahapralaya, cosmic repose.

Chapter 3

The Swans of Paradise

The Kalahamsa swan,[9] perched upon a lotus flower, floats on the pure, living waters. Hamsa means, "I am he, I am he, I am he." In other words, we can say,

"The Spirit of God floats upon the face of the waters."
—Genesis 1:2

Divinity breathes upon the sea of eternity. God is within us, thus we can find God only within ourselves: "I am he, I am he, I am he."

God is love. Love is found immanent and transcendent within each drop of the great ocean. God can only be found within sex and love.

The swan represents love. Love can only be enlivened with love. The swan was born in order to love. When one of a couple of swans dies, the other dies of sadness.

In Eden, swans assist at the table of the angels. Ineffable elixirs, which the gods drink in their diamantine cups, are elaborated within the immaculate, white craws of swans.

The combinations of this infinite substance are marvelous. The semen that we carry in our sexual glands is this infinite substance of the great ocean. The multiple combinations of this infinite substance are transformed into continents filled with plants, flowers, and fruits.

The multiple combinations of this infinite substance give rise to everything that is created: birds and monsters, human beings and beasts. Everything emerges from the seminal waters of Genesis. Love breathes upon those waters.

Parsifal, after having killed the swan in a wood near the castle of Monsalvat, remorsefully breaks his bow.[10]

---

9   Sanskrit. "... the Kalahansa, the Kala-ham-sa," and even the "Kali Hamsa," (Black swan). Here the m and the n are convertible... Hamsa is equal to a-ham-sa, three words meaning "I am he" (in English), while divided in still another way it will read "So-ham," "he (is) I" -- Soham being equal to Sah, "he," and aham, "I," or "I am he." -HP Blavatsky, *The Secret Doctrine*
10 From Richard Wagner's masterpiece *Parsifal*. Read *Parsifal Unveiled*.

THE CREATOR GODS ZEUS OF THE GREEKS (LEFT) AND BRAHMA OF THE
HINDUS (RIGHT) ARE BOTH ASSOCIATED WITH SWANS.

Tradition relates that the swan has the ability to separate milk from water, a clear
symbol of sexual transmutation: extracting the Mercury from the sexual energy.

Leda and the swan remind us about the enchantments of
love. The swan of love makes the waters of life fertile.

The fire of love makes life sprout from within the great
ocean. The water is the habitat of fire. The sexual fire is dormant within the pure, living waters. Fire and water, united in
a trance of love, originated the entire universe. The fire of love
breathes within our seminal waters. The fire of love makes the
waters of life fertile.

The swan symbolizes love. The swan can only be fed with
love. When one of a couple of swans dies, the other dies of
sadness.

Chapter 4

The Sexual Act in Eden

Chastity alone reigns in Eden. Sexuality in Eden is as pure as the light of the Elohim. Nonetheless, the sexual act also exists in Eden. Plants, flowers, trees, gods, birds, reptiles, animals, and human beings: everything emerges from sex. Creation is impossible without sex.

As human beings have body, soul, and spirit, so do plants. The souls of plants are the elementals[11] of Nature. Every plant, every tree, and every herb has its own particular individuality; thus, every plant is an individuality of body, soul, and spirit. These are the elementals of Eden; these are the innocent angels of Eden. These elementals are organized in vegetable families, which botanists have classified with Latin names.

Vegetal magic teaches us how to manipulate the elementals of plants.[12] In Eden, these vegetal families have their temples and their gods; the gods of Eden are the elemental kings (the Malachim) of Nature.

Not a single plant can produce fruit without love and sex. The elementals of plants also know how to love. The nuptial bed of these ineffable beings from Eden is made by the roots of plants and trees. The elementals of plants connect themselves sexually; yet, in order to suppress seminal ejaculation (fornication), they know how to opportunely withdraw from each other, since the seed always pass into the womb without the need of ejaculating the semen. Thus, the female becomes impregnated and her fecundated internal vitality makes the fruit sprout. The combinations of this infinite substance are marvelous. Thus, this is how the ether of life[13] serves as an instrument for the reproduction of plants.

---

11 "Nature spirits," called elves, dwarves, sprites, fairies, etc.

12 Read *Esoteric Medicine and Practical Magic* and *Igneous Rose* by Samael Aun Weor.

13 One of the four ethers of the ethereal /vital body. The ether of life is the foundation of the reproductive and transformative sexual processes.

The chemical ether[14] allows vegetal transformations. It transmutes, associates, and disassociates the chemical elements; this is how plants are filled with delicious fruits, and how life sprouts.

The luminous ether[15] dyes the flowers and fruits with ineffable colors.

Then, everything becomes resplendent under the light of the sun, since the reflecting ether[16] becomes like an ineffable mirror within which all of Nature is delighted.

Thus, this is how life surges forth from within the bosom of Eden.

The mountains in Eden are as blue as the sky and as transparent as crystal. Back when human beings lived in Eden, they reproduced themselves as the plants do; then, the rivers of pure living water flowed with milk and honey.

At that time, human beings uttered the great, universal language of life, thus the fire, air, water, and earth obeyed them. All of Nature kneeled before human beings and served them, since they did not ejaculate their seminal liquor. Man and woman united sexually, yet in order to suppress seminal ejaculation, they knew how to withdraw before the orgasm.

Then, during the sexual act, the lunar hierarchies utilized one spermatozoon in order to reproduce the species. One single spermatozoon easily escapes from the male sexual glands without the necessity of ejaculating the semen. This is how the woman was fecundated and human life sprouted. This is called an immaculate conception.

An ineffable virgin related with the constellation of Virgo dwells in Eden; this being works with the rays of the Moon. She is the immaculate conception. She is a primordial Elohim from paradise. Those who return to Eden know her, because this fully-pure Elohim governs the immaculate conception.

Blessed be love. God shines upon the perfect couple.

---

14 The chemical ether is related with all the processes of organic assimilation and nourishment.
15 The luminous ether is related with the processes of sensory perception.
16 The reflecting ether is intimately related with the faculties of memory, imagination, willpower, etc.

Chapter 5
Lucifer

If you have your lamp filled with oil, then the temple will always be filled with light.[17] Yet, if you spill the oil of your lamp, the fire will be snuffed out, and you "shall be cast out into outer darkness: there shall be weeping and gnashing of teeth."[18]

The semen is the habitat of fire; if you spill the semen, your lamp will be snuffed out and you shall sink into the luciferic outer darkness: in other words, the Lord Jehovah said:

> "Of every tree of the garden thou mayest freely eat: But of the tree of the knowledge of good and evil, thou shalt not eat of it: for in the day that thou eatest thereof thou shalt surely die" —Genesis 2:16-17

In Eden, the elementals do not spill the semen.

When we spill the semen, the lamp is without fuel; then the flame is extinguished, and we enter into the outer darkness of Lucifer. The semen is the fuel of the lamp; without fuel, a lamp cannot burn, and where there is no fire, there is no light. Then, only darkness reigns.

Woeful is the inhabitant of Eden that dares to spill his semen; his lamp will be snuffed out for lack of fuel, and he will sink into the luciferic outer darkness.

The Tree of the Science of good and evil[19] is sex. Human beings were driven out from Eden when they ate of the forbidden fruit. Adam was all the men of Eden, and Eve was all the women of Eden. In other words, when Adam and Eve spilled the oil of their lamps, they were darkened for lack of oil, thus they lingered in profound darkness. This how humanity exited Eden.

---

17 "And thou shalt command the children of Israel, that they bring thee pure שמן [semen] oil olive beaten for the light, to cause the lamp to burn always." —Exodus 27:20
18 Christian Bible, Matthew 8:12
19 The Tree of Knowledge described by Moses in Bereshit / Genesis.

The fire of the Holy Spirit is the igneous serpent of our magical powers. The fire of the Holy Spirit is the Kundalini,[20] the fountain of every life. This fire is secluded within our semen. Therefore, if we spill the semen, the fire will die and we will enter into the kingdom of darkness.

When human beings spilled their semen, they entered into the kingdom of Lucifers. Lucifer as a demon is terribly perverse. The Lucifers are his legions who obey and follow him.

Sexual passion is the foundation of the Lucifers. When human beings allowed themselves to be seduced by the Lucifers, they spilled the oil from their lamps and remained in darkness. Human beings exited Eden through the doors of sex, and through the doors of sex they entered into the kingdom of the Lucifers.

If human beings want to return to Eden, then what they must do is to fill their lamp with oil and to light it. This is how they will leave the kingdom of the Lucifers and enter again into Eden. This is how we leave the darkness and enter into the light.

---

20 See glossary.

Chapter 6
Jehovah, Lucifer, Christ

There are luciferic beings as well as Edenic beings. The luciferic being spills semen, but the Edenic being does not spill semen. This present humanity is luciferic, but the ancient humanities—namely the Polar, Hyperborean, and Lemurian root races—were Edenic humanities. Comprehend that the Edenic state is a state of consciousness, and that the luciferic state is just another state of consciousness.

Thus, just as any person has a body of bones and flesh, likewise a being from Eden can have a body of bones and flesh. Similarly, just as any person has a body of bones and flesh, likewise a luciferic being can have a body of bones and flesh, because the Edenic and luciferic states are just states of consciousness.

When human beings exited Eden, their consciousness was submerged into certain atomic strata or luciferic regions. Then the human soul sank into its own atomic infernos and lost its powers. This is how the soul exited Eden, how the Edenic being died, and the luciferic being was born. This is why the Lord Jehovah said,

> "Of every tree of the garden thou mayest freely eat: But of the tree of the knowledge of good and evil, thou shalt not eat of it: for in the day that thou eatest thereof thou shalt surely die." —Genesis 2

Within the gigantic patios of the temples of ancient Lemuria, men and women united sexually in order to create; at that time, the sexual act was guided by the Elohim. Man and woman (sexually united) knew how to withdraw before the orgasm in order to suppress the seminal ejaculation.

At that time, the Elohim utilized one spermatozoon and one feminine gamete in order to create, since only one spermatozoon and one feminine gamete are needed in order to create. A spermatozoon is so infinitesimal, so microscopic, that it can easily escape from the sexual male glands without the necessity of spilling the semen. This is how the Edenic being sexually reproduces. This is how the children of immaculate conceptions are born. This is what immaculate conception means.

Lucifer tempted the human being and the human being fell into temptation. Lucifer as a black magician wears a bloody colored tunic and covers his head with a red cap like the Bons and the Drukpas from oriental Tibet. The lustful forces of the Luciferics awoke animal passion within human beings; then men and women started to ejaculate their semen. This is why the Lemurian tribes were expelled from the temples.

Then, in those times of yore, the Kundalini—that had been victoriously lifted up in the medullar canal—descended to the coccygeal bone and there it lingered, enclosed within the chakra Muladhara. The lamp of the temple was snuffed out and the human being sank himself into profound darkness.

Thus, this is how the Edenic being died and the Luciferic being was born. Then, when the human being ate from the forbidden fruit, the Lord Jehovah said, "Behold, the man is become as one of US, to know good and evil" [Genesis 3:22].

If the human being had not eaten from the fruit of the Tree of Knowledge, he would have risen to the angelic state, yet he would have done it in a primeval innocence. In Eden, in relation to the Lord Jehovah, we were as the fingers of the hand are in relation to the brain.

However, Lucifer gave us independence. The forbidden fruit made us cognizant of the science of good and evil. This science is very profound. There is good in evil and evil in good. There is something evil within everything good; there is something good within everything evil. Crime is also hidden within the incense of prayer; crime is also hidden within the perfume of litany. There is much virtue in the evil ones, likewise there is much evil in the virtuous ones. Whosoever knows good from evil and evil from good receives the tremendous sword of cosmic justice.

Angels know the science of good and evil. Angels are perfect humans. Angels also exited Eden and returned into Eden; this is why they are angels. As we presently are, the angels were formerly.

Hence, we exited Eden; nonetheless, we knew good and evil.

So, we exited Eden; nonetheless, we acquired independence.

Jehovah, the governor of Eden, said,

> *"Of every tree of the garden thou mayest freely eat: But of the tree of the knowledge of good and evil, thou shalt not eat of it: for in the day that thou eatest thereof thou shalt surely die"* —Genesis 2:16, 17

Yet, Lucifer said unto the woman,

> *"Ye shall not surely die: For God doth know that in the day ye eat thereof, then your eyes shall be opened, and ye shall be as gods, knowing good and evil"* —Genesis 3:4, 5

Thus this is why, when the human being ate from the forbidden fruit, the Lord Jehovah said,

> *"Behold, the man is become as one of US, to know good and evil"* —Genesis 3:22

This is how we acquire wisdom; this is how we achieve independence. This is how we acquire cognizance of the science of good and evil.

Nevertheless, now we must return to Eden in order to become as gods, knowing the science of good and evil. We must enter into Eden through the same door from which we exited. We exited Eden through the door of sex, and only through that door can we return into Eden. So, let us return into Eden in order to become as gods.

Eden is sex itself. Therefore if we want to enter into Eden, we must return to the primeval sexual system of Eden. We must enter through the door of sex because that is the door from which we exited. There is no other door to enter into Eden. There is no other door to exit Eden. We must enter through the door from which we exited; this is the law.

After exiting Eden, the human being sank into the atomic infernos of nature. If it were not for Christ, it would be impossible for us to leave the abyss. Fortunately, a savior was sent to us; that savior is Christ.

We must now incarnate Christ within ourselves in order to return to the Father. No one comes to the Father but through the Son.

Only in the redeemer's blood can our robes be washed and made white, to clothe us so that we can enter into Eden exactly through the same door from which we exited. The supreme obedience of Christ opposed the supreme disobedience of Adam.

Jehovah gave us his commandments, Lucifer gave us individual independence, and Christ redeems us from sin. This is how the gods are lifted up from the mud of the earth.

Chapter 7

The Tree of Life

Thus, this is how the sentence of the Lord Jehovah was accomplished,

> *"So he drove out the man; and he placed at the east of the garden of Eden Cherubim, and a flaming sword which turned every way, to keep the way of the Tree of Life."* —Genesis 3:24

The two trees of Eden are the Tree of the Science of good and evil, and the Tree of Life. These two trees of the orchard even share their roots.

The Tree of Life is represented in our physical body by the spinal column, and the Tree of Knowledge is represented by our sexual organs; these trees of Eden even share their roots.

God placed Cherubim[21] and a flaming sword to keep the way of the Tree of Life. If the fallen human being could eat the delicious fruits of the Tree of Life, then now we would have fornicator gods. That would have been the damnation of damnations, the most terrible sacrilege, and the impossible.

This is why, menacingly and terribly, the flaming sword of cosmic justice blazingly turns every way, to keep the way of the Tree of Life.

The Tree of Life is "the Being."

Now then, we must know that the Innermost is our Spirit, the Being, the Tree of Life. The Innermost is the most beloved son of the "Inner Christ." The ray from which our very Innermost emanated is our inner Christ. The inner Christ is one with the Father.

Father, Son, and Holy Spirit[22] are a perfect triad. The Innermost was born from this triad. The Innermost is enveloped by six inferior vehicles, which interpenetrate without

---

21 Hebrew כרבים, angels, buddhas.
22 Christian symbol of the three primary forces, which are represented in every religion.

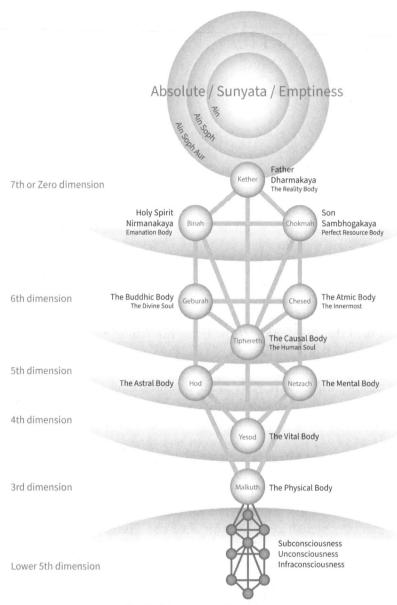

THE TEN SEPHIROTH OF THE TREE OF LIFE

confusion, thus forming the human being. All faculties and powers of the Innermost are the fruits of the Tree of Life.

Human beings will eat the fruits of the Tree of Life when they return to Eden; then, they will see God face to face without dying, the lightning will serve them as a scepter, and the tempests will be as carpeting for their feet.

There are ten tides of life that interpenetrate without confusion. These ten eternal emanations are the ten sephiroth of Kabbalah. These are the ten branches of the Tree of Life. Now, we comprehend why God placed ten fingers on our hands.

The twelve senses[23] of the human being are related with our spinal column. The physical exponent of the Tree of Life is our spinal medulla. These twelve senses are the twelve fruits of the Tree of Life.

---

23 The five (5) physical senses plus the perceptive abilities of the seven (7) awakened chakras / churches. "In the midst of the street of it, and on either side of the river, was there the tree of life, which bare twelve manner of fruits, and yielded her fruit every month: and the leaves of the tree were for the healing of the nations." –Revelation 22:2

The Ghent Altarpiece by Jan and Hubert van Eyck

Chapter 8
Initiation

Human beings fell into the abyss when they exited Eden. It is impossible for us to leave the abyss without the help of a savior.

The guardians of light and darkness are between Eden and the abyss. The guardians of Eden keep the way to the Tree of Life. The guardians of the abyss are the tempting Lucifers.

When we exited Eden, we entered into the tenebrous abysses of nature. We can only leave those abysses by means of cosmic initiation. Every initiation is a spiritual birth.

Whosoever wants to be born has to enter into the feminine womb in order to be gestated; thus, this is how the right to be born is acquired by the one who wants to be born. Initiation is totally sexual. Thus if we want to be born, we need to practice sexual magic[24] with our spouse.

The clue of sexual magic is the following: "Introduce the virile member into the feminine vagina and withdraw without spilling the semen (without orgasm)." This is the sexual act performed by the creatures who live in Eden.

When we were within the womb of our physical mother, we developed organs, viscera, glands, etc. Thus, when we are practicing sexual magic, we are in a process of spiritual sexual gestation; then, we develop the flowers of the soul. This is how we awaken the fire of the Holy Spirit[25] and transform ourselves into masters.

Thus, within the womb of the great Mother, we are gestated as gods. This is how to awaken the Kundalini and transform ourselves into gods.

When human beings ejaculated their semen, they sank into pain and lost their esoteric powers, because when the semen is ejaculated, the human consciousness submerges within

---

24 Magic is from magi, "priest," thus sexual magic is priestly or sacred sex.
25 The Christian name for the third aspect of the Holy Trinity, or "God." On the Kabbalistic Tree of Life, this is the third sephirah, called Binah, "intelligence." This force has many names in other religions.

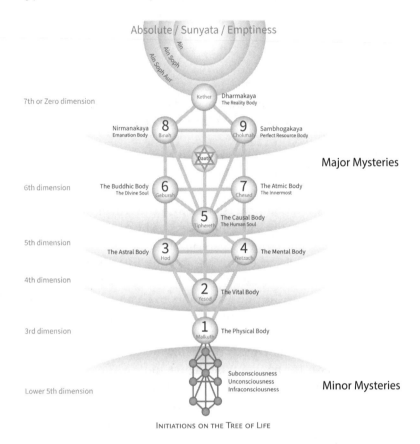

INITIATIONS ON THE TREE OF LIFE

the atomic infernos of nature, which is the kingdom of the Lucifers. This entire humanity dwells in the abyss.

One becomes aware of dwelling in the abyss only when one is prepared to exit it. We can exit the abyss only through initiation. There are eighteen initiations, which are eighteen cosmic births. They are constituted by nine initiations of Minor Mysteries and nine initiations of Major Mysteries.

Initiation pertains to your very life. Initiation pertains to the consciousness and to sex. Our consciousness is a spark, detached from the great cosmic consciousness. We had mineral, plant, and animal consciousness;[26] once we acquire human consciousness, then much later we can have Angelic, Archangelic, Seraphic, etc., consciousness.

---

26 See "Intellectual Animal" in the glossary.

To state that "this is good" or "that is evil" is an easy matter, yet to have cognizance[27] of good and evil is very difficult. Likewise, to state that 2 + 2 is 4 is very easy, yet to have cognizance that 2 + 2 is 4 is a matter that pertains to gods.

The drunkard knows that drinking alcohol is wrong, yet the drunkard does not have cognizance that drinking alcohol is wrong. If the consciousness of the drunkard became cognizant that drinking alcohol is wrong, then he would prefer that "a millstone be hung about his neck and that he be drowned in the depth of the sea"[28] than continue in the vice of alcoholism.

Our consciousness awakens by means of more elevated levels of the Being and life. Thus, knowledge that does not become cognizance is worthless. Millions of spiritual students study our books, yet the intellectual knowledge of the written truths alone is worthless, because having cognizance of these truths is what is important. Thousands of spiritual students believe they have cognizance of the truths they have read; wretched beings... they are mistaken... Only the great masters of Major Mysteries have cognizance of those truths. Students of spiritual schools are parroting chatterers who repeat what they read, that is all. Therefore, what is important is the awakening of the consciousness, because the intellect is just a function of the animal soul, yet the consciousness is a function of God.

There is a mountain: at the bottom of it is the abyss. Thus, the one who wants to exit the abyss has to climb the mountain. There are two paths that lead to the summit. The first path turns in a spiral way around the mountain, thus spirally it reaches the summit, yet the second is the straight, narrow, and difficult path that as a straight line reaches the summit.

The entire suffering humanity climbs along the spiral path that resembles a snail-shell shape, while few are the initiates that climb along the narrow path. The spiral path is very long, yet the narrow and difficult path is short. The latter is the initiatic path of woe and renunciation.

In the past, there were great schools of mysteries: these schools of mysteries were in Egypt, Eleusis, Troy, Rome,

---

27 Comprehension, conscious knowledge.
28 Words of Jesus from Matthew 18:6, Mark 9:42, Luke 17:2

Carthage, Babylon, among the Aztecs, Incas, Druids, etc. At that time, only the priests of privileged castes were allowed to enter into initiation. The entire drama of "the Passion of the Lord" was represented within those temples of mysteries. But then our Lord the Christ came and publicly opened the path of initiation for all human beings. Hence, what is remarkable about Jesus Christ is the fact of having publicly represented this drama upon the old roads of Jerusalem. This is how he opened the doors of the temple for all human beings.

> "Ask and it shall be given you. Knock and it shall be opened unto you. Because strait is the gate, and narrow is the way, which leadeth unto light, and few there be that find it." —Matthew 7: 7, 14

> "Among a thousand who seek me, one finds me. Among a thousand who find me, one follows me. And among a thousand who follow me, one is mine." —Bhagavad-Gita

When the black age dawned, the schools of mysteries were closed in the physical world. Now, we have to seek those schools within, very deep within our consciousness.

Only those who have ascended through the nine degrees of the Minor Mysteries can enter into the Major Mysteries.

People remember the Son of God, yet they do not remember the Son of Man.[29] Notwithstanding, the divine master is god and human. The divine master opened the path of initiation for all human beings. However, in order for him to open the path for everybody, he had to tread the path himself. Thus he became a perfect man: he became a god.

The path of perfection is a path of the terror of love and law.

---

29   "When the Beloved One [Christ] becomes transformed into the soul, and when the soul becomes transformed into the Beloved One, that which we call the Son of Man is born from this ineffable, divine, and human mixture. The great Lord of Light, being the Son of the living God, becomes the Son of Man when he transform himself into the Human Soul. The Sun-Man is the result of all our purifications and bitterness. The Sun-Man is divine and human. The Son of Man is the final outcome of the human being. He is the child of our sufferings, the solemn mystery of the transubstantiation." —Samael Aun Weor, *The Aquarian Message*

Chapter 9

Ages of the Consciousness

In the internal worlds, there is no chronological time. In the internal worlds, life is an eternal moment. Thus, when we cite time, we are referring to "states of consciousness."

In Kabbalah, the numbers of any given quantity are added together in order to extract a kabbalistic number; i.e. if we want to know the kabbalistic number of the year 1956, then we disarrange that quantity as follows: 1 9 5 6. By adding them together, we have 21, and 2 + 1 is equal to 3. Thus, the number 3 is the kabbalistic value of that year.

Likewise, if we say that a master has an age of 300 years, we disarrange the number as follows: 3 + 0 + 0: this addition is equal to 3. This means that master has completed the third initiation of Major Mysteries. Yet, if we say that this master has the age of 340 years, we are indicating that master has the third initiation of Major Mysteries plus 40 years or degrees of the fourth initiation of Major Mysteries.

So, if we affirm that a disciple is 80 years old, we disarrange that quantity a follows: 8 + 0 equals 8, thus this means that the disciple has the eighth initiation of Minor Mysteries.

The ages of Minor Mysteries are from 10 to 90, and the ages of Major Mysteries are from 100 to 900. Ages from 1000 and beyond are the ages of the gods. Thus, in order to enter into the ineffable joy of the Absolute,[30] it is necessary to acquire the age of 300,000 divine years.

Consequently, if a master has the age of 500 years and wants to acquire the age of 600 years, then he has to enter again into the female womb in order to have the right to be born; this is how he is born into the age of 600 years. This means that master has to practice sexual magic in order to develop as a 600 year old master.

As the sexual force has the power of forming organs, glands, viscera, nerves, etc., likewise the same sexual force has the

---

30 Abstract space, the unmanifested, also called sunyata, emptiness, void-ness. See glossary.

power of opening for us the powers of clairvoyance, clairaudience, telepathy, etc. The sexual force has the power to develop all of the lotus flowers of the soul. Thus, we attain the right to be born only by entering into the maternal womb.

We, the inhabitants of Eden, affirm that the right to be born is acquired only through sexual magic, thus anything that is not taught in this manner, in this way, is a worthless waste of time, because we exited Eden through the doors of sex, and only through the doors of sex can we enter into Eden again. Eden is sex itself.

The ages of the consciousness have their roots in sex.

Chapter 10

Astral Traveling

The human being is a triad of body, soul, and Spirit. The soul is the mediator between the Spirit and the body. A soul is acquired and a Spirit IS. The Innermost is the highest aspect within us; the Innermost is the Spirit. The *Testament of Learning* states:

> "Before the false dawn came over this earth, those who survived the hurricane and the storm gave praise to the Innermost, and to them appeared the heralds of the dawn." —Quoted from The Dayspring of Youth by M

Thus, the soul is between the terrestrial man and the Innermost. The soul is dressed with an ultra-sensible, material body with which it travels through space. This ultra-sensible, material body is the astral body.[31] Thus, the astral body has something of the human and something of the divine.

The astral body has its ultra-physiology and its ultra-pathology, which are intimately related with the grand sympathetic nervous system and our glands of internal secretion. The astral body is endowed with marvelous senses that we can utilize in order to investigate the great mysteries of life and death.

Mind, will, and consciousness are inside the astral body.

Our disciples must learn how to travel in their astral body.

The subject matter we are teaching in this chapter is a tremendous reality. Unfortunately, the brothers and sisters from all spiritual schools totally ignore the use and maneuvering of the astral body. We feel nothing but pain when we see that the brothers and sisters of those distinct organizations are so ignorant about the use and maneuvering of the astral body. The brothers and sisters from these distinct spiritual schools live in the astral plane with their consciousness asleep.

When a brother or sister enters into the path, the tenebrous ones from the lunar path attack them during their normal sleep. There, these brothers and sisters from the shadows

---

31 The form (body) we use in the fifth dimension, the world of dreams.

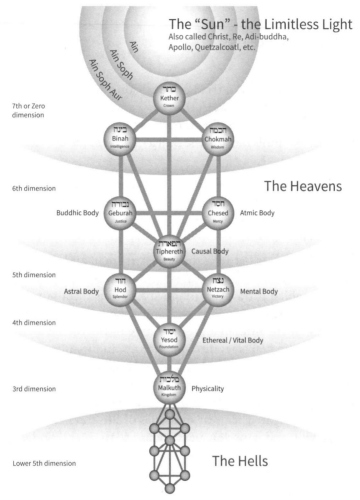

The "Sun" - the Limitless Light
Also called Christ, Re, Adi-buddha,
Apollo, Quetzalcoatl, etc.

Ain
Ain Soph
Ain Soph Aur

7th or Zero
dimension

כתר
Kether
Crown

בינה
Binah
Intelligence

חכמה
Chokmah
Wisdom

6th dimension

The Heavens

Buddhic Body

גבורה
Geburah
Justice

חסד
Chesed
Mercy

Atmic Body

תפארת
Tiphereth
Beauty
Causal Body

5th dimension

Astral Body

הוד
Hod
Splendor

נצח
Netzach
Victory

Mental Body

4th dimension

יסוד
Yesod
Foundation
Ethereal / Vital Body

3rd dimension

מלכות
Malkuth
Kingdom
Physicality

Lower 5th dimension

The Hells

SEVEN BODIES OF THE BEING ON THE TREE OF LIFE

assume the shape of the guru in order to divert these disciples. Now we can comprehend why it is a crime to not teach the disciples the practical use and maneuvering of the astral body.

It is necessary for our disciples to awaken their consciousness during the normal sleep so that they can defend themselves against the attacks of the tenebrous ones.

To acquire cognizance of the process of normal sleep is not dangerous; we must acquire cognizance of all of our natural functions.

Chapter 11

The Hill of Chapultepec

In this chapter, we see a fragment of a native Mexican codex depicting the Hill of Chapultepec. At the top of the hill, we see a grasshopper or cricket. In the august Rome of the Caesars, the cricket was sold in golden cages at costly prices.

There is an Aztec temple in "Jinn" state within the Hill of Chapultepec. The natives of Mexico would make long mystical pilgrimages to Chapultepec. We must now comprehend why the Aztecs considered this hill to be sacred.

THE HILL OF CHAPULTEPEC

By carefully observing the fragment of the Mexican codex of Chapultepec, we see two human beings floating above the hill. Those two beings are traveling in their astral bodies. A human head pronounces a note, represented by two beams of light that come out of his lips. That note is the sibilant and sharp sound of the cricket. That sound is the keynote of the Logos. The Logos sounds.

All of nature is the incarnation of the Word. The keynote of the cricket is the Word. That note is a chorus; our keynote vibrates within that ineffable chorus.

If a musician playing a musical instrument fortuitously played our keynote, we would instantly drop dead. Everything in nature has a keynote.

Whosoever wants to project in their astral body at will must enter into the state of slumber while mentally pronouncing the syllable "**LA**," mentally alternated with the syllable "**RA**." Pronounce these two syllables mentally and in an alternated and separate manner.

The student must try to listen to the sharp sound of the cricket. That sound emerges from within our brain cells. For this, it is necessary to have a serene mind, enough drowsiness, and focused attention on what one is doing.

If this exercise is performed well, then at the moment the student enters into the state of transition between vigil and sleep, the student will sense the sharp sound of the cricket within the brain. The student must then willfully enter a little more into the slumber state and increase the resonance of that sound. Then one will get up from the bed and exit the bedroom, heading towards the Temple of Chapultepec, or towards the Gnostic Church, or to any place one wishes to go.

When we state that the student must get up from the bed, this must be performed with action, since this is not a mental exercise. Indeed, this is not a matter of thinking that one is getting up; the disciple must perform it in action, without thinking. Thus, when getting up from the bed, the student must actually do it, because in order for the astral body to become free, the physical body must remain in the bed, and Nature will (as usual) perform the separation of the physical and astral bodies. This is why the student has to just get up from the bed, and that is all.

With this clue, our Gnostic disciples will travel in their astral body to the temples of mysteries of the White Lodge.[32]

If our disciples would like to have better concentration, it would be very appealing for them to have a little cricket in

---

32 The ancient collection of pure human beings who uphold and propogate the highest and most sacred of sciences. It is called "white" due to its purity and cleanliness (ie. the absence of pride, lust, anger, etc.). This "brotherhood" or "lodge" includes men and women of the highest order from every race, culture, creed and religion.

their bedrooms. The cricket can be kept in a small cage. This way, by focusing on the cricket's sound, it will resound within our brain sooner. With this clue, we can attend the great temples of the White Lodge.

Whosoever wants to learn esoteric science has to travel in the astral body, because esoteric science is studied in the internal worlds, and esoteric science is learned only by personally conversing with the masters.

The intellectual theories of this physical world are worthless; they only harm the mind and the brain.

The regent of the Temple of Chapultepec is the Master Rasmussen. Two guardians with flaming swords guard the entrance of the temple. Ancient wisdom is taught within this temple. The great masters of the White Lodge assemble in this temple.

Chapter 12

Clue for the Awakening of the Consciousness During Normal Sleep

There is no danger in the projection of the astral body, because everybody is projected in their astral body during normal sleep. Therefore, whosoever wants to awaken their consciousness during normal sleep must know the clue of **discernment**.

During normal sleep, every human being wanders in the internal worlds with their consciousness asleep. During normal sleep, the soul, enveloped by its astral body, abandons the physical body. This is how the ethereal body is able repair the dense physical body. We awaken from our natural sleep when the soul enters into the physical body.

In the internal worlds, the souls are occupied repeating their daily chores; there, they buy and sell like in the physical world.

During normal sleep, the souls of the living and the souls of the dead coexist. In the internal worlds, we see everything as in the physical world, i.e. the same sun, the same clouds, the same houses of the city: everything looks the same. Now, our Gnostic disciples will understand why the souls of the dead do not accept that they are physically dead. Likewise, our disciples will comprehend why the souls of the living buy and sell, work, etc., during their normal sleep.

By consciously projecting ourselves in the astral body, we can know about the mysteries of life and death, since every human being is unconsciously projected in the astral body during normal sleep. Therefore, if we awaken the consciousness during normal sleep, then we can know about the great mysteries of life and death.

There is a clue for the awakening of the consciousness during normal sleep. This clue for the awakening of the consciousness is that of discernment. Let us study it:

If while walking on a given street you unexpectedly find a friend or see objects that attract your attention, then perform a little jump with the intention of floating. Naturally, logic says that if you float, it is because you are wandering outside of your physical body. However, if you do not float, it is because you are doing the jump with your physical body.

During normal sleep, within the internal worlds, it so happens that we act the same way as we would within the body of flesh and bones, and if we add to this the fact that we see everything the same way as when we are in the physical world, then we will comprehend that it is only if we float or fly that we will be aware of the fact that we are in our astral body; we then achieve the awakening of our consciousness.

To that effect, this exercise must be practiced at every moment during the vigil state while in the presence of any intriguing matter, since what we perform during the vigil state we repeat during normal sleep. Thus, when through our subconsciousness we repeat this practice during normal sleep, then when performing the jump, the outcome will be that we will float in the astral body. This is how our consciousness will awaken and filled with happiness we will say, "I am in my astral body...!"

Thus, we can direct ourselves to the Holy Gnostic Church in order to converse with the angels, archangels, seraphim, prophets, masters, etc. This is how we receive instruction from the great masters of the White Lodge. This is how we can travel in the astral body throughout the infinite.

So, we do not need to destroy our minds with so many books and theories, since within the internal worlds we can receive the teachings from the masters.

When awakening from normal sleep, disciples must exert themselves to remember everything that they saw and heard during their normal sleep.

It is also necessary that our disciples learn how to interpret their internal experiences. To that effect, study the book of Daniel in the Bible; there, you will learn how to interpret internal experiences.

The slumber state and memory are the powers that allow us to know the great mysteries of live and death.

Dreams are "astral experiences." Dreams are reality.

Chapter 13
Negotiation

When the hour of death arrives, we abandon the physical body and enter into the internal worlds. After physical death, souls continue to believe that they are flesh and bones. After physical death, the souls do not accept even a little that they no longer belong to the world of the flesh. Only little by little are those souls of the dead awakening their consciousness, so that after a certain time those souls can enter into a new maternal womb in order to have the right to be born again in the world of the flesh. This is the law of metempsychosis through which all of us come to pay the evil deeds we performed in our former lives. Thus, if we performed good, we collect good, yet if performed evil, we collect evil.

"With what measure ye mete, it shall be measured to you again." —Matthew 7:2

The one who sows lightning will harvest tempests. Perform good deeds so that you can pay your debts.

By performing good deeds we can cancel our old debts from past incarnations. When an inferior law is transcended by a superior law, then the superior law washes away the inferior law.

The lion of the law is fought with the scale. The one who has capital can pay, and when he does, he is successful in his negotiation.

In the internal worlds, we can talk with the forty-two judges of karma. The chief of those forty-two judges is Anubis. The lords of karma reward or punish us.

We can also request credit from the judges of karma, but every credit has to be paid either with good deeds or with pain.

In order to arrange their negotiation, initiates must attend the palace of Anubis. In the internal worlds, our good deeds are symbolized by exotic coins. When we request the divine hierarchies for certain services, we then have to pay them with

WEIGHING OF THE HEART IN THE TEMPLE OF ANUBIS

those coins. If we want to replace those expended coins, we then have to perform good deeds.

The one who has capital in the internal worlds can perform marvelous things, because nothing is given to us for free: everything has its price. The true capital is made with good deeds. Thus, if we do not have capital, we then have to suffer the unutterable.

We must know the esoteric value of the coins. On a certain occasion we requested a service from the god of the wind, Ehecatl,[33] yet we had to pay him twenty-five esoteric cents for his service. Thus, if we add the numbers 2 + 5, we get 7. So, seven is the arcanum of expiation.[34] We had suffered a lot, patiently; thus we had earned that coin and we paid him with it. This is how a certain person that was making us suffer was sent away from us; this is how that miracle was performed. Yet, if we did have that coin, then Ehecatl would not have done that work, because nothing is given to us for free: everything has its price.

By working on behalf of humanity we can cancel our old debts. The only one who can forgive sins is Christ.

Only the most remarkable remorse, supreme internal repentance, and solemn oaths can lead us to forgiveness. Such a

---

33   Read *Aztec Christian Magic* by Samael Aun Weor.
34   Arcanum 7, Triumph, of the Tarot.

negotiation can only be arranged in the internal worlds with Christ.

Initiates must know the twenty-two Major Arcana of the Tarot[35] in order to arrange their negotiations. The numbers are added together as we already explained in the former example of Ehecatl.

A certain bodhisattva[36] whose mental body was sick was told: "Within 500 years you will be healed." Thus, 5 + 0 + 0 equals 5. At that time, the bodhisattva was recapitulating his first initiation of Major Mysteries, so when told that at 500 years he would be healed, he understood that he would be healed with the fifth initiation of Major Mysteries. Thus, when that bodhisattva reached the fifth initiation, he was told: "You have already suffered much for three years; now, you will be better dressed." Three is our triune Spirit.

That bodhisattva had spiritually suffered very much because he was fallen. Thus, when he spiritually rose again, his purple tunic was returned to him, and spiritually he became better dressed.

---

35 Read *Tarot and Kabbalah* by Samael Aun Weor.
36 An initiate on the straight path. See glossary.

The Magician

ARCANUM ONE OF THE ETERNAL TAROT

Chapter 14

The Twenty-two Major Arcana and Astral Projections

Arcanum 1: The Magician. The man.

Arcanum 2: The woman. Esoteric science.

Arcanum 3: The Heavenly Mother. Material and spiritual production.

Arcanum 4: The Emperor. Progress, success.

Arcanum 5: The law. Karma, the Hierophant.

Arcanum 6: The Lovers. Victory, good luck.

Arcanum 7: The Chariot of war. Expiation, pain, bitterness.

Arcanum 8: The number of Job. Ordeals and suffering.

Arcanum 9: The Hermit. Initiation.

Arcanum 10: The Wheel of Fortune spins. Retribution.

Arcanum 11: The tamed lion. Persuasion.

Arcanum 12: The Apostolate. Sacrifice.

Arcanum 13: Death and Resurrection.

Arcanum 14: Temperance. Matrimony, Association.

Arcanum 15: Typhon Baphomet. Amorous failure.

Arcanum 16: The Fulminated Tower. Punishment, terrible downfall.

Arcanum 17: The star of Hope.

Arcanum 18: Hidden enemies. Twilight.

Arcanum 19: Radiant Sun. Success.

Arcanum 20: Resurrection.

Arcanum 21: Insanity. Failure.

Arcanum 22: The crown of life.

The Hierarch

All internal calculations, all internal additions, are interpreted with these twenty-two major arcana. The divine Master Jesus told a disciple of ours that she would have to remain incarnated working in the Great Work for 32 more years. When the numbers of this quantity (32) are added, we get the Arcanum 5 of the Tarot: the law. This means that this sister will have to remain incarnated until her destiny is fulfilled in accordance with the Law.

The children of this perverse luciferic humanity are begotten with the Arcanum 15 and die with the Arcanum 13.

Passion

Immortality

Astral Projections

Astral projections and Kabbalah are an integral whole.

There is a state of transition between vigil and sleep; every human being is involuntarily projected out of the physical body in that moment. Yet, by paying attention, we can be voluntarily and consciously projected out of the physical body in that moment of transition between vigil and sleep. To that effect, what is important is to watch our sleep.

This is how we can astrally get up from our bed and leave towards the Gnostic Church. Our Lord the Christ officiates in the Gnostic Church.

So, all our disciples have to do is watch their sleep and get up from their bed in the moment when they enter into a slumber state. This must be performed with actions. Do not assume that this is a mental exercise, and do not think that you must get up mentally: we repeat again that we must get up with action. We must get up naturally, as when we physically do it every morning.

This is how we can transport ourselves in the astral body to the White Lodge in order to study at the feet of the master. This is not dangerous because everybody comes out in their astral body. This is better than stuffing our heads (like bookworms) with books and theories. Too many theories confuse; theories falsify the mind and damage the brain.

Esoteric science is studied in the internal worlds. Therefore, the one who does not know how to be willingly projected in the astral body does not know esotericism.

It is necessary to study the twenty-two major arcana and learn them by memory in order to understand the esoteric language of the initiates in the astral plane.

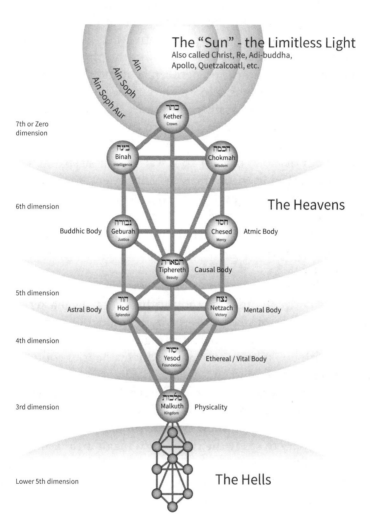

The "Sun" - the Limitless Light
Also called Christ, Re, Adi-buddha, Apollo, Quetzalcoatl, etc.

Ain
Ain Soph
Ain Soph Aur

כתר
Kether
Crown

7th or Zero dimension

בינה
Binah
Intelligence

חכמה
Chokmah
Wisdom

6th dimension

The Heavens

Buddhic Body

גבורה
Geburah
Justice

חסד
Chesed
Mercy

Atmic Body

תפארת
Tiphereth
Beauty

Causal Body

5th dimension

Astral Body

הוד
Hod
Splendor

נצח
Netzach
Victory

Mental Body

4th dimension

יסוד
Yesod
Foundation

Ethereal / Vital Body

3rd dimension

מלכות
Malkuth
Kingdom

Physicality

Lower 5th dimension

The Hells

DIMENSIONS ON THE TREE OF LIFE

Chapter 15

Jinn States

Human beings can bring their physical bodies out of this chemical region; meaning, human beings can place their physical bodies into the internal worlds.

The law of gravity reigns in this chemical region, yet the law of cosmic levitation reigns in the internal worlds.

In the internal worlds, we can float with the physical body.

The clue to enter with our physical body into the internal worlds is voluntary somnambulism.[37] Thus, while resting in his bed, the disciple will enter into a slumber state and will get up in the same way the somnambulist does. Somnambulists get up from their bed while maintaining their slumber state; thus, while in their sleepy state, somnambulists work and walk. Therefore, the disciple that wants to enter into the internal worlds with the physical body has to imitate the somnambulists. After getting up from the bed, the disciple will make a small jump with the intention of floating; if the disciple floats and if sees oneself as being excessively fat, it is because one succeeded.

This is how our disciples will walk upon the waters of the seas in the same way as Christ. When Christ walked upon the waters, he was carrying his body in the Jinn state. Precisely, this is what is called the "Jinn state."

If Peter had not doubted, he could have also walked upon the waters in the Jinn state. What is necessary is to have faith and to be a little sleepy; that is all.

Thus, with an intense faith and a little bit of sleep, we can place our physical bodies into a Jinn state. Peter became an expert of the Jinn state with the help of an angel and a little bit of sleep; this is how Peter liberated himself from the chains in his prison, to be safe and sound.

If we invoke the god Harpocrates,[38] he will come to our call. We can invoke this angel with the mantra **HAR PO CRAT IST**.

---

37 Also called sleepwalking.
38 See glossary.

JESUS WALKS ON THE WATER

"But the ship was now in the midst of the sea, tossed with waves: for the wind was contrary. And in the fourth watch of the night Jesus went unto them, walking on the sea. And when the disciples saw him walking on the sea, they were troubled, saying, It is a spirit; and they cried out for fear. But straightway Jesus spake unto them, saying, Be of good cheer; it is I; be not afraid. And Peter answered him and said, Lord, if it be thou, bid me come unto thee on the water. And he said, Come. And when Peter was come down out of the ship, he walked on the water, to go to Jesus. But when he saw the wind boisterous, he was afraid; and beginning to sink, he cried, saying, Lord, save me. And immediately Jesus stretched forth his hand, and caught him, and said unto him, O thou of little faith, wherefore didst thou doubt?"

—Matthew 14:24-31

We can place our physical bodies in the Jinn state with the help of this angel. We can also transport ourselves to any place of the world in a few moments with the help of this angel.

The egg has special powers that allow us to place the physical body into the Jinn state. Procedure: the disciple will slightly boil an egg in water; in other words, he will cook it for a very short time. Thereafter, he will make a hole in the egg on the narrow, conical side, then by means of a very thin device, he will extract the yoke and white. The shell of the egg possesses the powers of the god Harpocrates.

The forces of HAR PO CRAT IST are a variant of the Christic forces.

Sequentially, the disciple will place the eggshell on the bed next to one's head; then the disciple will imagine oneself inside that shell. The disciple will invoke HAR PO CRAT IST and will ask Harpocrates to transport one with the physical body to whatever place the disciple wishes to go. Thus, while keeping the slumber state as a somnambulist, the disciple must get up and hold the eggshell, and then one will leave the bedroom while saying: "Harpocrates, help me, because I am leaving with my physical body."

This is how the disciples of our Gnostic groups will place their physical bodies into the internal worlds. This is how they will go in bones and flesh to the Holy Gnostic Church. This is how they will receive the communion of bread and wine and attend the "Praetor." This is how disciples will know the great mysteries without the necessity of damaging their minds with the theories and sterile discussions of spiritual schools.

In the Jinn state, there are enchanted lakes, Jinn lakes; likewise, there are mountains, temples, towns, and cities. On the eastern prairies of Colombia, a city is in Jinn state named "Manoa." On all the mountains of the world, there are many temples of the White Lodge in the Jinn state.

Our Gnostic Sumum Supremum Sanctuarium on La Sierra Nevada of Santa Marta, Colombia will eventually enter into the Jinn state. Wherever there is an enchanted (Jinn state) temple, mountain, or lake, the forces of HAR PO CRAT IST are in intense activity.

Regarding Jinn states, Gnostic students must never get weary, since some will triumph immediately, yet for others it will take years in order to achieve success. Understand that tenacity and patience are the foundation of any progress.

With these practices of HAR PO CRAT IST, our disciples will accumulate within their vehicles that marvelous force of HAR PO CRAT IST.

Later in time, our disciples will organize those marvelous energies in order to place their physical bodies in Jinn state. Marvelous things can be performed with those forces.

Chapter 16
Clue to Invoke the Physical Body From a Distance

Those who know how to project their astral body can invoke their physical body from a distance. This is performed with the help of our Innermost. Pray to your Innermost as follows:

"Thou who art thyself, thou who art my real Being, I beseech thee, bring me my physical body."

This is how the Innermost will bring the disciple's physical body in the Jinn state. Thus, no matter how far away the disciple's astral body might be, the disciple's physical body will arrive there.

The physical body will humbly arrive before us. It will come dressed with its underwear or night clothes; it will come dressed with the same clothes as we left it in the bed.

The moments when we find ourselves face to face with our physical body are astounding. Since in those moments we are in the astral body, we must command our physical body to perform the following action: "Physical body of mine, jump, and hover over my head, and enter within me, through my pineal gland." Then, the physical body will obey and will enter through the pineal gland; this gland is situated in the superior part of the brain. This is how our physical body will come to our call.

This is how we can function with the physical body in remote places. While in the Jinn state, we can visit the temples of mysteries in order to learn the doctrine at the feet of the master. If you want special help, then when you are outside of your physical body perform the following invocation:

PRAYER

"I believe in God, I believe in Christ, and I believe in Samael.[39] *Samael, bring me my physical body. Samael, bring me my physical body. Samael, bring me my physical body."*

Repeat this prayer many times, and I, Samael, your humble servant, will come to your call in order to bring you your physical body in the Jinn state. This is how I will serve you, beloved disciples, with the condition of upright conduct. We the masters are willing to help all human beings to enter again into the internal worlds.

"Ask and it shall be given you. Knock and it shall be opened unto you." —Matthew 7:7

Disciples who want to learn how to willingly project themselves in the astral body will receive our help if they invoke this humble servant, Samael, the author of this book. At the moment of your practice, pray as follows:

"I believe in God, I believe in Christ, and I believe in Samael. Samael, take me out of my physical body."

Pray this repeatedly during the moments of falling asleep. Thus, when you feel a certain lassitude, in other worlds, when you feel lethargic and sleepy, it is because I, Samael, am helping you. At that moment, perform a supreme effort of will and get up from your bed; I, Samael Aun Weor, will take you to the Gnostic Church.

"Ask and it shall be given you. Knock and it shall be opened unto you." —Matthew 7:7

At these moments, evolution is returning towards the great light, and we, the humble servants of this wretched humanity, are resolved to help all the human beings who want to enter again into the internal worlds.

---

39 Samael is the Innermost Being of Samael Aun Weor. Samael is not a terrestrial person, but a Logos. Samael Aun Weor is his bodhisattva.

Chapter 17

Meditation

There are many disciples who, in spite of having known our clues for astral projection, have not learned how to project themselves at will. The failure of these students is due to the fact that they already lost the powers of their astral body. These students have no other choice but to be submit themselves to the discipline of meditation: this is how they will recover their lost powers.

Meditation is a technique in order to receive information. When the sage is submerged into internal meditation, it is because he is searching for information. The chakras enter into activity through meditation.

Meditation encompasses three steps:

First, concentration.

Second, meditation.

Third, Samadhi.[40]

Before starting our practice of concentration, we must sit comfortably; we can also perform our practice lying down in bed. All types of earthly thoughts must withdraw from our mind; thoughts must fall dead at the doors of the temple.[41] Before concentration, we must also empty our mind, to not think of anything. When these prerequisites have been fulfilled, we then start our practice of internal concentration.

Thus, we separate our mind from the things of the physical world, and we inwardly direct it towards our Innermost.

> *"Know ye not that your bodies are the temple of the living God, and that the Spirit of God dwells in you?"*
> —1 Corinthians 3:16

The Spirit of God within us is the Innermost. We must love the Innermost. We must adore the Innermost. We must render

---

40 See glossary.
41 "...so must all earthly thoughts fall dead before the fane." —The Voice of the Silence

cult to the Innermost. We must profoundly meditate on the Innermost.

Then, while immersed in profound meditation, we must provoke drowsiness: this profound drowsiness will lead us to the state of samadhi. Thus, we will leave the physical body without knowing how or at what time. This is how we will enter into the internal worlds. Dreams are legitimate internal experiences.

If we want to study a plant, we concentrate on it, we meditate on it, we provoke drowsiness, and we fall asleep; then in dream visions we see that the plant is transformed and becomes a beautiful child or a beautiful creature: this is the elemental of the plant. We then can converse with that vegetable elemental. This is how we can gather information about the properties of that plant, about its magical powers, etc. The vegetable elemental will answer our questions; this is how we will receive the requested information.

So, meditation will awaken our esoteric powers. Meditation provokes fundamental changes in the astral body. Then, during our normal sleep, there will be moments in which we will be conscious, and later in time we will say, "I am out of my physical body. I am in the astral body." This is how little by little we will acquire "continuous consciousness." Finally, the day will arrive in which the student will be able to utilize our clues in order to be consciously projected in the astral body at will. One will have then re-conquered one's lost powers.

During their hours of sleep, all human beings travel in their astral bodies. Their dreams are astral experiences. We must learn to remember our astral experiences. Thus when awakening from our normal sleep, we will practice a retrospective exercise in order to remember all those things that we did during normal sleep. During normal sleep, our disciples transport themselves to the White Lodges. During normal sleep, our disciples transport themselves to remote places.

Therefore, all our disciples must learn how to interpret their dreams, since even the most absurd dreams are absolutely symbolic.

Our internal experiences are interpreted based on the law of philosophical analogies, on the law of the analogy of contraries, on the law of correspondences, and on the law of numerology. The one who wants to advance in these studies must persistently study the book of Daniel in the Bible. The system of Daniel teaches us how to interpret our internal experiences.

DANTE BEING INSTRUCTED IN THE INTERNAL WORLDS. DRAWING BY BOTTICELLI.

Chapter 18
The Tenebrous Ones Disagree

The tenebrous ones disagree with our teachings; they state that it is not yet time to learn how to consciously project ourselves in the astral body. The tenebrous ones state that people must not yet enter into the internal worlds. These tenebrous ones sustain that we first have to dominate the physical body. This is how the tenebrous ones close the doors to the internal worlds for this wretched, suffering humanity. This is how the tenebrous ones close the doors to the superior worlds for the aspirants to the light, and after having closed the doors, they enslave them within their intellectual systems.

In the Middle Ages, the doors of access to the internal worlds were closed.[42] At that time it was necessary, so that humans would dedicate themselves to the physical world in order for them to acquire cognizance of their individuality.

Nirvana[43] has epochs of activity and epochs of profound repose. On February 19, 1919 at 3:40 PM, Nirvana entered into activity. From that moment the evolving life started its return towards the great light. So, basically, in these moments it is outdated to close the doors of access to the superior worlds.

In these moments, the hierarchies of Nirvana are struggling to make this humanity return towards the internal worlds.

At this moment, the planet Mercury is emerging from a cosmic night. Presently, the lords of Mercury are teaching human beings how to project themselves in the astral body. As the planet Mercury emerges more and more from its cosmic night, the lords of Mercury will become more and more active.

However, the tenebrous ones oppose this great cosmic law by stating that to project oneself in the astral body is "dangerous." They commit the crime of opposing the hierarchies of Mercury. This is how they close the door of access to the internal worlds upon this wretched, suffering humanity.

---

42 This was the Piscean era, which ended in 1962.
43 Sanskrit, here used to refer to the heavens, the superior regions of nature.

In the age of Aquarius,[44] all human beings will know how to consciously enter and leave their physical bodies at will. Yet, in order to enslave the souls within their intellectual systems, the tenebrous ones oppose this great law.

---

44 The Aquarian era begain February 4, 1962.

Chapter 19

The Tenebrous Ones Close the Doors of Eden

The tenebrous ones state that sexual magic must not be taught to humanity, alleging that humanity is not yet prepared for it. In this way, they close the doors of Eden to this wretched, suffering humanity. This is how the tenebrous ones close the doors of Eden to the souls who long for the light. Then, after having stated to the naive aspirants that sexual magic is "dangerous," the tenebrous ones enclose them within their complicated breathing systems. This is how they close the doors of Eden upon the suffering ones, and thereafter they enslave them within their intellectual systems. The tenebrous ones strive at any cost, no matter what, to avoid the sexual problem, because the tenebrous ones hate the doors of sex.

In ancient times, it was prohibited to divulge the Great Arcanum.[45] Those who intended to divulge it were condemned to penalty of death. Yet, today it is outdated to deny the Great Arcanum of sexual magic to humanity, because the divine hierarchies are teaching sexual magic so that humanity can return into Eden. Nevertheless, the tenebrous ones are opposed, and they make superhuman efforts in order to make humanity turn away from the doors of sex.

The tenebrous ones are enemies of the great law. The tenebrous ones defend their seminal ejaculation.[46] The tenebrous ones divert the wretched aspirants in order to enclose them within their intellectual systems.

---

45 The knowledge of sexual transmutation that was secret previous to the Aquarian era.
46 Orgasm, whether in males or females.

JESUS BLESSING THE "CHILDREN." IN ESOTERICISM, CHILDREN SYMBOLIZE
THE PURITY AND BEAUTY OF GENUINE MASTERS.

"Except ye be converted, and become as little children, ye shall not
enter into the kingdom of heaven." —Jesus, Matthew 18:3

Chapter 20

The Two Closed Doors

By uttering sublime and ineffable phrases, the tenebrous ones state that sexual magic is dangerous, thus this is how they divert wretched human beings away from the doors of Eden. By uttering words filled with sweetness, the tenebrous ones state that to project oneself in the astral body at will is dangerous. This is how the tenebrous ones close these two doors to liberation for the wretched souls. The tenebrous ones close the two doors of happiness, and thereafter they enclose their victims within their intellectual systems.

The tenebrous systems are usually filled with reasoning and philosophical words. The intellect is the most powerful weapon that the Luciferics use in order to impede their victims' escape from the abyss.

The abyss is filled with sincere, yet mistaken ones. The abyss is filled with people that have very good intentions. Many tenebrous ones from the abyss are sincere, yet mistaken.

Usually, the tenebrous ones believe that they can know God with their intellect. We, Gnostics, state that only God knows God. We need to abandon reasoning and intellect in order to attain union with God. We need to have the mind of a child in order to attain the union with God. We need sexual magic in order to enter into Eden.

We need to learn how to project ourselves in the astral body in order to converse with the Innermost. We need to study at the feet of the master.

Beginners must fall asleep while invoking the Lord Jehovah and pray to him to take them out in their astral body, thus the Lord Jehovah will take them out of their body. The student must get up in the moments of slumber. "Help yourself so that we can help you." Jehovah always helps us, thus let us help ourselves.

JUDGMENT OF CHRIST. NOTE THE DAGGER. ENGRAVING BY ALBRECHT DURER

"When we enter into the true path of
initiation, then all the spiritual devotees
turn against us. Christ was crucified by
the spiritual devotees of his time."

Chapter 21

Preparation for Initiation

1

The disciple who wants to enter the straight, narrow, and difficult path that leads us to the light has to withdraw from all spiritual schools. Those schools are filled with "sublime crimes." Those schools are golden cages filled with "very beautiful, poisonous vipers." Mystical evilness is very abundant in those schools.

The worst crimes registered in the penal code are committed under the shelter of the divine phrase "universal fraternity."

It is distressful for us to state this, but complacency with crime is also a crime. It is as bad to be silent when one must talk as to talk when one must be silent. We would like to be silent, yet one not only pays karma for the evil things that were done, but also for the good things that were left undone when these things could have been done. Therefore, we cannot be silent about this. We love humanity very much; thus, we need to point out crime, to touch the wound with the finger in order not to fall into the crime of being complacent with crime. If we would not say these things we would put a horrible karma (the karma of accomplices and cowards) on ourselves. So, the truth, although harsh, is our best friend.

All spiritual schools, orders, and lodges are delectable gardens within which are nests of dangerous vipers and poisonous flowers filled with perfume. Within those schools where the devotees are filled with hypocrisy and fanaticism, there are ineffable enchantments that lead us to the abyss, sublime theories that can lead us to the precipice, and sweet smiles that carry us to disgrace. Indeed, the opium of theories is more dangerous than death.

Spiritual devotees hug with one hand and with the other they stab the back with the sharp dagger of treason.

Spiritual devotees always cover their worst evilness with smiles and very sweet words. We do not have the intention of criticizing any person in particular because that is wrong; this is why we speak in a general manner for the good of the Great Work of the Father.

We have known horrible cases. We knew the case of a certain hypocritical pharisee[47] who passed himself off as Jesus Christ. He founded an order of black magic, and later he alleged that he was uniting all the schools, orders, sects, creeds, and lodges within a universal fraternity—and he was the center of it all, naturally.

We knew about another subject who took the name of K. H.[48] in order to declare that he was an avatar,[49] and that he would reunite all the schools under his scepter.

All these types of opportunist subjects usually found black lodges under the shelter of the beautiful phrase "universal fraternity."

We cannot remain silent about this, because complacency with crime is also a crime.

Almost all the spiritual devotees are totally petrified by their intellect. Almost all of them remain frozen in the spiritual theories of the nineteenth century, and filled with pride, fear, and arrogance, they reject the secret doctrine of our Lord the Christ.

Therefore, we advise our disciples to be very careful. It is better to withdraw from these types of ladies and gentlemen, because they are dangerous and deceitful. Whosoever betrays the Christ falls into the abyss.

In these times appear many false Christs,[50] and those who affiliate to them commit the crime of high treason.

Jesus Christ is the leader of all souls. This great master lives in oriental Tibet.

Do not forget that crime is hidden in the incense of prayer. Yes, crime is hidden in the mixture of perfumes and litanies.

---

47 Christian symbol of someone who appears pious, but is not.
48 This was not the authentic K.H. (Kout Humi), but an imposter.
49 Incarnation of divinity.
50 "Beware of false prophets, which come to you in sheep's clothing, but inwardly they are ravening wolves." —Matthew 7:15

False Christs have sublime appearances.

To state that "this is good" or "that is evil" is an easy matter, yet it is very difficult to have cognizance of good from evil and evil from good.

Black lodges are filled with sincere but mistaken people. The abyss is filled with people with very good intentions.

When we enter into the true path of initiation, then all the spiritual devotees turn against us. Christ was crucified by the spiritual devotees of his time.

Many enter the path and thereafter they no longer want to continue working in order to fulfill the needs of every good citizen. Those wretched beings neglect their duties towards their family, the world, and themselves. We have hear them say phrases like, "Money is vain," "This is the world of maya (illusion)," "I am no longer interested in the things of the world," etc. This is how these wretched disciples fail because they do not know how to fulfill their duties. This is how these devotees of the path move away from initiation, precisely because they do not know how to fulfill their duties as simple citizens.

Our disciples will now comprehend why we stated that crime is also hidden within the incense of prayer.

The one who enters the path must first be a model spouse, a model parent, a model child, a model citizen, a magnificent grandchild, and a patriarchal grandparent, etc. The one who does not know how to fulfill one's duties as a simple citizen cannot tread the path of the great mysteries.

Many disciples forget the good manners of a sincere and honorable gentleman or lady, and become truly irresponsible and even dangerous individuals.

People that had never stolen become thieves of books and money when they entered the path. The younger devotees who enter the spiritual path steal books, or they borrow them and never return them, etc. Others cheat their disciples; they borrow money from them and thereafter they steal it, etc.

Under the shade of the word "fraternity," all the crimes mentioned in the penal code are committed. There are those who take other people's money and allege that the money is for good deeds. There are those who criticize those who work, supposedly because everything is vanity, etc.

This is how devotees close the path that leads to the great mysteries to themselves.

On the path, there are many devotees who commit adultery, justifying themselves with phrases like these, "My spouse is refractory to the spiritual teachings." "The other partner I have agrees with my ideas." "The other is spiritual, and is the only one with whom I can practice sexual magic in order to attain in-depth realization," etc., and a thousand other mystical phrases. This is how adulterers shut the doors of the temple upon themselves.

Many devotees of the path use sexual magic as a pretext to seduce many naive devotees. This is how these mystical adulterers withdraw from the altar of initiation and fall into the abyss.

Sexual magic can only be practiced between husband and wife in legitimately constituted homes.

Many devotees steal the neighbor's spouse supposedly because the law of karma commanded it. All of these crimes have led thousands of spiritual devotees into the abyss.

When we went to a certain country to fulfill a mission, we were assaulted by certain spiritual elements who visited us in order to criticize our books, and to give us imperative orders and to insult us in our own home. In ordinary life, no gentleman or lady would dare to enter into someone else's home in order to give orders and to insult the owner of the house, because they would find themselves involved in a domestic scene and in a problem with the police. Unfortunately, the devotees of the path fall into these states of terrible irresponsibility.

Some even abandon the most basic laws of urban life and wander around the streets with their clothes dirty and in the most complete untidiness, and as a pretext they boast of being spiritual and rejecting of the vanities of the world. However, this is called degeneration. This is how, with their pessimistic exposure, the devotees of the path drive away many people from the path.

We must always dress in a decent manner, not because of pride or vanity, but simply out of respect to our neighbors.

The system to achieve in-depth self-realization has nothing to do with letting our beard or hair grow, or going around dirty on the streets. The one who wants to attain self-realization must start by being an upright and decent gentleman or lady.

The one who wants to attain self-realization has to practice sexual magic and tread the path of the most perfect sanctity.

Within most spiritual schools, devotees speak ill of their fellows, and argue like parrots. This is not right. No one has the right to judge anyone, because no one is perfect. Christ already told us:

> *"Judge not, that ye be not judged; for with what judgment ye judge, ye shall be judged: and with what measure ye mete, it shall be measured to you again..."*
> —Matthew 7:1-2

Thus, we do not have the right to criticize the neighbor's defects. Gossip and slander have filled the world with pain and bitterness. Defamation is worse than stealing.

2

Discussions and polemics have ruined many spiritual schools.

When two individuals argue, what they have is pride and arrogance in their minds. Both want to demonstrate their boasted superiority to one another. Both have Satan enthroned in their minds.

We must always respectfully express our concept, and allow our listener the freedom to accept or reject our concept. Everybody is free to think as they please, and we cannot exercise power over our neighbor's mind, because that would be black magic.

Intellectual discussion is luciferic and demonic.

We need to have the mind of a child in order to enter into the Major Mysteries. We need to be like children in our minds and hearts. We need to be perfect as our Father who is in heaven is perfect.[51]

The great mysteries are not achievable through vain intellectualisms. The Major Mysteries are achievable with the heart of a child. We have known great masters of the White Lodge who are totally illiterate.

Another danger that dishonors the devotees of the path is envy. Those who become filled with envy because of the progress of others become like "Judas,"[52] they sell their instructors for thirty pieces of silver. In spiritual schools and lodges, the envious people look at the clock and ring the bell in order to sabotage the lecture and the teachings of good lecturers. This is how crime is hidden within the incense of litanies.

On a certain occasion the venerable Master Morya told us: "The union with our Innermost is very difficult. The task is very hard. Out of two who attempt to achieve the union with their Innermost, only one achieves it," because as the poet Guillermo Valencia stated, "Crime is hidden amongst the poems."

Indeed, Master Morya was right, since crime dresses itself like a saint. Crime dresses itself as a martyr. Crime dresses itself as an apostle, etc.

This is why it is so difficult to achieve the union with the Innermost, since this is the path of the razor's edge.[53]

Our disciples must make an inventory of their defects and thereafter meditate for two months on each defect, successively; in this manner they will eventually be finished with all their defects. Whosoever wants to finish with all of their defects at the same time will not be able to finish off any of them.

This path is very difficult. Christ already stated it:

> "Among a thousand who seek me, one finds me. Among a thousand who find me, one follows me. And among a thousand who follow me, one is mine." —Bhagavad-Gita

---

51 "Be ye therefore perfect, even as your Father which is in heaven is perfect." —Jesus, Matthew 5:48

52 The disciple who betrayed Jesus.

53 "The path is as sharp as a razor, impassable and difficult to travel..." — Katha Upanishad

For every step that we take in the development of our esoteric powers, we must take a thousand steps on the path of
sanctity.

3

Those who want to enter into the Major Mysteries must
abandon the animal intellect. Animal intellect is luciferic and
demonic.

The great masters have minds like children. We must live in
great awe and tremble as if in the presence of God. We must
terminate our intellectual pride. We must have the innocent
and simple mind of an infant. We must not conceal crimes.

From time to time, disciples send us letters demanding that
we dominate the mind of this or that woman for them, alleging that they just want to bring these women to the right path.
This is how their lust is hidden within the incense of prayer.
By demanding enticement, by demanding of us works of black
magic, this is how they tempt the elder brothers.

No one has the right to violate the neighbor's mind, because
that is a crime. The neighbor's freedom must be respected.

Therefore, let us clarify this chapter by stating that the
entrance of the abyss has three doors: anger, covetousness, and
lust.[54] Anger disguises itself as a judge, covetousness is hidden
in good intentions, and lust wears a mystical robe.

Driven by lust, female spiritual devotees of the path sit on
the lap of male "devotees of the light" and use "innocence"
as a pretext in order to kiss and hug each other. This is how
crime is hidden within the incense of prayer.

Another critical crime is that of ingratitude. A dog is given
food and it is grateful, yet many devotees of the path are
ungrateful. If an authentic master teaches them, all that they
give back as payment are persecutions, hatred, and calumnies.

We know the case of a spiritual devotee who, when he was
hungry and unemployed, always met a charitable soul who
gave him food and shelter; however, soon after he got a new
job. Then, without regret, he turned against his charitable

---

54 Bhagavad Gita 16:21

supporters. Sometimes he publicly slandered them or attacked them. This is how this devotee paid with the coin of ingratitude. Nevertheless, he always found a philosophical excuse for his crime. Cynically, he stated, "I do not owe anything to anyone. Life is what provides everything. Thus, my charitable supporters are merely instruments of the great life. Therefore, I do not owe them anything."

Others abandon their mother or elderly father, saying, "All beings are my family. I do not care about my parents. I am a rebel, etc." This is how they hide their crime within the incense of prayer.

Others abandon their wretched wives and children, with the purpose, they allege, of following the spiritual life. This is how these hypocritical pharisees fall into the abyss of black magic.

Others allege that their mission is to unite devotees from all organizations in order to organize the great universal fraternity. However, school monopolizers are what these merchants of souls truly are.

Commonly, these monopolizers let their beards or hair grow, and thereafter, like hypocritical pharisees, preaching variety within unity, they boast of being like Jesus Christ and establish tenebrous orders "of Aquarius."

The cunning of these hypocrites is so refined that they skillfully place themselves in the center as living units. Then, as Jesus Christs in person and with the pretext of uniting all schools, creeds, and religions, they seduce the naive. Indeed, in the presence of these tenebrous swindlers, what we have to watch more closely is our money.

These bandits of the tenebrous orders of Aquarius have collected many real estate properties throughout America with the pretext of establishing "ashrams," initiatic colleges, etc. Naive, fanatical people, who deliver their lands to these tenebrous ones of Aquarius, are never missing. Thereafter, these tenebrous ones live very comfortable lives, even in Paris, supported by their enjoyable, mystifying income.

With flip-flops instead of shoes and long shirts falling to their knees, these tenebrous ones go arm in arm as roman curia, as missionaries of a horrible business. They aspire to have long beards when they receive the right of not shaving their face; thereafter they boast of being gentile gurus and major brothers and sisters. Some of them boast of being the reincarnation of Saint Peter, and their tenebrous followers of Aquarius even kiss their feet. How filthy those hypocritical loafers are!

Gnostics cannot simultaneously sit at the table of angels and the table of demons; we have to define ourselves.

If we want to enter into Eden, we have to enter through the same door that we exited; this door is sex. There is no other door. We have to enter through the same door we exited.

All the spiritual schools presently in the world are in the abyss, and their fleeting devotees are like school butterflies who prostitute spirituality.

On one occasion, we visited a spiritual temple. We then saw how a demon entered into a medium, and while passing as Jesus Christ, he spoke filled with sweetness, and all the listeners, full of a terrible fanaticism, worshiped him. This is what spiritism or spiritualism is: black magic. This is the abyss. It is difficult to state this, yet, it is the truth, and we must not be complacent with crime.

All the spiritualistic schools, organizations, and orders of this century are in the abyss.

4

The corruption amongst spiritual devotees is deplorable. On one occasion, when we were advising a spiritual devotee about the practices of sexual magic in the United States, she cynically told us — in front of her husband — that she would only practice sexual magic with her guru. We objected to her answer by telling her that sexual magic can only be practiced between spouses. Indeed, in the ordinary world, no profane adulterer would ever dare to give such a dimwitted answer in front of her husband. However, only the irresponsible spiritual devotees are driven to this type of whimsical, barbaric answer. What is worse is that the guru of this wretched devotee was only a charming impostor, a mystifying bandit, an executioner of souls.

On another occasion, we met a morbid mystic who sexually seduced many (female) devotees under the pretext of helping them. That wicked man fell in love with his wife's own daughter (his step-daughter) and seduced her. That wicked man was a fallen bodhisattva. Fallen bodhisattvas are worse than demons.

The majority of the tenebrous brothers and sisters of Aquarius are wicked men who are going around teaching black magic.

I know a fallen bodhisattva from Bogotá (Colombia), who formed a sect of imbecilic eunuchs who hate sex. Thus, through this awful way, this wretched brother harms homes and closes the doors of Eden for others.

So, in this day and age, it is very dangerous to just simply follow someone. What is best is to seek the inner master.[55] The best thing is to follow our "I am."[56] The best thing is to learn how to travel in the astral body in order to visit the temples of the White Lodge and to receive the teachings directly in the temple.

5

Preparation for initiation is very rigorous. Our disciples must live alert and vigilant like a watchman in the time of war. Cleanse your minds. Do not allow yourself to be deceived by the wicked.

Know, sisters and brothers, that modern intellectualism is of the wicked.

Scientism of these times:

> *"Even the wicked, whose coming is after the working of Satan with all power and signs and lying wonders..."*
>
> —2 Thessalonians 2:9

---

55   The Innermost, also called Atman, the inner buddha, etc.

56   Sanskrit सो ऽहम् "Soham" a very common phrase in the Tantras, Upanishads, etc. and a foundational expression of Vedic philosophy.

...airplanes, atomic bombs, false marvels in physiology, biology, medicine, chemistry, etc., all these miracles of science are false. Do not believe in those false miracles of the wicked.

> *"Let no man deceive you by any means: for that day (the day of the advent of Jesus Christ) shall not come, except there come a falling away first, and that man of sin be revealed, the son of perdition (this perverse humanity); Who opposeth and exalteth himself above all that is called God, or that is worshipped; so that he as God sitteth in the temple of God, shewing himself that he is God."* —2 Thessalonians 2:3-4

Brothers and sisters, I advise you: do not believe in the miracles of the wicked; these are lying wonders.

Modern scientists know nothing but mere illusory appearances. They do not know the human organism.

While in the Jinn state, the human body can fly, can pass through a wall from one side to the other without either the body or the wall getting hurt or dirty. It can also take the shape of plants, rocks, animals, and become small or large at will.[57]

About our former assertions, the wicked, the scientists of the Antichrist, do not know anything, since they base their entire physiology, pathology, biology, etc. on false appearances. Upon their false appearances they edify their science and perform their lying wonders.

This is how their materialism opposes and exalts itself above all that is called God, or that which is worshiped, so that they, as God, can sit in the temple of God.

When you Christify yourselves, you will know the true divine wisdom. Then you will preserve your bodies for thousands of years. Then you will heal the sick with the power of Christ, and you will walk upon the waters of the sea. You will perform marvels and wonders like the ones he performed in the Holy Land.

---

57 See "siddhi" in the glossary.

6

Spiritual schools are full of sincere but mistaken people. Crime is also hidden within the incense of prayer.

Christ was crucified between two thieves. Almost all organizations exploit the Christ. Some exploit him with good intentions and others exploit him with evil intentions; these are the good and the bad thieves.

In France, a scoundrel who devoted himself to carnival astrology and who was a connoisseur of fine beer suddenly let his hair and beard grow. He then traveled to Venezuela where he founded a renowned order of black magic of Aquarius. Thereafter he declared himself to be the very reincarnation of Jesus Christ. Later, another scoundrel followed his example and declared that he was Saint Peter, and shortly after had the impulse of wandering around in the streets wearing a tunic, cape, and sandals.

These scoundrels appear to be unbiased apostles, yet they exploit the name of Christ with evil intentions. Thus, with the pretext of founding their "ashrams," they get hold of real estate. The henchmen of these scoundrels are very sincere but mistaken people who, regrettably, commit the crime of betraying the lord of the souls. To exchange the Christ for an impostor is a crime of high treason.

Others think that by affiliating themselves with the black lodge called AMORC,[58] which sells "initiations" in the market,

---

58 Ancient and Mystical Order Rosæ Crucis (AMORC), also known as the Rosicrucian Order, founded by Harvey Spencer Lewis in the early twentiethc century. Do not confuse them with the genuine

they will become "Rosicrucians."[59] That lodge delivers the word "mathrem" to them as the final synthesis, as the non-plus-ultra of magic; nevertheless, this word is a mantra in order to enter into the planes of the black lodge. AMORC is a commercial institution. All those people exploit the Christ with evil intentions.[60]

Some devotees who are affiliated with the Theosophical Society do not understand the mystery of Christ. They are just petrified in the theories of the nineteenth century, which are packed with horrible fanaticism and fear. These devotees do not accept anything new, and based on pride, arrogance, fanaticism, and terrible fear, they think that the final word of knowledge is within their domain. They are people who dangerously and negatively end up exploiting the Christ with good intentions.

The Rosicrucians of Max Heindel[61] are sincere but mistaken devotees, because Heindel did not know the Christic mysteries; consequently they do not know the doctrine of the resplendent "I am." Heindel stated that "an exchange happened at the baptism of Jesus." He asseverated that Jesus himself, the Spirit, left that body, and that the Christ Spirit entered into Jesus' body, which was inhabited and used by Christ during his ministry. This is false, and enough proof that Heindel was absolutely ignorant about the doctrine of the resplendent "I am." Heindel did not know what the crown of life is, because he did not know about Christic esotericism. Therefore, Heindel is sincere

---

59 "The order of the Logos, the true Rosicross, does not have a visible or tangible organization in the physical world, it does not have a physical temple; this only exists in the superior worlds. The brothers and sisters of the Rosicrucian Order who have physical bodies here in this tridimensional world are all of them Resurrected Masters. They are Resurrected Masters who already incarnated the Christ. Those from distinct schools and orders in this physical world who denominate themselves Rosicrucian are false. The true Rosicrucian Order that the Logos has established upon the face of the Earth does not have any visible organization, it does not dictate courses by correspondence, nor does it collect fees, nor does it have juridical personality, nor does it have internal or external statutes." —Samael Aun Weor, The Kabbalah of the Mayan Mysteries

60 This is discussed in detail in *The Revolution of Beelzebub* by Samael Aun Weor.

61 1865-1919

but mistaken, and those who follow his mistakes tread on the path of error.

> *"And if the blind lead the blind, both shall fall into the abyss."* —Matthew 15:14

Moreover, the blind leaders of that institution are fornicators because they ignore the Great Arcanum. Any institution formed by fornicators is a black lodge. Consequently, they are sincere but mistaken ones who exploit the Christ with good intentions.

There are numerous people with mediumistic faculties within multitudes of spiritual temples, where multitudes of impostors manifest through the mediumistic faculties of these "channelers." All of them claim to be "channeling" Jesus Christ, and the wretched people firmly believe in such imposters. The abyss is full of tenebrous entities that manifest themselves through the faculties of the medium-channelers within these spiritual temples, where their wretched devotees are sincere but unfortunately mistaken people filled with terrible fanaticism. The leaders of those spiritual centers exploit the Christ with good intentions.

Multitudes of orders, lodges, schools, and spiritual centers follow the good thief, and others the bad thief.

Likewise, the wealth of the multitudes of religious sects has been amassed by the exploitation of the blood of Christ. The Vatican[62] is filled with riches, and the entire amount of wealth[63] of the Vatican has been amassed by the exploitation of the blood of the martyr of Calvary.[64]

Mystics illuminated by the Holy Spirit know by direct experience that Pope Pius XII[65] had the mark of the beast on his forehead and on his hands. Mystics illuminated by the Holy Spirit know by direct experience that Pope Pius XII was

---

62 Sacerdotal-monarchical state ruled by the pope who is the bishop of Rome and head of the Catholic Church.

63 The Roman Catholic Church is one of the wealthiest organizations on Earth, but there are no accurate assessments of its wealth.

64 The site where Jesus was crucified.

65 Catholic pope from 1939-1958, who orchestrated the Reichskonkordat, a treaty between the Vatican and Nazi Germany.

a demon from the abyss. Yes, he was an incarnated demon, a demon in a body of bones and flesh.

Within the ruins of many Catholic convents, skeletons of newborn children have been found. This is known by any stonemason who has worked within the ruins of those convents, where the cloistered devotees mystically killed, adulterated, and fornicated. These cloistered devotees gave birth with Arcanum 15 (carnal passion) and thereafter killed them with Arcanum 13 (death). It is well known that many priests fornicate and adulterate. Yes, they corrupt many damsels in their confessionary.[66]

Moreover, to demand payment for a wedding ceremony is a crime against the Holy Spirit, who as love dwells within the church of the heart. This is why it is a crime against the Holy Spirit to make a business of love. Those people follow the evil thief.

Multitudes of religious institutions, namely Protestants, Adventists, Jehovah's Witnesses, etc., all study the Bible literally, and exploit the Christ. They exploit the blood of the martyr of Calvary.

It so happens that since those wretched people do not know the secret doctrine of the "I am," they fall into the most terrible biblical misinterpretations, which are suitable only for Molière[67] and his infantile cartoons.

Multitudes of organizations are filled with spiritual intellectualisms. All these wretched people fornicate and are full of pride, fanaticism, and fear. All those people exploit the Christ; some exploit Christ as good thieves, and others as bad thieves.

They all adore the person of Jesus, but reject his doctrine, the secret doctrine of the "I am."

It is difficult to state all of this, yet it is the truth. It is as bad to talk when one must be silent as to be silent when one must talk. There are criminal silences as well as indignant words.

---

66 These statements were published in 1956, forty years before the public at large began to take the abuses of clergy seriously.

67 French comedic playwright Jean Baptiste Poquelin 1622-1673.

Notwithstanding, this is why there are many Rosicrucian and Theosophist[68] devotees that slander us for being compassionless because we state these truths. Nevertheless, these devotees are not cognizant of the crime called "prostitution of spirituality," which is committed when we mistake sanctity for sanctimoniousness, or when we mistake fraternity for complicity.

Indeed, this is why Sivananda[69] stated that this path is full of dangers within and without. This is the path of the razor's edge.

Regarding the Luciferic spirits: Max Heindel and Steiner[70] mistakenly believed that they were the stragglers of life, a wave between angels and men; they believed that their abodes were on the planet Mars (and one thousand other stupidities of the sort). Thus, if our disciples believe in these mistaken assertions of Max Heindel and Steiner, they will eventually confusedly consider that it is okay to become a demon.

The archdemon named Lucifer (the greatest black initiate from the lunar epoch) and his Luciferic followers are demonic hosts from the abyss; this was ignored by Steiner and Heindel.

Almost all spiritual schools teach how to develop mental force. They all want to fortify the mind. This is how many end practicing black magic. The mind is the donkey we must ride in order to enter into the Heavenly Jerusalem.

The mind (the manas,[71] the man) must debase itself before the majesty of the Innermost. This is ignored by spiritual devotees. Thus, what they always want to do is their own selfish will and never the will of the Father. This is the terrible truth of all these things.

---

68 The Theosophical Society, with which theosophy is now generally identified, was founded in 1875 by Helena Petrovna Blavatsky, author of *The Secret Doctrine* (1888).

69 Swami Sivananda (1887-1963), founder of The Divine Life Society.

70 Rudolf Steiner (1862-1925), founder of Anthroposophy.

71 The Sanskrit word manas is derived from the root मन् man, "to think." Manas is the root of the English term "man," for person, not gender.

Others deliver themselves to the practice of hypnotism,[72] and allege that it is for good. This is how crime dresses as a saint, because hypnotism is utter and legitimate black magic.

When a new school of black magic is opened, the first victim is the martyr of Calvary, since they speak in his name. Thus, their henchmen believe and raise money in his name, teach their black magic in his name, close the doors of Eden for others in his name, seduce naive young ladies in his name (so that their devotees can mystically commit adultery and fornication in his name), and obtain real estate in his name, etc.

Thus, Christ has been a bountiful business for Theosophists, Rosicrucians, etc., and all Aquarian spiritual devotees.

The greater part of esoteric writers write about what they have read. They repeat the theories of others like parrots. They speak about what they do not know. They say what they do not know. They explain things that they have never experienced. They are filled with intellectual pride, nevertheless they cynically state, "I am a child. I have no pride. I am very simple, etc." Hypocrites, pharisees, whitened sepulchers, generation of vipers. To the abyss! To the abyss! To the abyss!

We had the intention of sending this book to all those schools, yet one of our Gnostic brothers said, "Those schools would not accept it. They would conceal it because it is not to their advantage. Don't you see that the leaders of those schools are terribly jealous? They live off their schools and groups, and fear that their groups might collapse."

This is what our Gnostic brother told us. Naturally, logic was on his side and we had to accept his concept, since all those people live doing business with the Christ. They live off their business.

Some follow the good thief, and others the bad thief; that is the truth. Thus, this is how crime is hidden within the incense of prayer.

There is a great deal of virtue within the wicked, and a great deal of evil within the righteous. The saints have also committed a great deal of evil with their virtues.

72

Verily, verily, I tell you Gnostic brothers and sisters, that when we do not know how to use virtues, we can cause harm to others with those virtues.

"Love is law, but love with cognizance."

Complacency with crime is also a crime.

7

In this day and age, the Masonic Lodge grants its degrees based on money and social status. Many sell initiations. Many are bestowed with initiations. Yet, all of this is exploitation and black magic.

Authentic degrees and authentic white initiations are received in the consciousness. These initiatic ceremonies are performed within the superior worlds.

Initiations are intimate realizations of the consciousness, which must not be revealed, or spoken about.

No one can grant initiations to anyone. Initiation is attained through life itself.

In this day and age, everybody wants to be a master. Notwithstanding, we state that there is only one master;[73] this is the inner Christ that enlightens every human being who comes into the world. Thus, only Christ is the master. Only the resplendent "I am" is the master.

Therefore, all initiations of those Theosophical, Rosicrucian, etc., schools, orders and lodges are from the abyss.

Withdraw from all these dangers of the abyss, withdraw!

8

This is what the Lord Jehovah told us, "I have always helped you. I will always help those who withdrew from the schools of the Baalim." The Baalim[74] are the tenebrous ones.

Notwithstanding, in this century, all schools, organizations, lodges, religions, and sects fell into the abyss and became

---

73 "Neither be ye called masters: for one is your Master, even Christ." —Jesus, from Matthew 23:10

74 A Hebrew word ("mister, sir") used in the Bible to indicate black magicians.

schools of the Baalim, who eat (fornicate) at Jezebel's table[75] and consume things (theories, intellectualism, etc.) sacrificed unto idols.

There are Baalim sects where people end up believing that they "speak in tongues";[76] yes, their fanatic devotees believe that the Holy Spirit has entered into them. Nevertheless, they are only wretched victims of demonic entities who possess them.

> *"But he that is truly joined to the Holy Spirit must be necessarily pure and chaste, because every sin that a man does is without the body; but he that commits fornication sins against his own body. What? Do you not know that your body is the temple of the Holy Spirit which is in you?"* —1 Corinthians 6:18, 19

Those who resolve to lay the heavy cross of initiation upon their shoulders will find themselves persecuted and even hated by those spiritual devotees who live talking about initiation daily. Those Theosophists, channelers, and Aquarian devotees—who hate and despise chastity and who defend their beloved fornication with the most refined philosophies—are wolves dressed in sheep's clothing. When sexual magic is spoken about to them, they immediately reject it, because for them there is nothing better than to fornicate.

My brothers and sisters, if you want to lay the heavy cross of initiation upon your shoulders, do not allow the theories of those strayed souls to block your path. All those tenebrous souls crucified the Christ. All of those tenebrous souls live crucifying the Lord. All of them hide their feline claws within their felt gloves. They smile sweetly and speak ineffable and sublime words, but their thoughts are full of perdition.

---

75 "Notwithstanding I have a few things against thee, because thou sufferest that woman Jezebel, which calleth herself a prophetess, to teach and to seduce my servants to commit fornication, and to eat things sacrificed unto idols. And I gave her space to repent of her fornication; and she repented not." -Revelation 2

76 "And they [apostles] were all filled with the Holy Ghost, and began to speak with other tongues, as the Spirit gave them utterance." — Acts 2:4

"Woe unto you, scribes and Pharisees, hypocrites! for ye are like unto whited sepulchers, which indeed appear beautiful outward, but are within full of dead men's bones, and of all uncleanness." —Matthew 23:27

9

A great equilibrium in the consciousness is necessary in order to become an initiate. Thus, it is necessary to cultivate powers but to not covet them, to aspire to initiation but to not covet it, to know how to find virtues in the heart of the wicked, and to know how to find the evilness in the heart of the righteous.

People begin to practice sexual magic and then become weary. They fail due to the lack of tenacity and perseverance. If our consciousness has not yet acquired cognizance of what it is doing, then tenacity cannot be attained, and the consciousness cannot acquire this cognizance without suffering.

This humanity still needs to suffer more. They do not yet have moral responsibility.

People want to attain everything in a single day. Rare are they who persevere for their entire life.

People live flitting like butterflies from one school to another. This is why they fail.

The Gnostic who withdraws from the Gnostic doctrine is a totally "irresponsible individual," an embryo, a fetus without a complete, mature development whatsoever. Yet, the mature Gnostic would prefer death rather than to withdraw from Gnosis.

To achieve a perfect equilibrium between light and darkness is to achieve practical adepthood, and this perfect equilibrium cannot be achieved by any fanatic.

Great saints are born from the great wicked, yet saints can easily become demons.

The abyss is closer for the one who has already seen the light than for the one who still has not seen it.

10

In the world of the mind (the Devachan[77]), there are splendid halls filled with light and beauty. Here we find black magicians who resemble masters of ineffable light. These tenebrous Baalim only speak of divine things, yet by means of their most subtle philosophies, they advise us to spill the semen (to fornicate).

Many initiates do not know how to remain firm against the actions of those luminous temptations, thus they succumb and fall into the abyss.

Moses, the great initiate, condemned the spilling of the semen; he stated:

> *"And if any man's seed of copulation go out from him, then he shall wash all his flesh in water, and be unclean until the even. And every garment, and every skin, whereon is the seed of copulation, shall be washed with water, and be unclean until the even.*

> *"The woman also with whom man shall lie with seed of copulation, they shall both bathe themselves in water, and be unclean until the even."* —Leviticus 15:16-18

Therefore, Moses condemned the spilling of semen as unclean.

Nevertheless, the tenebrous Baalim teach how to spill the semen during the practices of negative sexual magic, because they haughtily ejaculate their semen during their practice of negative sexual magic. What cynicism! What a hoax!

This type of cult has its origin in the cult of the horrible Goddess Kali.[78] The order of Kula and its goddess Kali has its origin in the black magic of the Atlanteans. Yet, in this day

---

77 Theosophists use this word more or less like the "heaven" in most religions, describing a place where people go when they die.

78 "In India, Kali the Divine Mother Kundalini is adored, but Kali in her black, fatal aspect is also adored. These are the two Marys, the white and the black. The two serpents, the Serpent of Brass which healed the Israelites in the wilderness and the tempting serpent of Eden." —Samael Aun Weor, *The Perfect Matrimony*

and age, the order of this cult of the goddess Kali has its head-quarters in India.

Thus this is how, by means of this black tantric cult, the negative serpent (the tempting serpent of Eden) awakens and descends towards the atomic infernos of the human being, and becomes the Kundabuffer organ, the horrible tail of the demons. This is how the tenebrous Baalim deceive the naive.

These are "the deeds of the Nicolaitans, which I also hate" (Revelation 2).

The Canaanites, the inhabitants of Carthage, Tyre, and Sidon, perished because of these cults. Likewise, these horrible practices were the cause of the sinking of Atlantis.

Thus, Black Tantra is the cult with which people are transformed into the seven-headed beasts mentioned in the book of Revelation (Apocalypse). That is the hideous practice that transformed the Lemurian-Atlanteans into monsters.

Therefore, any instructor who teaches Tantra with the spilling of the semen is a black magician.

11

Many vain and stubborn people who join Gnosis believe that this is just another school amongst many others. Yet, such wretched people are lamentably mistaken, because Gnosis is the doctrine that gestates angels or devils. Yes, this is the outstanding reality of these studies. Therefore, those who dedicate themselves to the development of powers but do not strive for sanctification eventually transform themselves into demons. Likewise, those who want to make a business out of Gnosis transform themselves into demons.

When one enters into Gnosis, one has to die in order to live. However, proud intellectual people who have the habit of thinking in accordance to their whims, vanities, and prejudices are not good for these Gnostic studies. This is a very difficult enterprise for intellectual people, because they only want to stuff their minds with these Gnostic studies, and the reality is that Gnosis is a very deep functionalism of the consciousness.

What we have to do with the mind is to kill it, and thereafter resurrect it, totally transformed.

So, Gnosis is not apprehensible by means of reasoning or via the intellect, because Gnosis is a very profound functionalism that only concerns the consciousness. Regrettably, many Gnostic devotees are filled with versatility; since they quickly switch from firm and determined in Gnosis then immediately weak and doubtful, they are and are not Gnostic. These half-hearted Gnostics become Antichrists, because they listened to the word of Christ and thereafter fled; yes, those who have listened to Christ and thereafter return into the darkness because the word seems too harsh for them are the perverse traitors who go around scandalizing people.

Judas who sells Christ for thirty pieces of silver is epitomized by those lukewarm devotees that are full of faith when they listen to the word, yet when they allow the darkness to confuse them once again, then vociferate against the word of the Lord.

> *"But whosoever shall offend one of these little ones which believe in me, it had been good for that man if he had not been born, it were better for him that a millstone were hanged about his neck, and that he were drowned in the depth of the sea."* —Matthew 18:6

> *"It is the spirit that quickeneth; the flesh profiteth nothing: the words that I speak unto you, they are spirit, and they are life.*

> *"But there are some of you that believe not. For Jesus knew from the beginning who they were that believed not, and who should betray him. And he said, therefore said I unto you, that no man can come unto me, except it were given unto him of my Father. From that time many of his disciples went back, and walked no more with him."* —John 6:63-66

Therefore, those who flee are the lukewarm weaklings, who are and are not; they are the Judas-type, the tenebrous ones, the perverse Antichrists.

12

Our disciples must carefully avoid reading too many news-papers. At a banquet for journalists of an independent press in New York, a journalist clearly and forthrightly stated the following:

"We (journalists) are intellectual prostitutes."
  —John Swinton, New York, 1890

Therefore, it is not convenient to read too many newspapers, unless we want to prostitute our minds.

We need to have a simple and pure mind, like the mind of an infant. Only in this way can we enter into the Major Mysteries.

The intellect is so dumb that it can lose the entire meaning of a statement just because of the lack of one period or one comma, yet by means of intuition the Gnostic only needs to see a single letter in order to understand.

All of the modern academic punctuation and complicated grammar of the language, all of those intellectual compli-cations from the present time, serve only to complicate the intellect more; it only gratifies the intellect; it prostitutes the intelligence.

We need to liberate our intelligence from all types of sects, religions, schools, political parties, concepts of country and flags, theories, etc. All these things are the abominations and filthiness of the great whore (the intellectual animal mind) whose number is 666.

13

Our Gnostic disciples must be very careful with impostors. In Colombia, South America, in 1956, the leader of the ancient Rosicross Order alleged that some man named Bhekpati Sinha was a great master from India, a disciple of Gandhi, and thousands of more falsities of the sort. At that time, all of the spiritual people from Colombia kneeled before this gentleman, and a fanatic from the city of Cali, Colombia was even eating the leftovers of the food that this gentleman ate. Fortunately, intelligent people are never missing from the picture; thus, it occurred to one of our disciples to ask the beloved impostor for his address in India. So, the impostor gave him the address of Yogi Sivananda.

There is a common saying that states, "The lies of a charlatan fall faster than the speed of gravity."

So, the answer (which I hold in my archives) of the letter our student sent to that address, states the following:

Dr. Kattan Umaña Tamines. Cali, Colombia, S. A.

Beloved and immortal Being,

Greetings and adorations,

Regarding your amiable letter and attachment, through this we inform to your goodness that the gentleman Bhekpati Sinha, mentioned in your letter, does not have any connection with the activities of the Divine Life Society whatsoever, and he is completely unknown to me. The world is sufficiently broad in order to contain all types of people. The intelligent or wise has to discriminate within, and advance by himself towards his own goal, his own Self, while also searching for the emancipation of others.

The spiritual path is precisely called "the path of the razor's age," which is filled with obstacles within and without. Enter into the silence of your own heart and incarnate the Silent One, the Innermost.

May the Almighty One bless all of you with peace, good tidings, and supreme beatitude; with my considerations and meditation in OM.

Yours, Sivananda

Thus, we ask, where were the marvelous faculties of that Rosicrucian leader? Can such blind people be confident guides?

This is why we advise our disciples not to follow anyone. Let our disciples follow their own Self. Each of our disciples has to follow their resplendent and luminous inner Being. Each one has to adore their own "I am."

We beg, beseech, our disciples not to follow us. We do not want henchmen or followers. We have written this book so that you, our friends, listen to your own internal master, your resplendent "I AM." The Innermost is your master: follow Him.

First, take heed that none of the many false avatars who appear during these times deceive you, for many impostors appear in these times and deceive others.

Second, take heed of sexual temptations.

Third, do not ever attend spiritual centers; the medium-channelers can easily lead you astray from the path.

Many disciples have fallen horribly due to these three dangerous reasons. Flee from these three treacherous dangers so that you may not lose your initiations and degrees.

14

Esoteric discipline is very demanding, yet we must not confuse sanctity with sanctimoniousness, since the sanctimonious type of person has filled the world with tears. The fanatical, sanctimonious type of person becomes horrified at everything; i.e. a tenebrous, sanctimonious person saw the Mexican sculpture of the bat god[79] and said that it was related with black magic, since for the sanctimonious type of person even the most divine things are black magic.

Spiritual devotees criticized the Master Litelantes[80] because she did not comply with their sanctimoniousness. Yes, some sanctimonious women hated her because she did not share in their squawking, chattering like parrots that talk but do not accomplish anything, and which speak about things that they do not understand.

The sanctimonious types are like butterflies that only pay fleeting visits from one school to another, since they are always looking for flowery, comfortable armchairs to rest upon; they

---

79 Read *Aztec Christic Magic* by Samael Aun Weor.
80 Wife of Samael Aun Weor.

sanctimoniously hate sexual magic and go around always swarming with fear.

Boldly, the sanctimonious type of person goes inveigled with theories believing that he belongs in the kingdom of the super-humans. Yes, the sanctimonious type person is so imbecilic that he would dare to excommunicate Ghandi or even Jesus Christ, if he was to find them eating a piece of meat. This is what the sanctimonious type of person is: always fanatic, always fearful, always a fornicator.

These types of sanctimonious persons always assume that Jesus Christ was a simpleton filled with sanctimoniousness. Yet, those Theosophists, Rosicrucians, and spiritualist-channelers, etc., of Aquarius who assume this are mistaken.

Jesus Christ was a remarkable revolutionary, a very severe and solemnly sweet master. Because this is how sanctity is: severe and sweet.

The authentic saint is a perfect gentleman or lady who totally fulfills the ten commandments of the law of God, and who knows how to handle their sword when necessary in order to defend good, truth, and justice. The authentic saint never goes around boasting about it, since he is always known by his deeds.

"Ye shall know them by their fruits." —Matthew 7:16

15

The arrogant and proud clairvoyants slander their fellows and fill the world with tears. This is because the turbid waters of a swellheaded spirituality—that is, a mind filled with reasoning, pride, preconceptions, social prejudices, platitudes, anger, egotism, etc.—can only reflect the tenebrous images of the abyss.

The mind of the clairvoyant has to be as serene as a lake of Nirvana so that the entire panorama of the universe can be reflected upon that most immaculate lake.

The silhouettes of trees are reflected upon the surface of the waters, but inverted. Similarly, every master of glory has also a shadow in the abyss.

Thus, when the mind of the clairvoyant is filled with prejudices, one then takes the shadow for reality. This is how the great masters of the White Lodge have always been slandered by swellheaded clairvoyants.

The swellheaded clairvoyant rejects the leafy trees of life because the mind is filled with preconceptions and prejudices that keep him or her enchanted with the tenebrous shadows, which are outlined, inverted, like abysmal demons within the profound bottom of the waters.

This is why many clairvoyants who formerly praised us, later stoned, slandered, and crucified us, when their impressions about us changed due to this or that reason.

Indeed, when our imagination is disturbed by the tempests of reasoning, the starry heaven of the spirit becomes gloomy, and then our clairvoyance can take the shadows for reality.

When clairvoyant bodhisattvas fall, they become worse than demons, because the fallen, clairvoyant bodhisattvas believe themselves to be omnipotent and powerful; they become conceited. They confuse what they see clairvoyantly; they take the shadows for reality, and end slandering the great masters.

Fallen, clairvoyant bodhisattvas harm homes, state what they do not know, explain with authority what they do not understand, never accept their position as fallen bodhisattvas, and end even believing that they are superior to their master.

This is why esoteric discipline is very severe, and also why the clairvoyant must not go around boasting about visions to others because they will lose their powers.

The clairvoyant must be humble, serene, obedient, meek, chaste, respectful, and moderate in speech. The clairvoyant must be pure in thought, word and action. The clairvoyant must be like a child.

16

Many Rosicrucian, Theosophist, etc., devotees do not know how to live, and indeed, the only thing we need to know is how to live. Goethe said,

*"Every theory is gray, and only the tree of the golden
fruits of life is green."*

The White Lodge has informed us that many Gnostic devotees (who are consciously or unconsciously in black magic)
will take our statements in this book as too harsh. Thus, this
will be the cause for them to desert Gnosis and they will react
by slandering us. These deserters will spread their defamatory
gossip against us.

Therefore, we warn those who like to snoop around that
Gnosticism is not like the other schools they have attended.
Many become Theosophists and then they leave; they then
move into the "Rosicrucian Order" and also withdraw without
anything significant happening to them. Thus, this is how
they like to go around like butterflies from school to school,
in conformity with all of those Spiritualist, Theosophist,
Rosicrucian and pseudo-Aquarian, decadent doctrines, etc.,
and nothing happens to them when they switch schools.

However, if they think that they can do the same with
Gnosis, we warn them that they cannot, since whosoever enters
into Gnosis is internally subjected to the remarkable test of
the Guardian of the Threshold. If one succeeds in the test, one
then enters into the straight, narrow, and difficult path that
leads us to Nirvana. Then, the degrees, initiations, and other
tests, etc., come afterwards. Thus, the higher the disciple is,
the more terrible is the fall. Those who have not seen the light
ignore a great deal, and therefore, much is forgiven of them;
however, the greater the degree of cognizance, the greater the
degree of responsibility. Therefore, those who saw the light and
then leave become demons. This is how horns have grown on
the foreheads of the astral bodies of many bodhisattvas. This is
how these fallen bodhisattvas have become demons. Therefore,
from Gnosis one becomes either an angel or a devil.

After a false step, many continue rolling downward into the
abyss, and finally the horns grow on them and they become
demons. This is the remarkable reality in Gnosis.

*"For in much wisdom is much grief: and he that
increases knowledge increases sorrow."* –Ecclesiastes 1:18

Therefore, stay back, nosy people!

Therefore, stay back, profaners!

Gnosis is a two-edged sword; it defends and gives life to the humble and virtuous, yet it wounds and destroys the curious and impure.

17

Esoteric discipline is indeed remarkable. Some fanatic devotees of the Spiritualists of Aquarius commit the most horrible crimes within their mind, yet if they suspect something bad of someone else, they cynically attribute these feelings as warnings from their Innermost. Thus, this is how they slander people and thereafter they say, "My Innermost tells me everything." When they get enraged, they shout, "I am not angry! What I feel are strong intuitive impulses of my Innermost." Thus, they attribute every evil idea, every evil thought, as impulses from their inner God.

Such people confuse intuition with malice, and the voice of the silence with the voice of Satan. We Gnostics state the voice of the silence never utters atrocities, because it is perfect; whereas the voice of Satan always utters perversities.

Within the abyss, the black magicians adopt the shape of our friends, and thereafter they say and do horrible things before the initiates. Thus, if the initiates allow themselves to be deceived by those tenebrous entities, they then become slanderers of others. Defamation is worse than stealing.

Slandering initiates sink into the abyss. Slandering initiates lose their degrees and initiations, in other words, they fall.

Some of those initiates who in remote ages were demons of the abyss are now marvelous; they no longer allow themselves to be deceived by the tenebrous entities; they marvelously know how the demons behave. These types of initiates cannot be misled by any tenebrous entity, since they know what the abyss is. Their expertise is profound in that area; they know very well the Tree of the Science of Good and Evil.

However, the initiates who in ancient times did not know the abyss now become naive victims of the tenebrous entities;

such initiates are easily deceived by the tenebrous ones. These are the initiates that become slanderers of their fellowmen. These are the initiates who vociferate against others and who fall into the abyss.

In order to be as gods, we have to totally know the Tree of the Science of Good and Evil.

18

Hypocritical pharisees sit on Christ's seat.

"And if the blind lead the blind, all shall fall into the abyss." —Matthew 15:14

We knew a hypocritical pharisee who rejected the sacred wine because the grape juice had fermented. Someone hosted him in his home and he indignantly fled from this house because the owners of the house ate meat. That perverse pharisee was a follower of another horrible impostor, a black magician.

Hypocritical pharisees!

"Do not ye yet understand that whatsoever entereth in at the mouth goeth into the belly, and is cast out into the draught? But those things which proceed out of the mouth come forth from the heart; and they defile the man. For out of the heart proceed evil thoughts, murders, adulteries, fornications, thefts, false witness, blasphemies." —Matthew 15: 17-19

"Woe unto you, scribes and Pharisees, hypocrites,! For ye make clean the outside of the cup and of the platter, but within you are full of extortion and excess." —Matthew 23:25

When some pharisees criticized the venerable Master Litelantes because she ate meat, she answered, "First I will correct my defects, and after I have corrected them, I will then stop eating meat." Those pharisees then thundered furiously against this great guru of the law.

Many hypocritical pharisees hate us because we are not complacent with whoredom, because we condemn crime, yet they state that this is how we hate. This is how they imprecisely judge us.

What happens is that all of those hypocritical pharisees from Spiritualism, Theosophism, Rosicrucianism, Aquarianism, etc., yearn for a sanctimonious mastery where masters are complacent with crime; a type of spiritual whore-master who, complacent with crime, goes around from lodge to lodge, from school to school, from sect to sect. This is why we, those who truly love humanity, are hated by hypocritical pharisees.

We knew a hypocritical pharisee that let his hair and beard grow in order to deceive imbecilic people; that pharisee stated that he was bound by the Nazarite vow. Regrettably, his followers ignored that since the advent of Christ the ritual law was nullified. Thus, his questionable Nazarite vow only served him as a pretext in order to deceive naive souls.

At that time, a married woman resolved to abandon her sacred wife's duties in order to head out, she alleged, as a Magdalene following the beloved impostor.

> *"Woe unto you, scribes and Pharisees, hypocrites! for ye are like unto whited sepulchers. Ye serpents, ye perverse generation of vipers, how can ye escape the damnation of hell?"* —Matthew 23: 27, 33

To the abyss!

19

The unconscious state of many Theosophist, Rosicrucian and Aquarian Spiritualists is shameful; it grieves us to see them discussing and arguing about things of which they have no cognizance. They talk about karma, yet they have never conversed with a master of karma. They intellectually discuss the cosmos, yet they do not know how to consciously travel in the astral body. They have never personally conversed with an angel. They only argue because they have read; that is all.

Nevertheless, the most critical matter about this is that they believe that they know.

Wretched people... how swollen with pride they are... they are worthy of pity.

We have known powerful, enlightened masters who have never read a book. Notwithstanding, we have also known great male, learned, spiritual devotees who are total ignoramuses, yet they are very swollen with pride. To match them, there are female spiritual devotees who have read a great deal and are even worse; they are swollen with a frightening vanity. It is shameful to see them, how they speak, how they argue about things that they have never seen. They speak about reincarnation, yet they do not remember their past lives. They speak about karma, yet they have never visited the tribunal of karma. They discuss cosmogenesis, yet they have never been consciously present in the astral body at the dawning of a world in formation. They speak with authority about what they have never seen, and thereafter, swollen with pride, they sit in their comfortable armchairs within their living rooms. Usually, these female spiritual devotees end up adoring sublime, long-bearded and long-haired impostors.

When these spiritual devotees become involved with mediumism or channeling, they end up believing they are famous reincarnations; they all become Marie Antoinette, or Joan of Arc, or Mary Magdalene; not a single one of them wants to be insignificant. They all want to be "grandiose."

Nevertheless, the authentic female enlightened masters never go around boasting about it.

The true disciples and masters are those who know how to consciously travel in their astral body. The male and female devotees who remember their past lives and who can astrally attend the temples of mystery are true enlightened beings, yet they never go around boasting about it; these are the ones who really know.

20

Those who know how to consciously project themselves in the astral body, those who know how to settle their negotiations in the tribunals of karma, those who directly receive the teachings within the temples of mystery, those who remember their past reincarnations, are the ones who really know esotericism, even if they have never read a book of esotericism. Yes, these are the people who really know esotericism, even if in the world they are nothing but wretched illiterates, even if they are nothing more than simple cooks, or uncivilized Indians.

We knew two powerful enlightened beings who were absolutely illiterate. One was an uncivilized Indian (a Mama) of La Sierra Nevada of Santa Marta (Colombia). The other was the powerful guru Litelantes, a great master of karmic justice. These two powerful initiates enjoy the privilege of possessing continuous cognizance. In similar privileged conditions, these two initiates possess teachings that could never be written down, because if they were to be written down, such knowledge would be profaned.

The great intellectuals who met these two gurus looked at them with disdain, because these initiates did not talk like parrots, because they were not full of sanctimoniousness, because they were not intellectuals, because they never went around boasting about their esoteric affairs.

Notwithstanding, we have known others who have only sporadically, in other words, from time to time, awakened consciousness; these types of devotees are nothing but mere beginners in these matters.

What is important is to possess continuous cognizance in the astral plane. This is why we have delivered exercises and clues in this book.

Therefore, whosoever does not know how to consciously project oneself in the astral body does not know esotericism, even if they have the "33rd social degree of Masonry," even if they are Aquarian devotees, even if they are named Theosophists, or even if they qualify themselves as Rosicrucian Knights.

To read books of esotericism or to skillfully theorize about it can be done by anyone, yet for our consciousness to acquire cognizance of the esoteric wisdom is something else. To do this one needs to study the true esoteric wisdom within the internal worlds.

Again, whosoever does not know how to consciously project oneself in the astral body does not know esotericism.

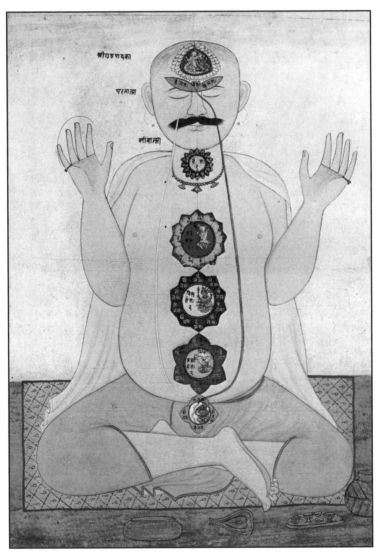

CHAKRAS AND CHANNELS

Chapter 22

The Two Witnesses

"And there was given me a reed like unto a rod: and
the angel stood, saying, Rise, and measure the temple of
God, and the altar, and them that worship therein."
—Revelation 11:1

That "reed like unto a rod" is our spinal column. There is
a canal[81] along that reed; through this canal ascends the fire
of the Holy Spirit that emerges from our sexual organs. This
Pentecostal fire[82] resembles an ardent and terrific divine serpent.

For a husband, what is important is to know how to love his
wife. For this it is important that during the sexual act they
learn how to withdraw without spilling the semen. This is how
the fire of the Holy Spirit is awakened. This is how the ardent
serpent from our reproductive organs is lifted up.

There is nothing more sublime than love, the kiss, and
the sexual act. So, when we do not spill the semen, it is then
transmuted into seminal vapors, and these seminal vapors are
transmuted into energies. The sexual energies are then bipolarized into positive and negative. The positive are solar and
the negative are lunar. These solar and lunar currents rise up
to the brain. The solar currents are related to the right nostril,
and the lunar currents to the left nostril.

The solar and lunar currents from our sexual gonads rise
up to the sacred chalice, which is the brain, through a pair
of canals. These canals that rise to the brain are two nervous,
sympathetic cords that entwine along the spinal medulla. Fill

---

81 Sanskrit sushumna.

82 "And when the day of Pentecost was fully come, they [the apostles] were
   all with one accord in one place. And suddenly there came a sound from
   heaven as of a rushing mighty wind, and it filled all the house where they
   were sitting. And there appeared unto them cloven tongues like as of
   fire, and it sat upon each of them. And they were all filled with the Holy
   Ghost..." Acts 2

up your chalice, brothers and sisters, with the sacred wine of light.

"And I will give power unto my two witnesses, and they shall prophesy a thousand two hundred and threescore days, clothed in sackcloth." –
Revelation 11:3

XILONEN

These two sympathetic nervous cords are the two witnesses.

These sacred cords are symbolized in the two braids of hair that hang from the back of Xilonen, the symbolic Aztec sculpture.

"These are the two olive trees, and the two candlesticks standing before the God of the earth. And if any man will hurt them, fire proceedeth out of their mouth, and devoureth their enemies: and if any man will hurt them, he must in this manner be killed." –Revelation 11:3-5

Our two sympathetic cords are terribly divine, because when their solar and lunar atoms unite in the coccygeal bone, the serpent of ardent fire awakens. This is why the two witnesses have such a remarkable power.

"These have power to shut heaven, and that it rain not in the days of their prophecy: and have power over waters to turn them to blood, and to smite the earth with all plagues, as often as they will." –Revelation 11:6

Behold how beautiful these two witnesses appear on the back of the Aztec goddess Xilonen!

So, the two witnesses awaken the serpent of fire, which is called Kundalini by the Hindus. Amongst the Aztecs the serpent of fire is called Quetzalcoatl, and they represent it with the rattlesnake. This is the fire of the Holy Spirit that is comparable to a fiery serpent, which when awakened hisses very similarly to the hiss emitted by any serpent of flesh and bone. Its hiss is like a still, small, divine sound, similar to the one produced by the rattles of the rattlesnake, or like the subtle chirp of the cricket.

This sexual serpent awakens with the ardent kiss and with sexual magic. This serpent is septuple in its internal constitution. This serpent has the power to open all the seven churches of our spinal column, and can transform us so that we can become as gods. Only the two witnesses have the power to awaken it, and to open heaven. The formula to awaken the serpent is the following, "Introduce the virile member into the feminine vagina, and withdraw without spilling the semen."

According to the practice of sexual magic and according to the purification performed by the student, one inevitably and systematically receives the nine initiations of Minor Mysteries in one's consciousness. These nine initiations are nothing but the probationary esoteric path. Nonetheless, it is possible that the student may not apprehend in the physical world the secret mysteries related with the nine initiations of Minor Mysteries, since these initiatic events occur in the consciousness, and if the student does not know how to bring the memories into the physical brain, logically, in the physical world one will be oblivious of those events, since these are very intimate matters that concern only the consciousness.

The two witnesses have the power to awaken for us the fire of the Holy Spirit. The serpent is lifted up little by little in accordance with our purification. This is how we prepare ourselves for the nine initiations of Major Mysteries. The Minor Mysteries are nothing else than the preparatory path for the Major Mysteries.

The Minor Mysteries are also a chain that we have to break. This chain is broken only when we arrive at the Major Mysteries, because in the Major Mysteries the two witnesses have the power to lift the fiery serpent up to the atom of the Father, which resides at the root of the nose, and when this happens our Innermost then receives the first initiation of Major Mysteries.

For this, transmute your sexual energies and withdraw from all those spiritual schools which are dens of fornication, sodomy, homosexuality, and mystical autoeroticism.[83]

In the city of Barranquilla, Colombia, we knew a man who boasted that he was a master. This man always lived surrounded by children, until the police discovered that he was an inverted corrupter of minors, a pedophile. This black magician boasted about being a Free Buddhist, and since he lived always surrounded by children, imbecilic people believed him and said to themselves, "This is indeed a great master," thus all of them bowed in reverence before this venerable phony master, who was a "sublime" pedophile.

At that time, in that city of Barranquilla lived a wretched, old spiritual woman who venerated this sublime pedophile master. This wretched granny claimed that she played chess with our very Jesus Christ. Yes, she hobnobbed with God, and directed an association of fornicators entitled "The Universal Fraternal Society."

Likewise, we knew a man who endured twenty-five years practicing mystical autoeroticism. He was a disciple of another impostor named Omar Cherenzi-Lind. Yes, he was a mystic that venerated the impostor Omar Cherenzi-Lind, the "troubadour of pleasant vices."

Pathetically, this is what the spirituality of the twentieth century is: a horrible and filthy mixture of mysticisms with fornication, lasciviousness, homosexuality, adultery, swindles, mystical robbery, exploitation, sexual corruption, etc.

All of these perverse, filthy, mobster fornicators boast about being "sublime masters," gurus, avatars, great reformers, etc. None of them wants to be insignificant. All of them believe they are great and powerful.

This is why we advise you to practice sexual magic and withdraw forever from those dens of iniquity. Seek your inner "I am," because He is the only one who can save you.

---

83 Masturbation.

*"I am Alpha and Omega, the beginning and the end,
the first and the last. Blessed are they that do his
commandments that they may have right to the Tree of
Life, and may enter in through the gates into the city;
For without are dogs, and sorcerers, and whoremongers,
and murderers, and idolaters, and whosoever loveth and
maketh a lie."* —Revelation 22:13-15

The two witnesses shut the doors of Eden to all those perverse spiritual devotees. The two witnesses are terribly divine:

*"These have power to shut heaven, that it rain not in
the days of their prophecy: and have power over waters
to turn them to blood, and to smite the earth with all
plagues, as often as they will. These are the two olive
trees, and the two candlesticks standing before the God of
the earth."* —Revelation 11:6, 4

In India, the two witnesses are known as Ida and Pingala;
these are their Sanskrit names.

Therefore, we must practice sexual magic with our spouse
and withdraw from those spiritual schools that tolerate mystical whoredom.

We knew of a good marriage within which, unfortunately, the wife had the absurd complex of combining schools.
Her husband, exhausted from his work, arrived to his house
and instead of finding peace, caresses, and repose, found
Theosophists, Rosicrucians, Aquarianists, Spiritualists,
Masons, etc. All of those people were an unbearable group of
chattering parrots who disturbed that wretched man's tran-
quility to the breaking point of finally terminating that marriage. Thus, the man married another woman and his ex-wife
kept her cage of chattering parrots.

Indeed, the spirituality of this century only provokes nau-
sea, since all those cage-like schools are filled with chattering
parrots, sublime whoredom, ineffable gossip, mystical thievery,
divine imposters, assassins of souls, etc. Those who engage this
type of spirituality are exposed to thievery. Those who host
this type of spirituality in their home can be sure that they
could lose their spouse or daughter or their goods.

There are very dangerous types of spiritual devotees who always find the word "hate" as an excusable door in order to escape, and thus avoid the very grave problems that we are exposing here. Yes, they always allege that we "hate," and thereafter they present to us a Christ invented by them, namely a weak, effeminate Christ who is complacent with crime, who is an accomplice of whoredom and Pharisees, a cowardly Christ who did not eject the merchants from the temple, a Christ that did not accuse the most "sanctimonious Pharisees" of hypocrisy, a Christ that did not condemn the doctors of the law, a Christ that did not qualify the tenebrous entities as a perverse generation of vipers, etc. This is the horrible sacrilege that these types of spiritual devotees do. They are the ones who daily thrash the Lord.

We Gnostics are not accomplices of delinquency. This is why we denounce crime, because we do not like to hide crimes.

We work for a decent, neat, clean, gentlemanly and honorable Gnosticism. We want less wordiness and more actions.

We want a practical Gnosticism without mystical autoeroticism, without "parrots," without filthiness. We must morally bathe and clean ourselves.

We must learn how to consciously travel in the astral body. We must resurrect our two witnesses by means of sexual magic, thus the fire of Pentecost will awaken. And when this fire burns the scum, the larvae, the filthiness, we then enter into the mysteries of fire. This is how we Christify ourselves.

Therefore, to want to unite and associate with schools of fornicators who are complacent with whoredom is the breaking point of absurdity. The new era signifies death to the spiritual schools of this century. The new era will be initiated by blood and fire.

We will end this chapter by clarifying that within the term "spirituality" we are including all those cage-like schools where futile, chattering parrots gather, namely Theosophism, Rosicrucianism, Spiritualism, Aquarianism, Martinism, Masonry, Mazdaznan, Circles of Communion of Thought, Anthroposophism, diverse independent groups, Brethren of Dharma, Krishnamurtianism, and thousands of religious sects or spiritual groups whose doctrines are filled with mystical fornication, useless intellectualism, and absurd fanaticism.

Understand that when we use the term "spirituality," we are addressing their fornicating spiritual devotees, because through that term we are embracing all those types of fornicating people who belong to the distinct schools, lodges, orders, halls, centers, etc.

PADMASAMBHAVA AND YESHE TSOGYAL DEMONSTRATE SEXUAL MAGIC OF TIBETAN BUDDHIST TANTRA

"Meditate on the supreme and unchanging [bliss, Eden]. With vajra [male sexual organ] placed inside lotus [female sexual organ], brings the winds [vital forces] into the drops [bodhichitta], the drops into the chakras [on the spine]; the movement of drops halted at the vajra [restrained, not emitted], always rigid [erect], the yogi continually raises fluid [never releasing it]. With the yoga of mahamudra [great Hermetic seal], the descent to the vajra, and by its blessing, the instances of supreme unchanging [bliss, Eden], completed at 21,600 [Arcanum 9, Initiation], will bring the great enlightenment, the attainment of Vajrasattva [diamond soul]."

—ORNAMENT OF STAINLESS LIGHT, AN EXPOSITION OF KALACHAKRA TANTRA,
BY KHEDRUG NORSANG GYATSO (15TH CENTURY AD).

Chapter 23

GAIO (ΓΑΙΟ)

Listen, both of you, man and woman who adore each other: when you are sexually united, vocalize the mantras, **DIS**, **DAS**, **DOS**.[84] Extend the sound of each letter; prolong that sound as much as possible. In this manner, children of mine, you will awaken your sacred serpent. During your sexual trance, as your kisses and caresses increase, you are charging yourselves with the elemental fire and electricity that seethes and throbs in all creation.

Woman, suppress orgasm during the sexual act, and in this manner you will awaken your Kundalini. Man, suppress your sexual climax and in this manner you will awaken your feathered serpent, Quetzalcoatl. Yes, if both of you withdraw before the spasm, if you do not spill your semen, then the sacred fire will awaken in both of you; and you shall become as gods.

> *"Because strait is the gate, and narrow is the way, which leadeth unto light, and few there be that find it."*

So, our Lord the Christ stated to us in Matthew 7:14 that there is only one strait gate and narrow path; nonetheless, the tenebrous ones asseverate that God can be reached through many paths. So,

> *"Enter ye in at the strait gate: for wide is the gate, and broad is the way, that leadeth to destruction, and many there be which go in thereat: Because strait is the gate, and narrow is the way, which leadeth unto life, and few there be that find it."*

We exited Eden through that strait gate, and through that gate we must enter into Eden again. The strait gate through which we exited is sex, and only through this same gate we must enter again. Eden is sex itself, thus, we cannot enter into Eden through false doors.

Nevertheless, my brothers and sisters:

---

84 The vowels are pronounced as in Latin. Dis as "tree," Das as "fall," and Dos as "go."

"Beware of false prophets, which come to you in sheep's clothing, but inwardly they are ravening wolves. Ye shall know them by their fruits. Do men gather grapes of thorns, or figs of thistles?" —Matthew 7: 15,16

Consider, can the fruits be good of those who neither go into Eden, neither allow them that are entering to go into Eden? The tenebrous ones advise seminal ejaculation and state that sexual magic is dangerous. They demand thousands of conditions in order to have the right to practice sexual magic. Yes, this is how the tenebrous ones shut the doors of Eden to this wretched, suffering humanity, and thereafter, through thousands of fallacies, they toss the wretched souls into the cages of their intellectual systems; behold, this is the crime of the Luciferics.

"Every tree that bringeth not forth good fruit is hewn down, and cast into the fire. Wherefore by their fruits ye shall know them." —Matthew 7:19, 20

"But woe unto you, scribes and Pharisees, hypocrites! For ye shut up the kingdom of heaven against men: for ye neither go in yourselves, neither suffer ye them that are entering to go in. Woe unto you, scribes and Pharisees, hypocrites! For ye compass sea and land to make one proselyte, and when he is made, ye make him twofold more the child of hell than yourselves."
—Matthew 23:13, 15

Take heed that no man deceives you, brothers and sisters of my soul:

"For many shall come in my name, saying, I am Christ; and shall deceive many." —Matthew 24:4

The tenebrous ones let their hair and beards grow long and thereafter they found spiritual societies and state, "I am the Christ." Yes, my brothers and sisters, "many false prophets shall rise, and shall deceive many" [Matthew 24:11]. Yes, the tenebrous ones with theories and more theories will shut the gate of sex to you.

We, the brothers and sisters of the White Lodge, advise you to study the seven churches[85] of the Apocalypse (Revelation) of St. John. There you will find the necessary conditions in order to open the seven churches of our spinal column with the blessed fire of sex. All prerequisites are written in the Bible. Thus, do not allow yourselves to be deceive by the dazzling intellectualities of the Luciferics.

In this book we have delivered the remarkable secret of sexual magic so that you can transform yourselves and become as gods. Indeed, we have delivered this book with immense sacrifice; nonetheless, we are absolutely sure that humanity will reward us with ingratitude.

The scoundrels will study this book not in order to learn, but in order to criticize, slander, persecute, blemish, and discredit us. Yes, the viperine tongues will propagate against us, the true elder brothers and sisters, many lies and defamatory remarks, since this is the payment that we always receive from this wretched, suffering humanity.

Nevertheless, all of us swear in the name of the Eternal Living God that there is no other path to redemption. Thus, whosoever states that there are other paths that lead to liberation, lies; such an individual is luciferic and demonic, or at the least, a sincere but mistaken soul.

"I am" the way, the truth, and the life. "I am" the sacred word of Eden. Eden is sex itself; through that door we exited and through that door we must enter again; this is the law.

---

85 Christian Bible, Revelation 1-3. Also read *The Aquarian Message* by Samael Aun Weor.

Adam and Eve in Eden

Chapter 24
The Sexual Problem

Those who despise sex reject Eden, since Eden is sex itself.
Yet, black magicians state that we must not consider sex
important whatsoever; thus, this is how they shut the doors of
Eden to weak souls.

We knew the case of a tenebrous one who went to the
extreme of telling another man, "Here I leave you my wife. You
can use her if you wish." That black magician abandoned his
wife and children, and went around the world preaching a doctrine of black magic.

> "Woe unto you, scribes and Pharisees, hypocrites! For ye
> compass sea and land to make one proselyte, and when
> he is made, ye make him twofold more the child of hell
> than yourselves." —Matthew 23:13, 15

To state that sex is not important is to renounce Eden,
because Eden is sex itself.

There are many ignoramuses who look at sex with disgust.
These wretched souls do not know that sex is the door to
Eden. Those wretched souls do not want to enter through the
strait gate. Those souls renounce paradise and sink into the
abyss. We cannot enter into Eden but through the door from
which we exited. This door is sex. Therefore, whosoever despis-
es the strait and difficult gate will not enter into Eden and will
sink into the abyss. The Luciferics exert terrible efforts in order
to drive us away from that gate.

This is why Christ rightly stated,

> "Among a thousand who seek me, one finds me. Among
> a thousand who find me, one follows me. And among a
> thousand who follow me, one is mine." —Bhagavad-Gita

Black magicians use the intellect as a weapon in order to
drive us away from the doors of Eden. Yes, the Luciferics have
dazzling intellects. The Luciferics despise sex, yet they are terribly wicked and hypocritical fornicators. Lo and behold that the
gravest hypocrisy of these tenebrous ones is the sanctimonious

countenance they display as they speak about love and charity under the light of the gospels. They present themselves as if filled with an apparent humility, and thereafter they state that sex is not important, that sex is low and gross, and that they only seek the purest spirituality. Thus, this is how they shut the doors of Eden unto this wretched humanity.

> *"But woe unto you, scribes and Pharisees, hypocrites,!*
> *For ye shut up the kingdom of heaven against men: for*
> *ye neither go in yourselves, neither suffer ye them that*
> *are entering to go in."* —Matthew 23:13

Chapter 25

The Seven Churches

The Kundalini enters through the inferior orifice of the spinal canal, which is closed in ordinary people. The pressure of the seminal vapors opens this spinal orifice so that the igneous serpent can enter through it. Along the spinal medulla is the "canalis centralis," and within this canal is another even finer canal, which in the East is called Brahmanadi. A third canal which is even finer is within the latter. This third canal is the Chitra nadi.[86] Seven lotus flowers, which are the seven chakras, are along this last nadi. The seven chakras are the seven churches referred to by the Apocalypse (Revelation) of St. John.

As the Kundalini ascends, it opens each of the seven churches from bottom to top of the spinal canal. These seven chakras resemble seven lotus flowers that protrude from our spinal column.

These lotus flowers hang down from the medulla when the sacred serpent is still enclosed within the Church of Ephesus. However, when the serpent is lifted up to the brain, these lotus flowers turn and face upwards, shining with the sexual fire of the Kundalini.

There are spiritual schools that incite fear in their disciples. They alarm them with thousands of obstacles and very complicated theories, supposedly in order for them to have the right to awaken the Kundalini. Thus, their disciples falter before so many complicated and difficult theories. This is how the tenebrous ones shut the doors of Eden to this wretched, suffering humanity.

Verily, verily, I tell you, my brothers and sisters, that practicing sexual magic is the only requirement necessary to awaken the Kundalini and open the first church, which is located in the coccyx.

---

86 A nadi is a nerve channel for subtle energies.

"He that hath an ear, let him hear what the Spirit saith unto the churches; To him that overcometh (in other words, the one who terminates with fornication) will I give to eat of the Tree of Life, which is in the midst of the paradise of God." —Revelation 2:7

In other words, by laboring in sexual magic you will enter the paradise of God (Eden) and there you will eat from the Tree of Life. So, patience, suffering, and laboring are necessary in order to awaken the Kundalini and to open the Church of Ephesus, which is related to the sexual organs.

The requirements in order to open the second church are filial love for the Father, and knowing how to endure great tribulations and poverty with heroism; this is the prostatic/ uterine church, the Church of Smyrna.

The third church is Pergamus, and it awakens with total chastity. Those who want to awaken the third church must not eat things sacrificed unto idols, namely: theories, intellectualisms, modern scientism, pleasures like gluttony, alcoholic drunken sprees, etc. This church is at the height of the solar plexus (stomach).

The fourth church is Thyatira; this church belongs to the heart. The requirements for the sanctity that are needed in order to open this church are the following: chastity, charity, service, faith, patience, and much love.

Ephesus, Smyrna, Pergamus, and Thyatira are the four inferior churches of our temple. The three superior churches —Sardis, Philadelphia, and Laodicea—are in the tower of the temple; that tower is the head of the human being.

The Kundalini opens the seven churches of our spinal column. The necessary requirements for the development, evolution, and progress of the Kundalini are written in chapters one, two, and three of the Apocalypse (Revelation) of St. John. Therefore, all the obstacles and intellectual complications that the tenebrous ones place allegedly in order to have the right to awaken the Kundalini are pointless, since the Bible is the word of God.

Now, let us continue with the tower of the temple.

The fifth church is Sardis and is related to the thyroid chakra; this is the church of the larynx. When the sacred serpent opens the Church of Sardis, we can then hear in the internal worlds, because the esoteric ear is opened.[87] Internally, we then speak the language of the Light[88] and can create with the power of the word. The larynx is a uterus where the word is gestated. The creative organ of the angels is the larynx. The necessary requirements in order to open this church are vigilance, repentance, and good deeds.

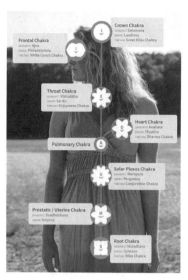

THE SEVEN CHAKRAS / CHURCHES

When the fire opens the sixth church called Philadelphia, clairvoyance awakens. This church is related with the chakra located between the eyebrows, which seems to protrude like a lotus flower from the pituitary gland. Clairvoyance allows us to see the ultra of all things; with it we see the internal worlds and the great mysteries of life and death. The moral requirements needed in order to open this church are sexual potency, veracity, and fidelity to the Father. When the marvelous door of this church is opened, the white dove of the Holy Spirit is sent forth to fly.

When the fire opens the seventh church called Laodicea, situated in the pineal gland, the crown of the saints then shines upon our heads. This is the diamond eye, the eye of polyvoyance, the eye of omniscience.

When the sacred serpent has passed from the pineal gland to the area between the eyebrows, then the high initiation—which is the first initiation of Major Mysteries—is attained.

---

87 Clairaudience.
88 The "golden language" spoken in the internal worlds.

In the first initiation of Major Mysteries, our Spiritual Soul[89] is united with the Innermost,[90] and this is how the masters of Major Mysteries of the White Brotherhood are born. Much humility is necessary in order to attain the union with the Innermost. The Apocalypse (Revelation) states to us,

> "To him that overcometh will I grant to sit with me in my throne, even as I also overcame, and am set down with my Father in his throne." —Revelation 3:21

When the Spiritual Soul is united to her Innermost, we (as Monads)[91] are dressed with the white robe of the masters of Major Mysteries. Then, the white five-pointed star glows with a radiant light upon the area between our eyebrows and, likewise, our seven churches are resplendent with glory.

We (as Monad) attend this great initiation without material vehicles of any kind. This great initiation is received out of the body within the superior worlds, and the new master (the Monad) receives a throne and a temple. Christ came to make of us kings and priests of nature in accordance with the order of Melchisedec.

The new master emerges from the profundities of our consciousness and expresses through the creative larynx. The new master is a remarkable divine potency.

> "And cried with a loud voice, as when a lion roareth: and when he had cried, seven thunders uttered their voices..."

These seven thunders are the seven keynotes of the seven churches that resound within our spinal column.

> "And the angel which I saw stand upon the sea and upon the earth lifted up his hand to heaven, and sware by him that liveth for ever and ever, who created heaven, and the things that therein are, and the earth, and the things that therein are, and the sea, and the things which are therein, that there should be time no longer."
> —Revelation 10:3-6

---

89 Divine Soul / Buddhi, corresponds to Geburah on the Tree of Life.
90 Chesed on the Tree of Life.
91 From Greek monas, "unity," the monad is the union of Atman - Buddhi - Manas, which are Chesed - Geburah - Tiphereth.

Chapter 26

Personages Who Do Harm

Regrettably, Yoga[92] has been misunderstood in the Western world.

Master Helena Petrovna Blavatsky, author of *The Secret Doctrine,* was a yogini. We all know that she did not live with the Count Blavatsky. Nevertheless, after having widowed the Count, she had to marry again. Yes, she had to remarry, yet a great yogini like her could not have married out of mere carnal passion. Besides, she married a venerable old man, therefore the reason for her to remarry is even deeper, more esoteric. Indeed, the Master Helena Petrovna Blavatsky needed marriage for her cosmic realization. She achieved something with Yoga, but not everything, since a yogi/yogini without sexual magic is like a garden without water. So, this is how by means of sexual magic she achieved the total development of her seven serpents.

Sexual magic is secretly taught within the schools of Eastern Yoga. Unfortunately, pseudo-yogis and pseudo-yoginis have spread in the Western world, and these ignoramuses have harmed many homes. These pseudo-prophets teach that sex is vulgar and perverse. They believe that they can jump over the walls of the Garden of Eden.

These pseudo-yogis/yoginis have ended the happiness of many homes, since they believe that they can enter Eden through false doors. They are the cause for the disgust and repugnance that many virtuous wives feel towards sex. Thus, by insulting the Holy Spirit these personages have ended the happiness of many homes.

We knew the case of a disciple of a cynical, demonic pseudo-yogi who rejected her husband sexually in order to follow the theories of that black magician, who naturally destroyed that marriage.

---

92 See glossary.

THE ANGEL RAPHAEL INSTRUCTS TOBIAS ABOUT SEXUAL ALCHEMY (FROM THE BOOK OF TOBIT)

"Sexual magic cannot in any way be harmful
since it is the normal, primeval way of
performing the sexual act by human beings."

Chapter 27

Fearmongers

There are many people who have the tendency of inciting fear in the devotees who begin to practice sexual magic. These fearmongers incite innumerable fears, i.e. fearmongers who state that sexual magic is harmful, or fear that the spouse might disagree and become angry, or that the Kundalini may flow through other canals, etc. All these and other types of fear have been invented by the black lodge in order to shut the door of Eden to this suffering humanity.

Sexual magic cannot in any way be harmful since it is the normal, primeval way of performing the sexual act by human beings. Seminal ejaculation is a vice that was taught unto humanity by the Luciferics, and any type of vice is harmful.

Where there is comprehension, anger cannot exist. An incomprehensive spouse is a problem for the initiate, yet that problem is resolved with silence, artfulness, and intelligence. Thus, before the incomprehensive spouse, it is better to be silent. In such cases, one practices in silence, vocalizes in silence, one transmutes the sexual energy, but does not say anything about it. The whole rite must be performed without saying it. Then, artfulness and love fill the void. Let those who have intelligence understand what we are stating here between the lines.

The other fear that the Kundalini may flow through other canals is false, because when the initiate begins to raise the first serpent, one is assisted by a master specialist, who has to direct the Kundalini of the disciple through the spinal canal. When the work is finished, the specialist receives a payment. Thereafter, when the initiate begins to work with the second serpent, one is assisted by another specialist, and so on successively. So, the disciple is not left alone.

Therefore, all these fears were invented by the fearmongers of the black lodge in order to shut the doors of Eden to this suffering humanity.

The Sacred Heart of Jesus

Chapter 28

The Church of the Holy Spirit

The church of the Holy Spirit is the church of Thyatira. This is the church of the heart. The priest who demands payment for a wedding ceremony commits a tremendous sacrilege, because a wedding is a ceremony that concerns the Holy Spirit, a wedding is a mystery of the heart. Therefore, to make of the heart a business is the same as to make the Holy Spirit a business.

Those who commercialize the sacrament of marriage profane the mysteries of the Holy Spirit in a horrible way. Love must not be bought or sold, because to do such a thing is to commit a serious crime against the Holy Spirit.

> *"Wherefore I say unto you, all manner of sin and blasphemy shall be forgiven unto men: but the blasphemy against the Holy Spirit shall not be forgiven unto men."* —Matthew 12:31

The one who commits suicide sins against the Holy Spirit, because the Holy Spirit gives us life through love and sex. When the soul of those who take their physical life by their own hand is reborn again, they get a pleasing life in their new physical body, yet they die against their will; this is their punishment.

The Judas-like person who betrays the master sins against the Holy Spirit because of ingratitude, since the love of the master abides in the church of the heart, and the fires of the heart control the Kundalini. The Kundalini develops, evolves, and progresses according to the merits of the heart.

So, the ascent of the Kundalini is very slow and difficult, because each vertebra demands certain conditions of sanctity. This is the terror of love and law. Thus, one single seminal ejaculation is enough in order for the Kundalini to descend one or more vertebrae. Afterwards, it is very difficult to recover the lost degrees related with those vertebrae; this is the punishment for the weak.

The man is one column and the woman is the other column of the temple of the living God. The two columns of the temple of the Holy Spirit are terribly divine. The man is the expansive principle, the woman is the attractive principle; the key of redemption is found in their union.

Love is nourished with love. The kiss is the mystical consecration of two souls who adore each other. While in the supreme trance of love, we forget about the theories of men.

The sexual act becomes the consubstantiation of love within the psychosexual human reality.

Man is strength; woman is sweetness.

Peter has the keys to heaven. Peter means "rock."[93] that rock is sex, and sexual magic is the key of Heaven. Upon the rock (sex) we must edify the church for our "I am."

Self-realization is impossible without the magic of love. Whosoever learns how to love will be transformed into a god. Sex is the philosophical stone, the cubic stone of Yesod.[94] Man and woman sexually united become as gods. It is better to love than to theorize.

Goethe said,

> "Every theory is gray, and only the tree of the golden fruits of life is green."

A home with playful children, a good garden, and a good wife are more valuable to a man than the accumulation of theories from all the spiritual schools of the world. A strong, loving, pure, and noble husband is more valuable to a woman than all the libraries of the world, because with the sacred fire of the Holy Spirit we become as gods, yet with theories we just become intellectual scoundrels.

Blessed be love. Blessed be the beings who adore each other.

---

93 Greek Πέτρος petros, "rock." "And I say also unto thee, That thou art Πέτρος, and upon this Πέτρος I will build my church; and the gates of hell shall not prevail against it." —Jesus from Matthew 16:18

94 Hebrew יסוד "foundation." The ninth sephirah on the Tree of Life, which corresponds to the sexual organs.

Chapter 29

The Seven Temples

The seven churches of our spinal column are intimately related with seven temples of Major Mysteries. These temples have their equivalent in the seven chakras of our spinal column. Therefore, these seven churches are seven temples within which reigns the terror of love and law. These seven churches are within the human being and within the universe, within the microcosm and within the macrocosm.

As we open our seven churches one by one in the spinal column, simultaneously one by one we enter each of the seven internal temples where only the terror of the great mysteries reigns. I.e., we experience a divine awe when we contemplate the cathedral of Sardis amongst lightning, thunder, and tempests, yet we can only enter into this cathedral when the laryngeal chakra (the church of Sardis) in our spinal column has been activated.

When the initiate has lifted the serpent upon the rod (spinal column), one receives the staff of the patriarchs, the rod of Aaron, the cane of seven knots, the golden reed, etc. We then enter into the church of Laodicea; that cathedral is made of pure gold. The initiate receives different rods according to one's works with the spinal fires. The cane of seven knots of Eastern yogis symbolizes the spinal column with its seven churches.

The Decapitated Man at the Museum of Aztec Culture of Mexico

Chapter 30

The Seven Serpents

Mexico always presents astounding surprises. In the Museum of Aztec Culture of Mexico, there is a strange stone upon which is chiseled the figure of a decapitated man. The head of this strange personage has been replaced by seven serpents. The virile phallus of this mysterious personage is shown in a state of erection; the shape of his phallus is modestly symbolized by a palm (symbol of victory). These types of phallic symbols are abundant in both the Aztec and Mayan cultures.

A very special veneration was rendered to the serpent in the Temple of Quetzalcoatl in Teotihuacán. Here we see the rattlesnake chiseled on the unconquered walls of that mysterious sanctuary. This is the Kundalini, the igneous serpent of our magical powers that Hinduism talks about.

On this strange stone, the Aztecs teach us two things: first, the Kundalini has seven degrees of power. Second, the Kundalini is totally sexual.

The Kundalini is the sum total of the seven serpents: two groups of three, with the sublime coronation of the seventh tongue of fire that unites us with the One, with the Law, with the Father. This is related to the septenary constitution of the human being, which Theosophy talks about.

Therefore, considering these issues under the light of these theosophical truths, we sustain that each organ is septuple in its internal, metaphysical constitution, and our spinal column is no exception; it is also septuple in its constitution.

There are seven nervous centers along our spinal canal. These are the seven churches referred to in the Apocalypse (Revelation) of St. John. These seven churches enter into activity with the sexual fire of the Kundalini. This is how the seven fiery serpents respectively open the seven churches in each of our seven bodies.

The Kundalini's sexual fire awakens with sexual magic. Yes, in the union of the phallus and the uterus is found the key of its power, on condition that the sacred wine (Exioëhary) is never ejaculated, not even a single drop.

Ancient Aztecs practiced sexual magic in order to awaken the Kundalini. Couples of man and woman underwent entire months caressing and loving each other and even in sexual connection within the sacred patios of their temples; however, they knew how to control their animal ego in order to repress seminal ejaculation. Thus, this is how they transmuted their pure waters of life into seminal vapors, and these vapors were transmuted into Christic energies. Then, these Christic energies were bipolarized into solar and lunar currents that ascended through Ida and Pingala.

When the solar and lunar atoms make contact in the coccygeal bone, then the Kundalini — Quetzalcoatl, the feathered serpent — awakens.

Seven serpents are represented in the figure of the decapitated man. The first serpent belongs to the physical body, the second serpent to the ethereal body, the third to the astral body, the fourth to the mental body, the fifth to the body of willpower, the sixth to the body of the consciousness, the seventh to the Innermost, our real inner Being. These are the seven portals of initiation. These seven serpents rise in successive order. These are related to the first seven great initiations of Major Mysteries.

We exited Eden through the door of sex, and only through that door can we enter once again. There are no other doors. Eden is sex itself.

The seven serpents grant us power over the earth, water, air, the universal fire of life; over the tattvas[95] of the ether.

Within us, the seven serpents awaken telepathy, intuition, the esoteric ear, clairvoyance, intuitive vision, and omniscience. The seven serpents transform us into gods.

The figure of the decapitated man found in the Museum of Mexico is a remarkable treasure of ancient wisdom.

Love is the foundation of practical magic. Thus, in the Aztec temples, men and women adoring each other awakened Quetzalcoatl, the sacred serpent, the terrific igneous serpent of our magical powers.

---

95   The subtle aspect of the elements.

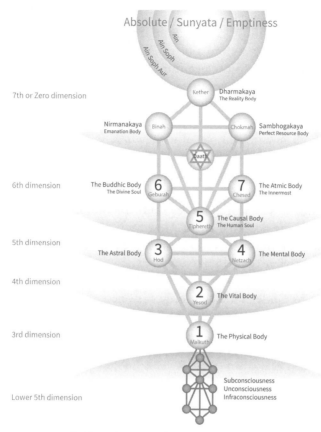

THE TREE OF LIFE AND THE INITIATIONS OF MAJOR MYSTERIES

Our destiny is to love; our destiny is to adore. There is nothing in the world that can overcome the force of love. When two beings (male and female) adore each other, intellectual theories are forgotten. Thus, it is better to love than to read. Yes, the ardent kiss of a man and a woman who love each other has more power than the theories of spiritual schools.

When a man and a woman unite sexually in a trance of love, they have the power to awaken the Kundalini and to open the seven churches of their spinal column. Even the gods are children of a trance of love. Blessed be love.

The one who has never loved does not know anything about life.

The flame of the spirit must be enlivened with the power of love. For this, we must kill the animal ego.

In the beginning, we must be intensely sexual. Thereafter, we must renounce sex. In the beginning, we have to develop powers. Thereafter, we have to renounce them.

Some people do not understand the former statements, and act awkwardly, as when someone wants to take part in a horse-race without having a horse, or if they have it, they want to begin the race facing towards the rear of the horse instead of its head. Yes, some wretched people understand everything in reverse; in other words, they want to renounce sex without first having awakened the sacred fire, or they want to renounce powers without first having acquired them. How foolish they are, renouncing something that they do not have, yet they are incapable of renouncing what they do have.

Indeed, this path is very difficult. This is the path of the razor's edge. Understand that only the one who has become christified can renounce sex, and only the one who is already prepared to enter into the Absolute can renounce his powers. Yet, the pseudo-Theosophist, pseudo-Rosicrucian Aquarianists, etc., do not understand this.

Jesus Christ said,

"I AM the way, the truth, and the life" —John 14:6

Yet, people do not understand this.

People are not concerned with their resplendent "I am," because instead of seeking within themselves, they prefer to follow impostors. Yes, instead of seeking their resplendent "I am" within themselves, they become henchmen of mystical thieves who disguise themselves as Christs. They follow bandits who disguise themselves as saints, who exploit them and lead them to the abyss. This is how people are. How foolish they are: they despise their "I Am the way, the truth, and the life." What an unwise behavior: they disregard their "I am" in order to follow the wicked, nonetheless they say that they are seeking the truth.

Understand that when Jesus said, "I Am the way, the truth, and the life," when he said "I Am," he was not addressing his persona, since to proclaim his own person is more than ludicrous, it is unwise. Thus, to think of Jesus in this manner is beyond stupidity. Through the phrase "I Am," the master taught us that the inner "I am" is the only way. Thus, through this phrase he did not talk to us about many ways in order to reach the truth, but only one. In none of the four gospels do we find him showing us many ways. He only said, "I Am the way, the truth, and the life."

Let us then enter the strait and narrow path that leads to light. That door is sex.

We met a terribly mystical, wretched old woman who looked at sex with repugnance, as something vulgar, dirty, and gross. She considered herself to be totally chaste and pure. When we studied her Satan (her Guardian of the Threshold) in order to know her purifications, we were surprised and had to defend ourselves, since her Satan attacked us in a horrible manner. The sexual appetite of that wretched soul was terrible. What happened is that the body of that sick old woman was no longer functional for her passionate satisfactions, that was all.

Many state, "Sex is vulgar. I am chaste and pure. I am very spiritual. I am no longer enticed by the lewdness of sex," etc. Yet, when we examine the Satan of those "super-transcended mystics," we verify that those souls are filled with a terribly suppressed sexual appetite. Within the fornicators, Satan is very robust and strong.

Only those who manage to ride the donkey, only those who tame the beast, are capable of transforming their Satan into a beautiful child filled with beauty. But we have to ride the donkey. We must practice sexual magic, to really face the beast in order to tame it and overcome it. This is the only way to attain chastity.

So, those wretched souls who look at sex as something repugnant, what they are really doing is defending their Satan, keeping it fat, robust, and strong. Indeed, when these type of male and female mystics return, reborn in new physical bodies, they get involved in the most horrible carnal passions.

Of what use is boasting about being an ineffable mystic if within us Satan is huge, robust, and strong, and waiting for opportunities to satisfy its passions? This is like the devil celebrating Mass.

Therefore, let us work with our seven serpents. Let us Christify ourselves, and only when we become as gods, then we will go beyond the sexual act. Then, we will enter into the Heavenly Jerusalem riding the donkey. Then we will really be chaste because we will have killed the beast.

So, chastity is the foundation of sanctity. However, some most-holy sanctimonious pseudo-masters of many orders of Aquarius are fornicators and adulterers. They have been the cause of many broken marriages. Naturally, these hypocrites of Aquarius keep silence about this. Why do they keep silent about it? Indeed, we should not put our nose into what is not our business, nonetheless we must never hide crimes because then we become accomplices of crime. Many preachers of Aquarius hide their crimes while publicly preaching doctrines that must be examined. We must examine the fruits of all preachers. We must not hide our crimes. All cases are fruits that must be carefully examined:

> *"For there is nothing covered, that shall not be revealed; neither hid, that shall not be known. Therefore whatsoever ye have spoken in darkness shall be heard in the light; and that which ye have spoken in the ear in closets shall be proclaimed upon the housetops."* —Luke 12:2, 3

> *"Verily, verily, I say unto you, whosoever committeth sin is the servant of sin."* —John 8:34

Christ said,

> *"Ye shall know them by their fruits."* —Matthew 7:16

Thus, the fruits of the tenebrous ones are tenebrous, like the tenebrous one who left his wife and his children and told another tenebrous one, "Here I leave you my wife; you can use her if you wish." Can such a man be an initiate? Can people who take communion and perform such things be initiates? Can a school lead by a sanctimonious hypocrite be of a white order?

Generally, these pseudo-masters and henchmen abandon their wives and children; thereafter, they declare themselves "saints of Aquarius." Hence, upon which moral bases do these Aquarian devotees stand in order to boast of being white initiates?

SECOND PART

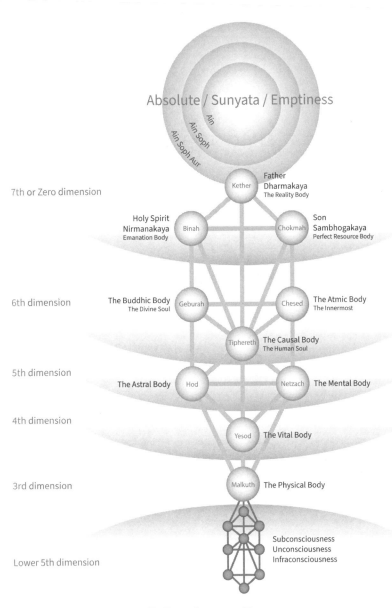

Absolute / Sunyata / Emptiness

Ain
Ain Soph
Ain Soph Aur

7th or Zero dimension — Kether — Father / Dharmakaya / The Reality Body

Holy Spirit / Nirmanakaya / Emanation Body — Binah

Chokmah — Son / Sambhogakaya / Perfect Resource Body

6th dimension

The Buddhic Body / The Divine Soul — Geburah

Chesed — The Atmic Body / The Innermost

Tiphereth — The Causal Body / The Human Soul

5th dimension

The Astral Body — Hod

Netzach — The Mental Body

4th dimension

Yesod — The Vital Body

3rd dimension

Malkuth — The Physical Body

Subconsciousness
Unconsciousness
Infraconsciousness

Lower 5th dimension

THE TREE OF LIFE AND THE MONAD

Chapter 31

The Birth of Jesus

*"Whosoever is born of God doth not commit sin; for his
seed remaineth in him: and he cannot sin, because he is
born of God."* —John 3:9

Master Jesus was a fallen bodhisattva who upraised himself
again with supreme sacrifices. Since many spiritual devotees
do not know what a fallen bodhisattva is, here we give the following explanation.

The Innermost has two twin souls: the Divine and the
Human. The bodhisattva is the Human Soul. Thus, when a
master (the Innermost) wants to reincarnate, he sends his
Human Soul (or bodhisattva) ahead to reincarnate. Then his
Human Soul enters the maternal womb and is born like any
ordinary child; nonetheless, we understand that such a child
is a bodhisattva (Human Soul) of a master. If these bodhisattvas want to incarnate their Innermost (divine master) within
themselves, then they have to prepare themselves in order to
achieve it.

The inner master is a perfect amalgamation of the
Innermost with the Divine Soul; these are already integrally
fused within him. The Innermost is masculine, and his Divine
Soul (the consciousness) is feminine. The outcome of this mixture is a perfect, divine hermaphrodite. This perfect hermaph-
rodite-spirit is the internal master. This is the master who
sends his Human Soul ahead to reincarnate and prepare. Thus,
when the bodhisattva is prepared, the inner master enters into
him. When this happens, we state that the master has been
born.

Therefore, when we state that Jesus was born in a manger,
we are esoterically affirming the spiritual birth of Jesus. The
manger of Bethlehem is only a symbol. The spirit of wisdom[96]
always reincarnates in this manger of the world in order to

---

96 Hebrew Ruach Chokmah-El which is Christ, Vishnu, Quetzalcoatl, etc.

CHRIST IS BORN AMONGST THE ANIMAL DEFECTS IN OUR MIND.

save the wretched, suffering humanity from the animals of the manger: the human passions.

Often, it happens that when the bodhisattva (Human Soul) of any given master falls, then that master cannot reincarnate.

The master never falls, yet his bodhisattva is human and can fall (sin). So, when a bodhisattva allows himself to fall, he, as a fallen bodhisattva, is then sent to reincarnate again in a new body in order to pay his debts. However, if he does not successfully upraise himself again, he is then sent to reincarnate again and again, each time in increasingly difficult conditions. When he finally upraises himself again, then the inner master enters within him in order to fulfill a great work.

Understand that Jesus is the bodhisattva of a master who was born in a temple. Jesus was a fallen bodhisattva, yet he upraised himself again with supreme efforts and sacrifices.

Thus, the birth of Jesus relates to his spiritual birth, which is the birth of

> *"The sons of God... which were born, not of blood, nor of the will of the flesh, nor of the will of man, but of God."*
> —John 1:12, 13

Chapter 32

Spiritual Birth

In order for the Being (the Innermost) to be born in us, we have to terminate with the process of the human "I." For this, we must not commit the error of dividing ourselves into a superior "I" and an inferior "I." That which spiritual students call "superior I" is not the Being, but rather a refined form of the human "I," a subtle modality of self-defense that the human "I" utilizes in order to persist and remain alive. Yes, that division is just a subtle evasion that the human "I" utilizes. It is just a refined concept of Satan.

We have to die in order to live. We have to lose everything in order to win everything. In order to have the right to live, we must die through the death of the cross, because the Being (the Innermost), full of glory and power, is only born upon the cadaver of the human "I."

Regrettably, our human "I" wants to appear everywhere. Our human "I" wants to be applauded and admired by everyone. The human "I" lets his hair and beard grow and wears strange clothes in order to appear publicly on the streets, so that the naive can call him master, elder brother, etc. Thereafter, like a harlot the human "I" publicly undresses in order to show off his powers, qualities, and lineage.

Yes, the human I's...

> "...love the uppermost rooms at feasts, and the chief seats in the synagogues, and greetings in the markets, and to be called of men, Master, Master" —Matthew 23: 6, 7

The human "I" has no humility. It boasts about everything. It swaggers about everything. It shows off everything without any modesty whatsoever. The human "I" is an actor who works in order to be applauded and admired by others.

> "Vanity of vanities, saith the Preacher, vanity of vanities; all is vanity." —Ecclesiastes1: 2

The human "I" is filled with jealousy. This is why the human "I" loves to be disguised with the cloak of Aristippus. Tradition tells how Aristippus, a great Greek philosopher, wanting to show his wisdom and humility, garbed himself with an old cloak, full of patches and holes. Thus, grasping the staff of philosophy and filled with a great humility, Aristippus walked through the streets of Athens, and in this fashion Aristippus arrived at the home of Socrates. When Socrates saw him coming, he exclaimed, "Oh, Aristippus, I see thy vanity through the holes in thy cloak."

The human "I" knows how to conceal anger within receptacles made of ice. Yes, within cold receptacles filled with beauty and ineffable perfume, the human "I" hides the fire of anger. This is how when driven by jealousy he declares that he is prudent, and he states that his anger is just confusion and stress, etc. Indeed, crime is hidden within the incense of prayer.

The authentic master never boasts of being a master. The true master is unknown. He dresses like any ordinary citizen and goes around anonymous and unknown.

Therefore, in order for the Being to be born in us, the "I" must completely die. The Being is what is, what has been, and what shall always be. The Being is the life that throbs in each atom, the Most Exalted within us. The Being is impersonal; it is the Innermost, the Most Exalted within. The Being is beyond desire, beyond the mind, beyond the will, even beyond consciousness.

The Being is beyond intelligence. The reason for the Being to be is to be the Being itself. The Being is life, "I am," the Being.

Chapter 33
Origins of the Human "I"

The human "I" is a monstrous larva that came into existence when we exited Eden. First, the "I" became the gross or vulgar man of the earth. Then the "I" evolved and manifested as a learned, intellectual man. Finally, the "I" makes a last effort in order to subsist; here, it declares itself to be a lofty selected one, a master, and enjoys being called by people, "Master, Master." The "chosen I" enjoys undressing like a harlot in order to show its figure, qualities, and divine powers to others. Subsequently, that monstrous larva develops into a "prophet" in order to exhibit its powers and virtues and thus be venerated by others. Thus the "I," dressed with the robe of Aristippus, goes around boasting of humility as long as no one touches its egocentricity; yet, when this is touched, it reacts filled with sublime anger.

The "I" enjoys boasting about its books and marvelous deeds. Moreover, with an ineffable pride, that monstrous larva disguises itself as a saint and martyr, and boasts of being a master, and even an angel.

In the nights of yore, the "I" was simple. Yet, throughout the centuries it became increasingly complicated and difficult. Some call this complicated process "evolution" and "progress," yet indeed, the complication and strengthening of that horrible larva called "I" is not evolution.

The human "I" suffers innumerable and subtle transformations. Sometimes it looks like a demon; sometimes it looks like a child-god.

In synthesis, we affirm that the "I" undergoes three successive stages of complication: the first is the gross or vulgar man of the earth, the second is the evolved or learned man who develops the intellect, and the third is the lofty selected or chosen ones who dwell in the highest. This third stage is the most dangerous. When the "I" reaches this third phase, it becomes very subtle and dangerous, since here it transforms itself into a divine or angelic "I." It adopts the characteristics of an angel and wants everyone to recognize its merits. This angelic "I" is more subtly dangerous than the human "I."

The "I" disintegrates when it enters into the house of the dead. The gods who want to enter into the Absolute have to kill the "I." They have to enter the house of the dead.

> *"Neither be ye called masters: for one is your master, even (the inner) Christ."* —Matthew 23:10

An authentic guru does not go around boasting about it. The authentic guru is the inner Christ. A true master goes around everywhere anonymously and unknown. He does not exhibit his deeds or powers, and is filled with modesty. A true master is before anything else an upright citizen. The authentic master is never an intellectual, since the intellect is an animal function of the human "I." The true master is like a child, pure, holy, simple, and natural. The true master is the inner Christ:

> *"That is the true Light, which lightens every man that comes into the world."* —John 1:9

After death, through successive periods of internal evolution the soul is undressed from the astral and mental bodies. Thereafter, the soul submerges in the ineffable joy of the infinite, where the marvelous harmonies of the fire resound. Unfortunately, at the threshold of mystery, the human "I" (within which linger the roots of evil and suffering) remains waiting for us for our new rebirth.

When the human "I" is about to die, the Being is born in us filled with glory and majesty. Thus, in each initiation, something dies within us, and something is born within us. This is how the human "I" dies little by little. This is how the Being is born little by little. This is why we call every initiation a birth.

Nature does not make any leaps. Thus, it is necessary for the human "I" to die in order for the Being to be born in us. It is urgent for the Being to receive his crown, which is the resplendent and luminous "I Am."

> *"Be thou faithful unto death, and I will give thee a crown of life."* —Revelation 2:10

After receiving the crown of life, the "I" metamorphoses itself into a "deity," then, internally, this dangerous divine "I" enters into the house of the dead, and little by little is definitively disintegrated. "The house of the dead" is an internal school where the human "I" dies little by little.

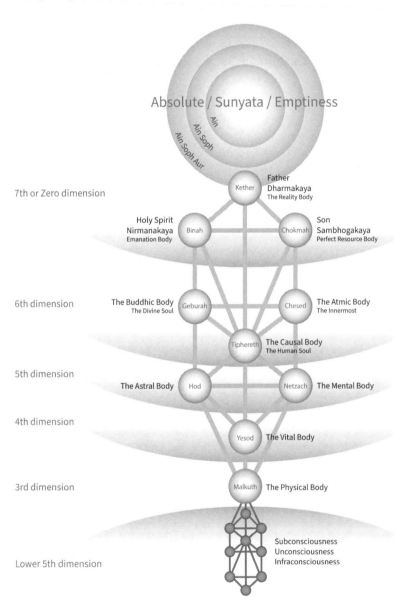

Absolute / Sunyata / Emptiness

Ain
Ain Soph
Ain Soph Aur

7th or Zero dimension — Kether — Father / Dharmakaya / The Reality Body

Holy Spirit / Nirmanakaya / Emanation Body — Binah — Chokmah — Son / Sambhogakaya / Perfect Resource Body

6th dimension — The Buddhic Body / The Divine Soul — Geburah — Chesed — The Atmic Body / The Innermost

Tiphereth — The Causal Body / The Human Soul

5th dimension — The Astral Body — Hod — Netzach — The Mental Body

4th dimension — Yesod — The Vital Body

3rd dimension — Malkuth — The Physical Body

Subconsciousness
Unconsciousness
Infraconsciousness

Lower 5th dimension

THE BODIES OF THE BEING ON THE TREE OF LIFE

Chapter 34

The Guardian of the Threshold

The Guardian of the Threshold is the human "I" which later metamorphoses into a divine angelic "I."[97]

After death, following the course of his inner development, the Being abandons the astral and mental bodies. Thus, the Being submerges himself in the starry infinite. Unfortunately, the Guardian of the Threshold (which is the "I") remains at the threshold of mystery. When the Being returns in order to enter into a new womb, the "I" then comes and continues to build our lunar, inferior astral body.

Upon rebirth, the Being is enveloped anew within mental, astral, ethereal, and physical bodies. These four bodies form a new, innocent personality;[98] unfortunately, little by little the human "I" takes over this new personality until totally controlling it.

The Being is pure, yet the human "I" is a horrible larva. The Being is transparent like crystal, yet the human "I" is monstrous like Satan. The Being is never offended by anything, yet the human "I" is offended by everything. The Being is indifferent before pleasure and suffering, before praise and insult, before victory and defeat, yet the human "I" is offended by everything; it suffers and cries, enjoys and seeks pleasures.

The human "I" always seeks for security, yet the Being is never afraid, and this is why he never seeks for securities. The human "I" is afraid of life, afraid of death, afraid of hunger, afraid of misery, etc. The "I" of humans exploit each other because of fear. They go to war because of fear. They steal and accumulate because of fear. They kill because of fear. They arm themselves because of fear.

The Being is beyond desire, beyond attachment, beyond yearning and fears, beyond death and the intellect, beyond human will, beyond intelligence. The Being is the Tree of Life.

---

97 This "divine, angelic I" is how the ego appears in saints; it appears to be beautiful, but is the many defects in the "gods": envy, pride, anger, etc.
98 See glossary.

The human "I" becomes intellectual and suffers because of its attachments and fears, because its jealousies and passions, its egotisms and hatreds.

Let us not confuse the human "I" with the "I am" of which Jesus speaks to us. The human "I" is the larva of the threshold, whereas the "I am" is the crown of life, the resplendent crown[99] of the Being.

The human "I" speaks of honors, seeks satisfactions, is subject to like and dislike. All imperfection in us is related to the horrible human "I." The Being is beyond like and dislike, pleasure and suffering, intellect and reasoning.

We have to kill our human "I" in order for our Being to be born in us.

The human "I" enjoys exhibiting powers. Wretched are the initiates who go around prophesying to people; they shall die assassinated because of not knowing how to be silent. The clairvoyant must not get involved with the lives of others, because he can be assassinated.

Gradually, the human "I" dies, and the Being is being born according to the ascension of the Kundalini through the spinal canal. Each of the thirty-three spinal vertebrae demands certain virtues. This means the death of specific defects in each vertebra. This is how the Being is being born in each vertebra, and how the human "I" is dying in each vertebra, little by little. In each initiation, something is born within us. In each initiation, something within us dies.

This is why we call every initiation a birth, because to be born is impossible without dying. It is impossible to be born if it is not through sex. Therefore, whosoever wants to be born has to enter into the womb of a woman, and only in this way is the right to be born attained.

The mere knowledge of the process of the human "I" is useless in terminating the "I." The Being cannot be born without fire, and fire cannot awaken without sex. The "I" only dies under the blazing edge of the flaming sword. That sword is the Kundalini, and it awakens only by practicing sexual magic with our spouse.

---

99 Hebrew Kether, the first sephirah on the Tree of Life.

We have to kill our "I" with the terrific sword of cosmic justice. Thus, the majesty of God can be expressed through us only with the death of the "I." The sword of justice is the Kundalini. Let us awaken the Kundalini with our spouse.

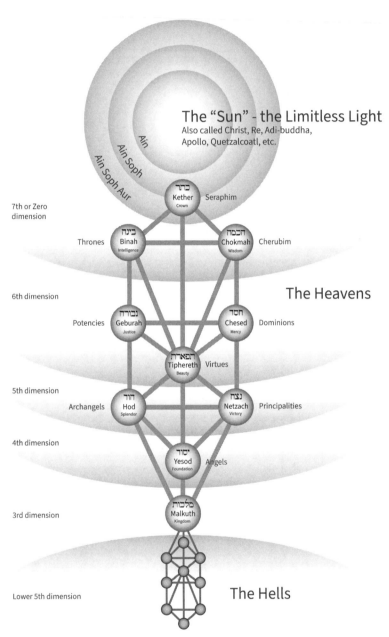

The "Sun" - the Limitless Light
Also called Christ, Re, Adi-buddha, Apollo, Quetzalcoatl, etc.

Ain

Ain Soph

Ain Soph Aur

כתר
Kether
Crown

Seraphim

7th or Zero dimension

בינה
Binah
Intelligence

Thrones

חכמה
Chokmah
Wisdom

Cherubim

6th dimension

The Heavens

גבורה
Geburah
Justice

Potencies

חסד
Chesed
Mercy

Dominions

תפארת
Tiphereth
Beauty

Virtues

5th dimension

חוד
Hod
Splendor

Archangels

נצח
Netzach
Victory

Principalities

4th dimension

יסוד
Yesod
Foundation

Angels

3rd dimension

מלכות
Malkuth
Kingdom

Lower 5th dimension

The Hells

CHRISTIAN NAMES OF RESIDENTS OF THE HEAVENS ON THE TREE OF LIFE

Chapter 35

The First Great Birth of the Christ Jesus

The first great initiation of Jesus was as natural and simple as the humble and innocent birth of a lotus flower. The bodhisattva Jesus did not covet initiations, powers, titles, degrees, hierarchies, masteries, social or divine positions, kingdoms, gold, or silver. Being higher than all angels, archangels, seraphim, potentates, etc., he preferred only to be a good man.

It is stated, "It is better to be a good man than a bad angel."

When apprehending the most complicated characters of the "I," we perceive that it becomes subtly covetous. Here it no longer covets noble titles, but divine titles, and wants everyone to call it master. It covets hierarchic and esoteric titles, and thus, one loses very long, infinite eternities entangled in the karma of the worlds. Here it no longer covets gold or silver, but esoteric powers; it no longer covets honors and greatness, but initiations and degrees. Here it no longer covets lordships or earthly kingdoms, but internal kingdoms, lordships, and majesties within the superior worlds. Here it enjoys governing paradises, and moreover, although this may seem incredible to you, it even become jealous of its own divine hierarchy and thus, it transforms itself into an ineffable tempter who enjoys governing worlds and suns, and thus offers its Edens to the bodhisattvas of compassion. Here, it no longer wants to rest on cushy beds in comfortable earthly mansions, but it longs to rest in the ineffable bliss of Nirvana. Yes, the "I" of the Nirvani[100] does not like the narrow, hard, and difficult path. It enjoys itself in Nirvanic, celestial rests, while wretched humanity suffers and cries. Notwithstanding, the Nirvanis offer the bodhisattvas of compassion their seductive paradises in order to impede the entrance into the Absolute.

---

100 Resident of Nirvana.

Verily, I tell you, beloved disciples, that it is better to renounce the bliss of Nirvana and to follow the path of long and bitter duty.[101]

The path of duty leads us directly to the Absolute. This is better than the bliss of Nirvana. Let us not fall into these divine, Nirvanic temptations.

Know that the bodhisattva who renounces the Nirvanic temptations, the planetary kingdoms (offered by the tempting gods), and renounces Nirvana (heavenly bliss) for the sake of this suffering humanity, is confirmed and "thrice honored," and after eternities gains the right to enter into the Absolute.

The Absolute is life free in its motion. It is the supreme reality, the abstract space that only expresses itself as absolute, abstract motion, happiness without limits, complete omniscience. The Absolute is uncreated light and perfect plenitude, absolute happiness, life free in its motion, life without conditions, without limits.

We have to terminate the process of the "I" in order to absolutely be.

In its most subtly refined shape, the "I" transforms itself into a dangerous child. The "I's" of many Nirvanic masters tempt us, saying, "Abandon the difficult path and come to Nirvana. Here, we are happy." Feeling compassion for our pain, they tempt us with nirvanic bliss.

The "I's" of angels, archangels, seraphim, potencies, virtues, thrones, and hierarchies of different splendors always have the innocence characteristics of children full of beauty. That divine "I" covets degrees, initiations, powers, divine titles, nirvanic majesties, and divine lordships. This divine "I" is the same human "I," yet completely refined.

Listen to me, you humans and gods; listen to me, you angels of Nirvana! Listen to me, oh planetary gods, happy beings, divine Nirvanis, listen to what we, the bodhisattvas of compassion say: the long and bitter path of duty that leads us directly to the Absolute is better than Nirvanic bliss. Those of us who follow that path of duty do not want to leave this path.

---

101 The path of the bodhisattva, also called the straight path.

Woe unto those who leave the difficult path; they will be entangled in the karma of the worlds. We, the bodhisattvas of compassion who love humanity immensely, state: as long as there is a single tear in any human eye, as long as there is even one suffering heart, we refuse to accept the happiness of Nirvana.

Therefore, instead of coveting degrees, powers, initiations and divine lordships, we must exert the effort of becoming useful beings to this suffering humanity.

We must exert great efforts in the law of great service. We must seek the fertile work in the Great Work of the Father. We must seek the means to become more and more useful to this wretched, suffering humanity. This is better than coveting internal titles, initiations, esoteric degrees, and planetary kingdoms.

Personality, individuality, and the "I" are the hard chains that bind us to the hard rock of suffering and bitterness. Gods and humans are submitted to the suffering of conditioned life.

Notwithstanding, in the Absolute we go beyond karma and the gods, beyond the law. The mind and the individual consciousness are only good for mortifying our lives. In the Absolute we do not have an individual mind or individual consciousness; there, we are the unconditioned, free, and absolutely happy Being. The Absolute is life free in its movement, without conditions, limitless, without the mortifying fear of the law, life beyond spirit and matter, beyond karma and suffering, beyond thought, word, and action, beyond silence and sound, beyond forms.

The Absolute is abstract, absolute space, abstract absolute movement, absolute freedom, without conditions, without restrictions: absolute omniscience and absolute happiness.

We have to cease the process of the "I" in order to enter into the Absolute. The human "I" must enter the house of the dead. It must go to the common grave of astral rubbish. The "I" must be disintegrated in the abyss in order for the Being, full of majesty and power, to be born.

The "I" of many masters enjoys its powers and lordships. It boasts being divine, and garbs itself with ineffable majesty and

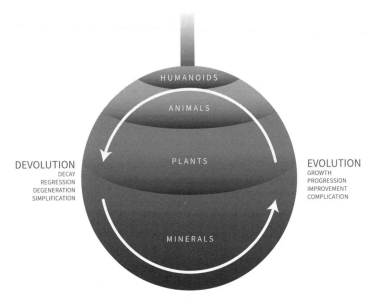

DEVOLUTION
DECAY
REGRESSION
DEGENERATION
SIMPLIFICATION

EVOLUTION
GROWTH
PROGRESSION
IMPROVEMENT
COMPLICATION

HUMANOIDS

ANIMALS

PLANTS

MINERALS

THE EVOLUTION AND DEVOLUTION OF CONSCIOUSNESS. ENTRANCE TO THE CONSCIOUS KINGDOMS IS THROUGH THE HUMANOID KINGDOM.

beauty. The "I" of many masters divests itself like a prostitute in order to show its forms and powers to others. It enjoys boasting about visions so that others will admire and venerate it. It speaks about its initiations and tells its secrets. Yes, it is like the miserly person who lives for counting his money, or like the scoundrel who goes around full of pride, constantly boasting about his high lineage and great wealth.

Listen to me, you humans and gods! Initiations are the awakenings of the consciousness, intimate matters of the consciousness. So, let us learn how to be silent, to be humble, and modest.

Authentic evolution relates to the consciousness, not to the "I." The "I" does not evolve; it only complicates itself, and that is all.

Mineral consciousness evolves when it awakens as plant consciousness. Each mineral atom is the physical body of an elemental creature filled with beauty. These mineral elementals have their language, their consciousness. They gather in tribes or families; they resemble innocent children.

The sublime kingdom of the plants is above the mineral kingdom. Plant consciousness also evolves until awakening as animal consciousness. Each plant is the body of an elemental child that aspires to enter into the animal kingdom.

Animal consciousness also evolves until awakening as human consciousness. Much later, the human awakens as an angel, archangel, etc.

Yet, the human "I" is merely a larva. It is the same larva of the threshold that becomes more and more complicated. The human "I" is the internal beast that controls the four bodies (physical, ethereal, astral, and mental bodies); upon this the monster called "personality" is constituted.

The human "I" of many masters no longer wants political positions, but longs for spiritual positions; it enjoys being a leader and fights for high hierarchical positions in schools, lodges, and spiritual movements.

Therefore, we have to conclude the process of our "I" and personality in order to have the right of Being. We have to terminate individuality in order to have the right to receive the crown of justice.

Only impersonal life and the Being can give us the legitimate happiness of the Great Life, free in its movement.

JESUS OF NAZARETH

Chapter 36

The Ceremony in the Temple

A festival was celebrated in the temple. A precious lamp
burns on the altar. A tri-colored banner victoriously fluttered
in the sacred precinct. The blue of the Father, the yellow of the
Son, and the red of the Holy Spirit flashed on that banner. The
three king-magi (Malachim) lingered in the chamber of reflection; they came to the temple guided by the mystical sun, the
star of Bethlehem. Jesus, the sublime bodhisattva, sat in front
of the altar, dressed in a white linen garment, a white cloak
covering his head. The sky was overcast with heavy clouds
and copious showers. This is how it is written by the prophet,
Micah 5:2:

> "But thou, Bethlehem Ephratah, though thou be little
> among the thousands of Judah, yet out of thee shall he
> come forth unto me that is to be ruler in Israel."

Lo and behold, here is that shepherd attending his spiritual
birth. This is the nativity of the heart. Suddenly, Jesus, the
good shepherd, rose and went towards a sacred precinct of the
temple. Then, a remarkable lightning bolt, a terribly divine
lightning, sparkled in the darkness; it was the inner master
who in those remarkable moments entered his bodhisattva.
Since he had already lifted his first serpent upon the pole, the
bodhisattva Jesus was prepared.

The three king-magi (the Malachim) came to worship the
man-child whose name is Jesus Christ. This is the birth of a
master. This is the nativity of the heart of...

> "...the sons of God... which were born, not of blood, nor
> of the will of the flesh, nor of the will of man, but of
> God" —John 1:12, 13

The three king-magi (the Malachim) worshiped Jesus in the
temple. Jesus then uttered these sublime words. "Oh, Jehovah,
God of mine, how remarkable was that thunderbolt that
fell from heaven!" This happened when Jesus went up into
a mysterious precinct of the temple; that precious precinct

was surrounded by beautiful balustrades. There, the master removed his cloak and sat on a chair. It was in those moments that a divine thunderbolt fell from heaven, and his Inner Being entered him.

> *"That which is born of the flesh is flesh; and that which is born of the Spirit is spirit."* —John 3:6

When Jesus was born in spirit and in truth, a chorus of angels chanted filled with happiness...

> *"Glory to God in the highest, and on earth peace, good will toward men."* —Luke 2:14

And the three king-magi (the Malachim) fell down, and worshiped the good shepherd.

Jesus was a man of medium stature with fair skin, lightly tanned by the rays of the sun. Jesus had black hair and a beard of the same color. Jesus had black and penetrating eyes like two ineffable nights. He had a wide forehead and straight nose (the word Nazarene comes from Nazar, meaning "a man with a straight nose") and fine, strong lips. The mystical birth of Jesus is the first initiation of Major Mysteries.

Chapter 37

The Sacred Family Flee to Egypt

"Now when Jesus was born in Bethlehem of Judaea... for thus it is written by the prophets" [Matthew 2:1,5] the college of initiates gathered in a great hall at the palace of Herod the king with the purpose of communicating unto the monarch the spiritual birth of the savior of the world.

Herod was a man of medium stature, a thin and svelte body with a rosy and youthful face. He wore a garment fashioned according to that epoch, and covered his head with a brilliant warrior's helmet.

Thus, Herod, seated at his working desk, listened to the report from the initiates of the temple, yet he did not believe it. He did not acknowledge Jesus as the promised Messiah, and with a lot of arguments, he indignantly rejected the report from the initiates.

Jesus said unto Herod, "You are a Justinian; you are just. What happens is that you have never liked me."

Then, exceedingly wroth, Herod spoke to the council and said, "Do not eat the Moon." Herod meant with this phrase that they must not abandon their lunar[102] cult. Since all racial religions are lunar, the Jewish religion is lunar.

Herod was totally conservative, and as such, he defended the ancient, traditional Jewish religion. Yes, Herod defended the ancient sacerdotal caste of the people of Judah. This is how Herod rejected the savior of the world.

Thus, the council at the palace of Herod was transcendental, since the new period of solar, Christic development in the world was announced in this initiatic council. Nevertheless, since Herod was strikingly conservative, he seized on to the lunar past and racial prejudices, and did not acknowledge Jesus as the savior of the world. Therefore, this council of initiates was a failure.

Herod then sought after the initiates in order to destroy them. He sent forth his soldiers to slay all the "children" that

---

102 See glossary.

were in Bethlehem,[103] since initiates are esoterically called "children." Therefore, the children are the initiates whom Herod ordered to be slaughtered.

This is how the soldiers went around the streets of Bethlehem and in all the coasts thereof, killing the initiates. Then was fulfilled that which was spoken by the prophet Jeremiah 31:15 saying,

> *"Thus saith Jehovah; A voice was heard in Ramah, lamentation, and bitter weeping; Rachel weeping for her children refused to be comforted for her children, because they were not."*

Nevertheless, Jesus managed to save himself by fleeing into the land of Egypt. This happened in winter and it rained a great deal. Thus, Jesus had to heroically prevail over the storms of the time. When this happened, Joseph and Mary were already old. They greatly suffered because of their son Jesus.

The sacred family departed to the land of Egypt by land and water.

---

103 Christian Bible, Matthew 2:16

Chapter 38

Jesus in Egypt

Inside a pyramid in the land of Egypt, Jesus was initiated as a student into the mysteries. A vestal dressed in a white robe gave him the first papyri to study.

The trees of Eden are two: the Tree of the Knowledge of Good and Evil, and the Tree of Life. The Tree of Knowledge of Good and Evil is sex. The Tree of Life is the Being. Every authentic cultural doctrine has to carefully study these two trees, because to study one tree while ignoring the other gives only an incomplete and useless knowledge. Of what use is it to study the Being if we do not know sex? Of what use is it to study sex if we do not know the Being? Both trees are from Eden, and they even share their roots.

These trees are the two great basal pillars of the White Lodge: wisdom and love. Wisdom is the Tree of the Knowledge of Good and Evil, and love is the Tree of Life.

The doctrine of these two trees was deeply studied in Egypt. The fatal shadow of the Tree of Life is the "I." The fatal shadow of the Tree of Knowledge is fornication. People mistake the shadows for reality.

Whosoever terminates the process of the "I" attains the Self-realization of the Being within oneself. Whosoever terminates with fornication is transformed into a Christ.

Jesus was submitted to remarkable purifications within the temple. A master instructed him daily. On a certain day, when descending a staircase, he was tempted by a woman, yet Jesus overcame temptation, thus he was victoriously approved. The master was tested many times. The fight against his "I" was remarkable. The bodhisattva had fallen in previous reincarnations; this is why Jesus had to lift up his five fallen serpents.

The sixth and the seventh serpents belong to the master (Atman-Buddhi); the master never falls. The bodhisattva is the one who falls; the bodhisattva is the will-soul (Human Soul); the Human Soul is dressed with the four bodies of sin, which are, the physical, ethereal, astral, and mental bodies.

Jesus had the serpent of each of these four bodies of sin fallen, thus Jesus had to lift them up. The fifth serpent that belongs to the Human Soul was also fallen, so Jesus had to lift up this serpent as well.

Jesus had reincarnated thousands of times on our Earth, and he had fallen. So, the Son of God was full of glory, yet the Son of Man was fallen, but he raised himself up again.

The Son of God is the Inner Christ, which enlightens every man that comes into the world.

Jesus studied in the College of Initiates. During those times, a tenebrous personage of the shadows waged war against the initiates of Egypt, nevertheless those initiates remained firm in the Light.

An instructor taught Jesus the great mysteries of sex. Within the pyramid there was a royal nuptial chamber, and within that chamber Jesus practiced sexual magic with his wife. His priestess-wife was a white woman with blonde hair and a beautiful soul. She was a very high initiate of the temple.

Yes, Jesus Christ encompasses a man joined to God, and as a man he was complete, since he had a wife.

During the trance of sexual magic, Jesus vocalized IN-RI, EN-RE, ON-RO, UN-RU, AN-RA.[104] He prolonged the sound of each letter of these sacred syllables in the following order:

IIIIIIINNNNN... RRRRIIIIIII

EEEEENNNN... RRRREEEE

OOOONNNN... RRRROOOO

UUUUNNNN... RRRRUUUU

AAAANNNN... RRRRAAAAA

So, Master Jesus vocalized these syllables by prolonging the sound of each of the letters of each syllable.

The mantra INRI awakens the sixth sense located between the eyebrows. This is how initiates can read other peoples' thoughts and see all the things from the internal worlds.

---

104 Mantra pronunciations are on page ix.

The mantra ENRE awakens the magic ear; this is how humans can hear over distances of thousands of miles and can hear the voices of the internal worlds.

The mantra ONRO has the power to awaken intuition located in the heart. Intuition is the seventh sense that resides in the heart and in the pineal gland. The voice of the silence is in the heart, and polyvoyance or intuitive sight is in the pineal gland. The intuitive sees everything and knows everything, is omniscient and powerful.

The mantra UNRU awakens in us the sense of telepathy; this is how we can perceive the thoughts of people at a distance. It is located above the navel in the solar plexus.

The mantra ANRA awakens in us the pulmonary chakra, with which we can remember our past reincarnations.

In the astral body these senses look like lotus flowers, and this is how during sexual magic Jesus made these lotus flowers spin.

Man and woman become filled with electricity and cosmic fire during the moments when they are sexually united. In these precise moments they can awaken the Kundalini and can make the chakras, discs, or magnetic wheels of their astral body to spin. We can awaken all the powers of the astral body with the sexual force. We can become angels with the sexual force.

Master Jesus also vocalized the great mantra **AUM**. Esoterically, this mantra is vocalized AOM. The mouth is broadly opened with the A; it is rounded with the O and closed with the M.

The A engenders everything, the O gestates everything, and everything is born with the M. The one who wants to be born has to enter into the womb of a woman in order to have the right to be born. Each letter of the mantra AOM has to be prolonged and sustained.

The mantra **IAO** was also vocalized by Master Jesus during the trance of sexual magic. He knew how to withdraw in time from the sexual act in order to avoid seminal ejaculation. This is how Jesus awakened all of his esoteric powers.

The mantra IAO is vocalized by breathing separately and prolonging the pronunciation of each of its three vowels. Do not pronounce its three letters in one breath. IAO has the power of awakening the sacred serpent.

Jesus knew how to love his wife, and this is how he awakened the sacred fire of the Holy Spirit in order to traverse the 33 holy chambers of the temple.

God shines upon the perfect couple. There is nothing more beautiful than the woman. The delights of love convert us into gods. When the woman knows how to love, she is transformed into a goddess. When the man knows how to adore, he is transformed into a god.

However, carnal passion stains the aura with a dirty, bloody color. Yet when we dominate passion, that color is transmuted into an incarnadine rosy color.

It is better to love than to theorize. It is much better to adore, love and kiss than to read complicated theories. However, kill your "Satan."

Goethe said, "Every theory is gray, and only the tree of the golden fruits of life is green."

Chapter 39

The Thirty-three Chambers of the Temple

In Egypt there was a certain subterranean passage that had thirty-three chambers. Each of these thirty-three chambers of the temple corresponds to one of our thirty-three spinal vertebrae. In the internal worlds, the vertebrae are called "canyons." The fire of the Holy Spirit rises from canyon to canyon like a serpent through the spinal medullar canal, yet with a single ejaculation of semen this serpentine fire descends one or more canyons; it returns downward according to the magnitude of the fault. Thereafter, it is extremely difficult to re-conquer lost canyons. This is why our Lord the Christ told us:

> *"Disciples must not allow themselves to fall, because those who allow themselves to fall have to struggle very much in order to recover what they have lost."*

Sexual magic can only be practiced between husband and wife in an established home. The man who practices sexual magic with different women, and the woman who practices sexual magic with different men, commit adultery,[105] and no adulterer achieves anything.

Yes, there are men and women who commit adultery by practicing sexual magic with many. As a pretext, they allege that they are helping others, yet they utilize these teachings in order to justify adultery, and this is a horrible crime against the Holy Spirit. The adulterer sinks into "outer darkness where only crying and the gnashing of teeth are heard."

Sexual magic can only be practiced in homes that are properly constituted and organized. Woe to those who utilize sexual magic in order to justify adultery.

Jesus was born mystically in Bethlehem, because he lifted up his first serpent (the fire of the Holy Spirit in his physical

---

105 See glossary.

body). Now, in Egypt, he began his work with the second serpent (the fire of the Holy Spirit in his ethereal body).

Thus, thanks to his priestess-wife, he worked with the second serpent, and as his serpentine fire ascended through the spinal medullar canal of his ethereal body, the Master Jesus passed from chamber to chamber through the subterranean passage. Each vertebra has its special conditions, namely virtues and tests, temptations and dangers. Thus, in each vertebra we are attacked by the tenebrous ones.

So, Jesus studied remarkable mysteries and received secret powers in every one of the thirty-three chambers of the temple.

When the serpent of the ethereal body reached the area between the eyebrows of Jesus of Nazareth, then the sun of the Father flashed in the rainy night, and the star of initiation with one eye in the middle suspended itself upon his head. The church of Philadelphia between his eyebrows became as

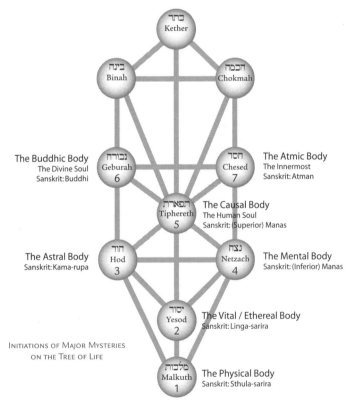

כתר
Kether

בינה
Binah

חכמה
Chokmah

The Buddhic Body
The Divine Soul
Sanskrit: Buddhi

גבורה
Geburah
6

חסד
Chesed
7

The Atmic Body
The Innermost
Sanskrit: Atman

תפארת
Tiphereth
5

The Causal Body
The Human Soul
Sanskrit: (Superior) Manas

The Astral Body
Sanskrit: Kama-rupa

הוד
Hod
3

נצח
Netzach
4

The Mental Body
Sanskrit: (Inferior) Manas

יסוד
Yesod
2

The Vital / Ethereal Body
Sanskrit: Linga-sarira

INITIATIONS OF MAJOR MYSTERIES
ON THE TREE OF LIFE

מלכות
Malkuth
1

The Physical Body
Sanskrit: Sthula-sarira

resplendent as the sun shining in all its beauty. Then, Jesus dressed himself with a white linen garment and the initiates placed a cloak of immaculate whiteness over his head.

An ineffable cosmic festivity made the glory of the temple shine resplendently, and the starry heavens of the spirit were filled with the cosmic happiness of delightful symphonies.

This is how the bodhisattva Jesus finished the recapitulation of the second initiation of Major Mysteries. This is how Jesus received his second birth. Thus, his second serpent completely opened the seven churches in his ethereal body, making this marvelous vehicle shine resplendently with glory.

Yes, Jesus accomplished all of this with love and the woman. Blessed be the woman. Blessed be the man who knows how to love with wisdom.

> *"All of you will be as gods if you leave Egypt and pass over the Red Sea."*

A human being enters Eden and becomes an inhabitant of Eden (the Promised Land) when the ethereal body is Christified. The Christified ethereal body is the wedding garment of the soul, the golden body.

The second serpent opens for us the powers of the ethereal body, and grants us the power to travel in the ethereal body.

The woman achieves all of this by suppressing the sexual impulse and thus avoiding the spilling of the semen.[106] Likewise, the man achieves all of this by knowing how to withdraw in time from the sexual act and thus avoiding seminal ejaculation. This is how the Kundalini develops, evolves, and progresses within the aura of the Solar Logos.

The ethereal body of Jesus was crucified and received its five stigmata. We have to live the entire drama of Calvary in each great initiation.

When the seven churches of the ethereal body of Jesus shone resplendently with glory, the ethereal body of Jesus became a Christ.

---

106 The loss of sexual energy through orgasm.

The Ascension

Chapter 40

The Third Serpent

After having finished his work with the second serpent, Master Jesus began his work with the third serpent of fire. The third serpent belongs to the astral body. The labor with each one of these serpents is very long and difficult. The Kundalini rises slowly through the central canal of the spinal medulla; this is a laborious work of great patience.

The conditions and moral requirements of sanctification that each one of the thirty-three vertebrae demands are plentiful; this is the terror of love and law.[107] Consequently, the ascension of each serpent means entire years of work and sanctification. Thus, to gain access to a single vertebra is a heroic realization.

The third serpent opens the chakras of the astral body. The astral body of Master Jesus was totally transfigured when this serpent of fire ascended and sequentially opened the seven churches of the central canal of the spinal medulla of his astral body. This third serpent descends from between the eyebrows into the heart by following a secret path that ends in the third holy center of the heart. The heart has seven centers.[108] Likewise, there are seven remarkable chambers in this secret path located between the eyebrows and the heart. All of this is the terror of love and law.

When the third serpent opens the Church of Thyatira in his astral body, the initiate is endowed with two small, igneous wings. These igneous wings grant us the power to instantaneously enter into any plane of cosmic consciousness. The spirit of movement teaches us how to maneuver the astral body and also about the laws of cosmic movement.

---

107 Note that in Hebrew, love is Gedulah, an alternative name for the sephirah Chesed (Atman, the Innermost), and law is related to the sephirah Geburah (the Divine Soul). These works are performed by Tiphereth, the Human Soul.

108 Read *Igneous Rose* by Samael Aun Weor.

When the third serpent reached the heart of Master Jesus, he then entered into a great luminous room of the temple, and while moving around the room, his astral body, filled with divinity, sparkled; thus filled with glory, filled with majesty and power, Master Jesus shone most exceedingly. Thereafter Master Jesus passed, within his astral body, through the initiatic process of death, resurrection, and ascension.

By means of fire, we extract from the astral body a psychic extract, which is the conscious soul (the cognizant or Sephirothic values of the astral body), which resembles a beautiful child. For three days this beautiful child remains within his holy sepulcher. On the third day this child resurrects and fuses with the Innermost, the inner Being.

After this esoteric resurrection, Jesus descended into the atomic infernos of nature, since we have to recapitulate within the abyss all the evils of our past reincarnations; this is why Master Jesus remained in the abyss for forty days. Before the ascension, the door of the abyss that is located in the lower abdomen opens up and we are examined by fire; here we are educated about the internal zodiac. Our evolution began in the constellation of Leo and ends in Leo.

During these forty days, within a closed temple the masters sing in a sacred language. They do this in order to help us to become detached from the abyss. The power of the word is terrifically divine. This is how, in the abyss, we bid our last farewell to the darkness.

During these forty days, the initiate abstains from the practice of sexual magic, and only after those forty days can one resume the performance of their rites of sexual magic.

When we exited Eden, all human beings sank into the abyss. However, we do not realize that we dwell in the abyss until we are ready to come out of it. So, all religious and spiritual organizations, namely Theosophism, Spiritualism, Aquarianism, etc. are from the abyss. It is distressing to state this, yet it is the truth.

The ascension of Master Jesus happened when the forty days ended. Then Jesus ascended unto the Father and received the Holy Spirit.

In the temple, four angels blow their trumpets, announcing the ascension of the initiate. The white dove of the Holy Spirit—with its majestic head of an elder—awaits us; we then enter into the temple full of glory and happiness. The Holy Spirit fills us with powers, wisdom, and majesty.

When Jesus received the third initiation of Major Mysteries, he entered the temple, whose altar was adorned with all types of flowers. The masters attended dressed with their white linen garments and covered their heads with long cloaks of immaculate whiteness, whose ends touched their feet. The cosmic music resounded majestically within the sacred environment of the temple. Indeed, this initiatic ceremony was majestic. So, this is how Jesus finished the recapitulation of the third great initiation of Major Mysteries.

In very ancient ages and within worlds of yore that disappeared eternities ago, Jesus Christ passed through nine great initiations of Major Mysteries. Nevertheless, he had to recapitulate all of them. The bodhisattva had fallen in past reincarnations, thus he had to re-conquer what he had lost. These great initiations are granted within the internal worlds.

Lo and behold, oh brothers and sisters, how many things are accomplished with love!

Women, behold the ineffable things of love! Jesus attained his third great mystical birth thanks to the priestess of the temple. The seven words are received in the third initiation.[109]

Sexual magic is the Great Arcanum, the arcanum of love. Therefore, do not let retarded[110] people confuse you, nor fearmongers to hinder your path. Understand that you will not attain anything by reading theories from those theoretical, fearful spiritual devotees who crowd all spiritual schools. Do not let yourself be convinced by them; flee from them, they are dangerous.

Practice sexual magic and you will become as gods. This is the doctrine of the Aquarian Age. This is Gnosticism. This is

---

109 Read *The Seven Words* included in *The Divine Science* by Samael Aun Weor.
110 Literally "delayed or held back in progress."

THE PHALLIC STONE OF JACOB

the Fifth Truth.[111] This is the doctrine that Jesus taught in secrecy to his seventy disciples.

The secret of all secrets is hidden within the Shem Hammephorash stone.[112] This is the cubic stone of Yesod. This is the philosophical stone. This stone is sex. This is sexual magic, love. Blessed be love.

The Bible tells us in Genesis 28:16,18:

> *"And Jacob awaked out of his sleep and he said, surely Iod-Havah is in this place; and I knew it not. And Jacob rose up early in the morning, and took the stone that he had put for his pillows, and set it up for a pillar, and poured oil upon the top of it."*

Indeed, it was from that moment that Jacob began to practice sexual magic. Later on, he incarnated his inner master, his real Being. Jacob is the bodhisattva of the Angel Israel.

Jesus became almighty with the Shem Ham-mephorash stone.

---

111 The teachings of the fifth archangel, the Logos Samael.

112 (Hebrew המפורש השם "Hashem Hamephorash") The "separated name," or the "name of extension, or "the blessed name." Specifically, a name of God that has 72 aspects and is hidden in the original Hebrew of Exodus 14:19-21.

Chapter 41
The Fourth Serpent

When Master Jesus awakened his fourth serpent, he knocked three times on a door and entered into a luminous room filled with delightful flowers and ineffable music. Four masters distributed in two groups received him; those masters were resplendent with majesty and each one had a sword of cosmic justice in his right hand. They rested the hilts of the swords over their hearts, thus the bare swords filled with a terrific power pointed up to the loft. Master Jesus placed himself between two of the masters while ineffable music resounded in the environment.

The serpent of the mental body of Jesus awoke by intense practice of sexual magic with the beautiful priestess of the temple. Yes, without the woman, nothing is attained. Likewise a woman without a man does not achieve anything. By means of sexual magic, everything is attained; nothing can replace the joy of love.

Thereafter, the master entered a classroom. All the disciples were seated at their writing desks. Here, all of them were studying the wisdom of the cosmic mind. Thus Jesus, filled with humility, joined the classroom as one more student.

The mental body is the donkey upon which we must ride in order to victoriously enter into the heavenly Jerusalem (the superior worlds), where we are greeted with branches of palm trees, praises, and feasts. The mental body is a material, dense body. The four bodies of sin (the physical, ethereal, astral, and mental bodies) are material bodies. The mind is the most stubborn animal that we have within; we have to crucify that mind over the sacrificial altar. The mind is the den of desire and wickedness.

If we fling a stone into a lake, we see then waves surfacing from the center of the impact to the periphery. Those waves are the reactions of the water against the impact of the stone; our mind is similar. Incessantly, the mind is reacting to the impacts that come from the exterior world. If we are insulted, we want to respond with a blow. If we are sexually tempted, we react filled with carnal passion. If we are flattered, we display smiles. Yet, if we are insulted, we reply with wickedness. The mind is like the donkey that walks faster if beaten, yet if it is not beaten, it walks even slower.

Krishnamurti addresses the mind a lot, nonetheless his mind is not yet Christified, since the thirty-three spinal chambers of his mental body are filled with darkness because his fourth serpent is not yet lifted up; he needs sexual magic. Yes, all desires, egotisms, crimes, and perversities dwell within the mind of man. However, only the fire can burn the scoriae of the mind.

Reasoning is a crime against His Majesty the Innermost. Many times the Innermost, the Being, gives us an order, yet our mind rebels against him with its reasoning. The Innermost speaks in the form of hunches or unprompted thoughts, yet our mind rebels by means of reasoning and comparison.

Reasoning is based on opinions, on the struggle of antithetical concepts, on the process of conceptual selection, etc. A mind divided by the struggle of reasoning is a useless instrument for the Being, the Innermost.

The voice of the heart is the voice of the Innermost; intuition is the voice of the Innermost. Action without reasoning is upright action; intuitive action is a just, right, and perfect action. Humanity in Aquarius will become intuitive.

Intellectual culture is purely a function of the animal "I." Intellectuals are puffed up with pride, arrogance, and sexual passion. The intellect is based on reasoning, and reasoning is luciferic and demonic. There are people who believe that they can know God by means of reasoning. We Gnostics state that only God knows himself.

Instead of wasting time reasoning, it is better to practice internal meditation. By means of internal meditation we can converse with God, the Innermost, the Being, the Most High. Only in this manner can we learn from the inner master. Only in this manner can we study divine wisdom at the feet of the master.

The intellect nourishes itself by means of external perceptions. That source of information is incomplete, since the external senses are the sources of that information and the external senses are totally deficient. Microbes cannot be studied with a deficient microscope, and the stars cannot be studied with a deficient telescope. Therefore, we have to awaken all the twelve senses of the consciousness.

Thought must flow silently and integrally without the battle of the antithesis that divides the mind between opposed concepts. A fragmented mind is a useless instrument for the Innermost.

We have to terminate with our reasoning and awaken our intuition. Yes, it is only in this manner that we can learn the true wisdom of God. It is only in this manner that the Innermost hands over the reins of the mind.

The true positive function of the mind is art, beauty, love, music: the mystical art of loving divine architecture, painting, singing, culture, techniques placed at the service of humans, but without selfishness, without wickedness, without hatred, etc. The intellect is the negative function of the mind; it is demonic.

The fourth serpent transmutes the mind matter into Christmind. This serpent rises through the spinal medulla of the mental body.

As his fourth serpent ascended from vertebra to vertebra, Jesus entered into each of the thirty-three chambers of the mental world. This is how he transmuted his mind matter into Christ-mind. Understand that without the fire of the Holy Spirit it is impossible to Christify the mind, and this fire can be awakened only by means of sexual magic and love.

The human mind is controlled by the Guardian of the Threshold of the mental body. This demonic creature is the mental "I" that we have to eject and expel from the mental body in the ordeal of the Guardian of the Threshold of the mind. This guardian is Satan in the mind. This is the intellectual, arrogant, and intensely fornicating, reasoning demon of the mind. Now we understand why the human mind is indeed perverse. The most dangerous demons have a sanctimonious mind and boast of being saints.

Jesus became triumphant in all the ordeals as he overcame the Satan of the mind. Jesus illuminated his thirty-three spinal chambers with the fire of the Holy Spirit, and studied the remarkable divine wisdom in each one of them. He learned that the most dangerous black magicians of the cosmos dwell in the mental plane.

The black magicians in the mental plane have sublime appearances. They speak ineffable and beautiful things, and thereafter they subtly advise the ejaculation of the semen. This is how they cause great initiates to fall. All the weaknesses of this humanity are in the mental world.

We must not divide our mind into superior and inferior parts.

As the physical body is an organism, likewise the mental body is another organism. If our Innermost hands over the reins of it, we can become as gods, yet if Satan handles the reins of the mind, we become demons.

Therefore, we must dominate the mind with the whip of willpower. We must ride on the donkey in order to enter the Heavenly Jerusalem. It is only in this manner that we become worthy of receiving the Body of Liberation elaborated with the purest atoms. The Body of Liberation has a Christic appearance. It exudes the aroma of perfection. This body replaces the physical body; it is made of flesh, but it is not the born from the flesh of Adam. This is the body of paradisiacal beings; this body is not submitted to illnesses or death.

When the fourth serpent of Jesus reached the fourth center of the heart, there was a feast in the temple. Then all the masters dressed in their white garments and cloaks occupied their seats and granted unto Jesus the title of buddha.[113] Dressed in a white garment and cloak, Jesus was within a precious sanctuary waiting for his entrance into the temple.

Thus, this is how, thanks to love and sexual magic, Jesus was able to liberate himself from the four bodies of sin. Yes, thanks

---

113 Sanskrit, literally "awakened." Buddha is not a name, but a state of being and title earned through initiation, as explained here.

to sexual magic, he was transformed into a dragon of the four truths: a buddha.

The fourth serpent totally opened the seven churches of Jesus in the world of the cosmic mind, and the cosmic feast of this event was magnificent. A precious lamp burned over the pyramid. Then, a great march with flags of victory was celebrated on the streets of the city, and the Egyptian masses, aroused with mystical enthusiasm, hailed the master. The guards of the city made a street of honor for the parade, and they had to struggle a lot in order to maintain order in all the stopping and going of the enthusiastic multitudes.

In this day and age, when our disciples receive the degree of buddha, then the blessed goddess, mother of the world, presents them in the temple of the mind and says, "Lo and behold, my most beloved child. Behold, here is a new buddha." Then, she places upon her child the diadem of Shiva and the cloak of the buddhas.

Then, Sanat Kumara[114] exclaims, "You have become liberated from the four bodies of sin, and you have entered into the world of the gods. You are a buddha. When a human becomes liberated from the four bodies of sin, he becomes a buddha. You are a buddha." Thereafter, Sanat Kumara delivers unto the initiate the globe of the imperator; this is a globe with a cross on top. Then, there is a solemn feast in the superior worlds.

Nevertheless, in Egypt, these initiatic ceremonies were performed in the physical plane. At that time, the initiatic colleges had not yet been closed. So, the feast of Jesus, the new buddha, was solemn, and the holy land of ancient pharaohs shook with glory. The solemn, initiatic march was an apotheosis.

Carrying a great cross over his shoulders, Jesus led the parade. Indeed, the cross belongs to the great mysteries.

Jesus represented this drama within the temples. Before Jesus Christ, the entire drama of the Lord's Passion was represented inside the temples of mysteries. However, later, Jesus painfully lived this drama in the beloved city of the prophets.

---

114 The founder of the College of Initiates of the great White Lodge. This adept lives in the Gobi desert in an isolated oasis. The body of this great being is more than 18 million years old.

The first teacher of Jesus was Elhanan. The second was the Rabbi Jehosuah ben Perachiah.[115] These were his preceptors in Palestine. However, when Jesus victoriously carried his cross in Egypt, he had already exceeded his previous instructors, since Jesus had become a Buddha.

A psychic extract is removed from the mental body. This psychic extract is then fused with the Innermost. This is performed within the temple.

This is how Jesus victoriously finished his fourth initiation of Major Mysteries.

The sexual fire burns remarkably in the temple of the mind.

---

115 These names are given by H.P. Blavatsky in Isis Unveiled, apparently as quotes from Hebrew sources.

Chapter 42

Jesus' Fifth Serpent

It was in winter when Master Jesus went into the wilderness. The weather was cold in Egypt, and there it was: an ancient, solitary, worn and eroded Egyptian temple of mysteries. Master Jesus entered the atrium, and while kneeling with all humility before the great hierophants, he requested to be admitted into the remarkable mysteries of the fifth serpent of burning fire.

The great Egyptian sages granted him admission. Then Master Jesus left the room and entered a small sanctuary of the solitary temple. In winter, the masters customarily wrapped themselves with blue and white religious shawls in order to be protected from the cold weather.

Thus, this is how Master Jesus entered into the mysteries of the fifth serpent, which ascends through the central canal of the spinal medulla of the will-soul (the Human Soul, Tiphereth).

We have already stated that the Innermost has two souls, namely, the will-soul and the cognizance-soul (Divine Soul, Geburah). The sixth serpent relates to the cognizance-soul; the seventh pertains to the Innermost itself.

There are seven serpents; two groups of three with the sublime coronation of the seventh tongue of fire which unites us with the One, with the Law, with the Father.

Therefore, the Innermost with his two twin souls is a pure and ineffable spirit (Monad). Thus, the four material bodies are the temple of the eternal triune Spirit. This is why Paul of Tarsus wrote in 1 Corinthians 3:16:

> "Know ye not that ye are the temple of God, and that the Spirit of God dwelleth in you?"

The Spirit of God is the Innermost in us. The *Testament of Learning* states:

> "Before the false dawn came over this earth, those who survived the hurricane and the storm gave praise to

the Innermost, and to them appeared the heralds of the dawn." —Quoted from The Dayspring of Youth by M

The human personality is the chariot, the mind is the animal that hauls the chariot, the Innermost is the coachman, the reins are the consciousness, and the whip is willpower. Woe unto the coachman who does not know how to hand over the reins! Woe unto the coachman who does not know how to handle the whip, because he will keep his whip and reins in hand and will not be able to use them! The beast without control will drag the chariot into the abyss, and the Innermost will lose his chariot.

In this day and age, there are many perverse people who are severed from their Innermost. These are crowds who follow a terribly tenebrous devolution in the abyss. All these devolving people have horns on their foreheads. Some of them are demons endowed with sparkling intellects, who boast of being prophets and avatars. Thus, shrouded within fine manners and exquisite culture, they often establish spiritual schools. Yes, within the privileged ranks of aristocracy are thousands of learned, educated, and intellectual people, who even follow mystical traditions, yet they are already totally severed from their Innermost. These are souls who have horns on their foreheads; they are tenebrous demons. These types of souls possess only the four bodies of sin (physical, ethereal, astral, and mental bodies). Unfortunately, their triune immortal Spirit is no longer linked within them. They live in the physical world, yet internally they dwell within the abyss.

The mind has to be lashed with the whip of willpower. It is necessary to learn how to use the whip. The Will-soul has to be Christified by means of the transmutation of human will into Christ-will; these are the mysteries of the fifth serpent.

Only Christ-will knows how to do the will of the Father on earth as it is in heaven. The majesty of Christ-will is portrayed in the nine symphonies of Beethoven. Yes, Christ-will is ineffable music that echoes the majesty of the Word.

Nevertheless, humans place their will at the service of the beast, and therefore they fail. This is why the divine Master Jesus said in Luke 22:42:

"Father, if thou be willing, remove this cup from me: nevertheless not my will, but thine, be done."

Subsequently, thanks to his priestess-wife, the divine Master Jesus managed to lift his fifth serpent upon a pole.[116]

When the initiate awakens his fifth serpent, he then enters into the temple, whose altar is adorned with the sacred shawl of Veronica. The divine face with the crown of thorns stained on the shawl is the living symbol of Christ-will. This symbolizes total sacrifice on behalf of the wretched, suffering humanity. All initiates carry their cross here, within the world of the will (sixth dimension).

Christ-will only knows how to comply with superior orders. It respects the free will of others. It does not exercise coercion over others, not even in teasing, because that is black magic.

In the world of the will, the soul is crucified in order to save humanity.

The ascension of the fifth serpent through the spinal medulla of the will-soul is very slow and difficult. Thus, when the fifth serpent reached the fifth holy center of the heart of the Buddha Jesus of Nazareth, he then entered a sacred precinct where a great Egyptian initiate priestess told him, "Among many, the master is disputed." Indeed, my brothers and sisters, all sects and religious ministries debate a great deal about Master Jesus.

Subsequently, Master Jesus entered into a great hall of the temple. Here, many aged masters were practicing sexual magic with their wives. They were heroically struggling in order to lift their fifth serpent under the guidance of a great hierophant who, smiling, contemplated the venerable elders performing sexual magic, which is the unutterable secret of the Great Arcanum.

In ancient Egypt, those who dared to divulge the Great Arcanum were condemned to the death penalty. Their heads were severed, their hearts were snatched from their bodies, and thereafter their ashes were tossed into the four winds. In the Middle Ages, those who divulged the Great Arcanum were killed, sometimes by the poison-stained tunic of Nessus, or the

---

116 As Moses was instructed to do in Numbers 21.

dagger, or the scaffold. Nevertheless, now we publicly deliver the Great Arcanum in order to initiate the new Aquarian Age. The Great Arcanum is sexual magic.

When Jesus lifted up his fifth serpent, he totally upraised himself again, since previously he was fallen.

The initiatic feast of the Buddha Jesus was majestic. Then the sacred female dancers happily danced in the temple. The sacred dances and its music enclose clues of immense esoteric power.

Thus, this is how the soul Jesus, by adoring the woman, by loving her and practicing sexual magic with her, upraised himself in Egypt.

He did not need to lift up his sixth and seventh serpents because those fires belong to the internal master, and he never falls. The one who falls is the Human Soul, which is the bodhisattva of the master.

In this dark age, there are a great number of fallen bodhisattvas. One of them is Andrameleck who became a horrible demon, presently incarnated in China. These bodhisattvas are common and ordinary people. Many of them are puffed up with vices and wickedness like Javhe, who is the genie of evil, a fallen angel. These types of bodhisattvas reincarnate incessantly in order to pay karma, They suffer and enjoy life, since they are like other people. Obviously, the internal master cannot enter into them until they upraise themselves from the clay of the earth. Daniel, Solomon, and many others are fallen.

This age of Kali Yuga[117] was fatal for many bodhisattvas who, when fallen, are worse than demons. For example, feeling compassion for a prostitute, an archangel sent his bodhisattva to assist her, yet his weak bodhisattva fell sexually with her, thus the bodhisattva lost his sword and sank into the clay of the earth. Logically, this bodhisattva remained disunited from his Innermost, and only after many painful reincarnations the bodhisattva upraised himself once again. Finally he became fused anew with his god.

---

117 Sanskrit, "dark age."

Chapter 43

The Last Moments of Jesus in Egypt

Once the Buddha Jesus lifted up his five fallen serpents, he shone resplendently, filled with glory. Thus, he did not need anything else but to be crowned. The coronation of Jesus is a primordial historical event that is older than the world. In fact, truthfully, this is why,

> *"Jesus said unto them, Verily, verily, I say unto you, before Abraham was, I am."* –John 8:58

Apocalypse (Revelation 2:10) states,

> *"Be thou faithful unto death, and I will give thee a crown of life."*

The crown of life is the Being of our Being. It is the authentic and legitimate "I am."

It is necessary for our "I" to die within, in order for the Being to be born within us. Thereafter, our Being receives the crown of life, which is the resplendent and divine "I am."

As the day differs from the night, as winter differs from summer, as God differs from the demon, likewise, the "I am" differs from the "I."

Therefore, those who speculate about having an inferior "I" and a superior "I" are just looking for an escape in order to avoid the process of their "I." We, the Gnostics, are not looking for any escape, because we know that the "I" is the horrible larva of the threshold, thus the only thing we want is to finish with that larva in order to have the right of Being. Yes, only through the termination of that larva can the crown of life be granted to us. Only in this way can the resplendent "I am" be incarnated within us.

In Egypt, Master Jesus learned how to project himself in the astral body by vocalizing **FARAON**. This is how he consciously projected himself in his astral body at will. For this, Master Jesus laid down on his bed in exactly the same manner as the Chac Mool, the Aztec god of rain. Jesus rested his head on a pillow and got sleepy by vocalizing the mantra FARAON.

When this mantra is vocalized is must be divided into three syllables. The first is "FA," which is the note that resounds in all of nature. The second is the Egyptian "RA." The third is the "ON," which reminds us of the famous Sanskrit mantra OM from India.

CHAC MOOL

Thus, Master Jesus got sleepy by mentally vocalizing this mantra, and thus he consciously projected himself within his astral body at will. It is important to prolong the sound of each one of the letters of the mantra FARAON so the physical body falls asleep, and the soul, the awakened consciousness, detaches from it and submerges itself within the internal planes with cognizance, thus traveling within the astral body at will.

Jesus was awarded by the pharaoh of Egypt with a sacred esoteric decoration, which had the shape of two small wings that symbolize the igneous wings. This award was placed over his heart.

In those times in Egypt, there was an initiate who was going astray. He intended to swerve Jesus as well, yet he failed in his attempt. Jesus with wisdom admonished that man. However, it was to no avail, since he had already very much gone astray.

Behold, here is the esoteric wisdom of Jesus that we, the Gnostics, are spreading in order to initiate the Aquarian Age. We are, therefore, the initiators of this new era.

> "But we speak the wisdom of God in a mystery, even the esoteric wisdom, which God ordained before the world unto our glory: Which none of the princes of this world knew: for had they known it, they would not have crucified the Lord of glory. But God hath revealed them unto us (the Gnostics) by his Spirit: for the Spirit searches all things, yea, the deep things of God."
> —1 Corinthians 2: 7-10

All religions and schools of this century adore and exploit Jesus' human personality, yet they reject the secret doctrine of the "I am." Yes, no one wants to seek internally his own resplendent and luminous "I am." Understand that the doctrine of the "I am" is the doctrine that Jesus taught to us, nevertheless people reject Jesus' teachings because:

> "...*The animal man receives not the things of the Spirit of God: for they are foolishness unto him: neither can he know them, because they are spiritually discerned.*"
> —1 Corinthians: 2:14

> "*Howbeit we speak wisdom among them that are perfect: yet not the wisdom of this world, nor of the princes of this world, that come to nought.*"
> —1 Corinthians: 2:6

After these events passed, Master Jesus left the pyramids. Thus, riding a camel, he went towards the sacred lands of Hindustan and Tibet, where he entered into the schools of mysteries.

In India and Tibet, Master Jesus made great prophecies, and it was there, on the snowy summits of Tibet, where the master entered a great temple of mysteries, where a great council of masters was held.

Indeed, Jesus became a true hierophant of the great mysteries. Thus, after his journey, he returned towards the Holy Land; by that time, Herod was already dead.

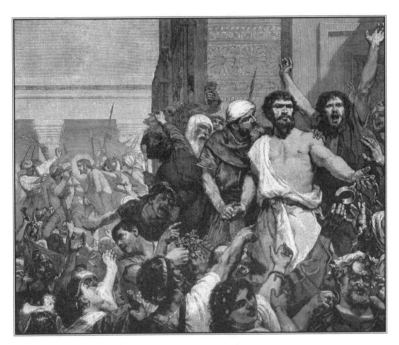

THE JEWS SAVE BARABBAS

"Do you want me to release to you the king of the Jews?" asked Pilate, knowing it was out of envy that the chief priests had handed Jesus over to him. But the chief priests stirred up the crowd to have Pilate release Barabbas instead.

"What shall I do, then, with the one you call the king of the Jews?" Pilate asked them.

"Crucify him!" they shouted.

"Why? What crime has he committed?" asked Pilate.

But they shouted all the louder, "Crucify him!"

- MARK 15:9-15

Chapter 44

Jesus in the Holy Land

The great Buddha, Jesus of Nazareth, returned to his own land in order to accomplish the greatest mission of all time. Nevertheless, it is very true that,

> *"A prophet is not without honor, save in his own country, and in his own house."* —Matthew 13:57

Even the natural birth of Jesus hides a moral and very painful tragedy:

> *"A virgin named Mariam, betrothed to a young man of the name of Iohanan, was outraged by another man named Ben Panther [Pandira] or Joseph Panther, says "Sepher Toldos Jeshu." "Her betrothed, learning of her misfortune, left her [for Bablyon], at the same time forgiving her. The child born was Jesus, named Joshua."*
> — H.P. Blavatsky, Isis Unveiled [1877]

So, the painful tragedy of Jesus starts from the beginning: his own physical conception. The angels who assisted his natural conception suffered terribly.

> *"For he hath made him to be sin for us, who knew no sin; that we might be made the righteousness of God in him"* —2 Corinthians 5:21

Jesus upraised himself from the darkness to the light. He passed through all human sufferings, and therefore he is the only one who can redeem us from all human pains.

The people of Israel were chosen in order to surround the master and thus to redeem the world. Now we comprehend why so many prophets and so many saints where born amongst the people of Israel. The glory of Solomon, son of David the King of Zion, shone resplendently on the unconquered walls of Zion. This is why the face of Jehovah resplendently shone upon the unconquered walls of Jerusalem. Likewise, Isaiah, Samuel, Jeremiah, Ezekiel and many other prophets shone filled with light on the streets of Jerusalem. These were the prophets chosen to accompany the Lord.

Regrettably, at the supreme hour of the final test, their Sanhedrin liberated Barrabas (Javhe) and sent their Christ, their promised Messiah to be crucified. Thus, when their people had to choose between Christ and Javhe, they crucified the Christ and adored Javhe, who is the chief of the black lodge. Javhe is a fallen angel, the genie of evil. Javhe is a terribly perverse demon.

This is how the people of the prophets of Judah crucified their promised Messiah, Christ; this is how their people, the nation of Israel, failed. This is how the people that had been chosen by the prophets of Judah in order to spread the Christic wisdom upon the entire face of the earth chose the abyss. Now, that nation follows Javhe and totally failed its prophets, because that nation betrayed its master and crucified him. If the Lord had not been crucified, the destiny of the Western world would have been another. We would now have sublime enlightened rabbis[118] everywhere, preaching Christic esotericism.

The union of Christic esotericism, secret Jewish Kabbalah, and holy alchemy would have completely illuminated and transformed the entire world. Yes, the mysteries of Levi would have shone with the light of Christ. Gnosis (Da'ath) would have magnificently shone everywhere. Then, the world would not have fallen into the dead Christianity of Roman Catholicism. Then, we would have been saved from the horrible darkness of the dark age (Kali Yuga). Regrettably, the people chosen by the prophets of Judah failed, and the entire humanity sank into the abyss.

> *"And, behold, the veil of the temple was rent in twain from the top to the bottom; and the earth did quake."*
> —Matthew 27:51

Then the Ark of the Covenant became visible for all, as the only hope of salvation. This ark represents the sexual organs, within which is the Great Arcanum, sexual magic, the supreme key of redemption.

---

118 Hebrew, literally "masters."

Chapter 45

The Baptism of Jesus

Albeit the Buddha Jesus was full of majesty, nonetheless he needed only one thing: his coronation. Consequently, Jesus went towards Jordan where John had his haven. Since John is a great master of the White Lodge, John officiated in his temple located at Jordan. At the door of the temple, John wrote an inscription that stated, "Profane dances are forbidden." John was a white bearded, venerable elder of medium stature. When officiating inside the temple, he dressed in his royal priestly robe; however, outside the temple, he dressed modestly, enveloping his body with camel's hair. Thus, this venerable elder was full of majesty. His half-naked body full of strong muscles and his wide forehead reflected the majesty of his resplendent Being, thus everyone respected him.

As it is written in the books of destiny, John had to live until the arrival of the Messiah. John had to be the great initiator of the Buddha Jesus.

When Jesus entered the temple, John was dressed in his priestly garments, thus he commanded Jesus to remove his vestures. Jesus undressed and only his sexual organs remained covered with a white cloth. Thereafter, Jesus came out of the vestibule and entered the sanctuary. There John anointed the Lord with pure oil and poured water over his head. It was in those moments when three stars resplendently shone within the internal heaven of the Spirit, and through the third star, red as living fire, from that heaven of the Spirit, descended (Chokmah) the spirit of wisdom. Yes, this was the supreme moment in which the spirit of wisdom entered in Jesus through his pineal gland.

The Father, only visible to the eyes of the Spirit, did not enter in those moments in the body of Jesus; he only attended the coronation of the Buddha Jesus riding his royal chariot of fire. Thus, this is how the coronation of the Buddha Jesus happened.

Apocalypse (Revelation 2:10) states,

*"Be thou faithful unto death, and I will give thee a
crown of life."*

Jesus was faithful and therefore he received the crown of life.

The crown of life is the eternal breath, profoundly unknowable to itself. It is a breath of the Absolute within us. It is
that pure ray from which the Innermost of each human being
emanated. It is the Atmic thread of the Hindustanis. It is our
"I Am."

*"Whosoever knows, the word gives power to, no one has
uttered it, no one will utter it, except the one who has the
word incarnated."*

Jesus incarnated the Word in the baptism.

*"In the beginning was the Word, and the Word was
with God, and the Word was God. The same was in the
beginning with God. All things were made by him; and
without him was not any thing made that was made.
And the light shineth in darkness; and the darkness
comprehended it not."* —John 1:1-3, 5

The Cosmic Christ is called Christos by the Greeks, Osiris by
the Egyptians, Vishnu by the Hindus, Kuan Yin, the Melodious
Voice by the Chinese, Avalokiteshvara by Tibetans. The Cosmic
Christ is the Army of the Voice, the great breath, the central
sun, the Solar Logos, the Word of God.

Sequentially, after this Gnostic baptism (Da'ath), like a
radiant sun, the Christ, filled with glory, resplendently shone
with an immaculate divine white light within Jesus. Thus, this
is how Jesus incarnated his resplendent and luminous "I am,"
and it was from that moment that the Buddha Jesus became
Jesus Christ (the Son of Man).

*"And the Word was made flesh, and dwelt among us...
full of grace and truth." "That was the true Light, which
lighteth every man that cometh into the world."* —John 1:
14, 9

Within Christ there are no hierarchical differences. Within
him we are all one.

"John bare witness of him, and cried, saying, This was he of whom I spoke, He that cometh after me is preferred before me: for he was before me." —John 1: 15

"And of his fullness have all we received, and grace for grace." —John 1:16

Thus, whosoever incarnates the inner Christ will become him as well.

Many buddhas incarnated Christ in the past, and in the future, many buddhas will incarnate the Lord.

Understand that no one can receive the crown of life without first having lifted his seven serpents upon the staff.

Anyone who says, "I received the crown of life" lies, because the one who receives it does not boast about it. The one who receives it is only known by his deeds. The crown of life is a remarkable secret.

We have to become dwellings of the Lord.

"And as Moses lifted up the serpent in the wilderness, even so must the Son of man be lifted up." —John 3:14

Understand that (like Jesus) we have to incarnate the Christ within us in order to ascend to the Father. Christ is not an individual. Christ is the Army of the Voice, the Word of God. No one comes to the Father but through the Son (the Cosmic Christ).

Within Christ we are all one. Within the Lord there are no differences between one person and another, because we are all one within him. Thus, there is no individuality within him. So, the one who incarnates Christ becomes him, him, him.

"Variety is unity."

Therefore, we have to finish with the personality and the "I" for in order for the Being to be born within us. We have to terminate our individualism.

If a mystic in a state of ecstasy abandons all seven bodies in order to investigate the life of Christ, one will then see the Self (the Glorian) represented in the drama of the passion of the Lord. One will then be one's Glorian performing miracles and marvels. One will experience the Self dead and resurrected on the third day. That mystic will occupy the place of Christ, and in those moments one shall be Him, Him, Him, because in the world of the Christ there are no individuals. Within the Christ there is only one Being that expresses Self as many.

When the "I" and the individuality are terminated, then only the values of the consciousness remain. These are the attributes of eternal Absolute Abstract Space, who only can say, "I Am the way, the truth and the life. I Am the Light. I Am the Life. I Am the good shepherd. I Am the door. I Am the bread. I Am the resurrection."

This is how the Being receives the Being of his Being, the "I Am," which is a breath from the Great Breath within each one of us, our particular ray, He, He, He. The "I am" is the Inner Christ of every human being, our divine "Augoides," the Logos. Whosoever receives the crown of life has the right to say, "I Am He. I Am He. I Am He."

Theosophists talk about the Monad, yet the Glorian is not the Monad, and nevertheless, the Monad emerges from him. He is our particular ray. That ray is a perfect triad. Only he can liberate us from the law of karma. He is the Logoic Ray of each human being. The end of the law is Christ.

The law of karma is merely the stepmother, the healer that cures us, that is all. Yet, in Christ we are free. Christ is the Logos, the Word. He makes of us free and powerful kings nad queens and priests and priestesses. Whosoever receives the crown of life liberates the Self from the law of karma.

He is the Army of the Voice, our resplendent dragon of wisdom. He is the crown of life, faith, the Word, the crown of justice, the Christ. Under the law we are slaves, yet in Christ we are all free because the end of the law of karma is Christ.

> *"Be thou faithful unto death, and I will give thee a crown of life."* —Revelation 2:10

The attributes of the eternal "I am" are within the Army of the Voice. Therefore, discard all of your idolatries, religions, schools, sects, orders, and lodges and seek your resplendent and luminous "I am" who dwells within the depths of your Being. He is your only savior.

Christ is the Army of the Voice, who is the unique Being, the Being of all Beings, the sum total of all the attributes of eternal Absolute Abstract Space. It is the total, impersonal, universal, and infinite Cosmic Christ... Christ is a multiple perfect unity.

> *"And the light shineth in darkness; and the darkness comprehended it not."* —John 1:5

Christ is the Solar Logos, is the Army of the Voice, which is an eternal, unconditioned, and multiple perfect unity. He is the creative Logos. He is the Word of the first instant. He is the Great Breath emanated from within the bosom of the Eternal Absolute Abstract Space. Christ is the Army of the Word, the Eternal Absolute Abstract Space, which is the Being of the Being within all Beings. It is the Absolute, the Unutterable Name, the Limitless Space. Whosoever incarnates his Christ becomes Christified and thus enters into the ranks of the Army of the Voice.

In Egypt, the Christ was called Osiris, and whosoever incarnated him was an Osirified being. Among the Aztecs, the "I am" is named Quetzalcoatl.

> *"And the light shineth in darkness; and the darkness comprehended it not."* —John 1:5

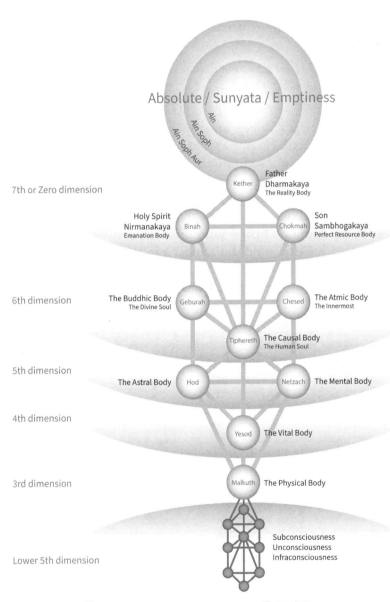

Absolute / Sunyata / Emptiness

Ain
Ain Soph
Ain Soph Aur

7th or Zero dimension — Kether — Father / Dharmakaya / The Reality Body

Holy Spirit / Nirmanakaya / Emanation Body — Binah   Chokmah — Son / Sambhogakaya / Perfect Resource Body

6th dimension — The Buddhic Body / The Divine Soul — Geburah   Chesed — The Atmic Body / The Innermost

Tiphereth — The Causal Body / The Human Soul

5th dimension — The Astral Body — Hod   Netzach — The Mental Body

4th dimension — Yesod — The Vital Body

3rd dimension — Malkuth — The Physical Body

Subconsciousness
Unconsciousness
Infraconsciousness

Lower 5th dimension

THE CROWN OF LIFE IS THE FIRST TRIANGLE ON THE TREE OF LIFE

Chapter 46

The Three Aspects of the Crown

The crown of life has three aspects:

First, the Ancient of Days, the Father

Second, the beloved Son of the Father

Third, the very wise Holy Spirit

Father, Son, and Holy Spirit are the perfect triad within the unity of life. Therefore, this triad plus the unity of life are the holy four; the four eternal carpenters, the four horns of the altar, the four winds of the sea, the holy and mysterious Tetragrammaton[119] whose mantric word is יהוה Iod Hei Vav Hei, the outstanding name of the Eternal.

Each human being has one's own original crown, which is our own ray that connects us to the Absolute.

The Innermost is the beloved son of the crown of life.

The entire theosophical septenary[120] emanated from our original crown, which is the "I am" that theosophists fail to notice.

---

119 (Greek) Literally "four lettered name," which refers to Hebrew יהוה.
120 The seven bodies.

Immortality

ARCANUM 13 OF THE ETERNAL TAROT

Chapter 47

The Ancient of Days

The Ancient of Days is original in each human being, He is the Father. There are as many Fathers in Heaven as there are humans on earth. The Ancient of Days is the hidden of the hidden, the mercy of mercies, the goodness of goodness, the root of our Being, the "Great Wind." The hair of the Ancient of Days has thirteen ringlets; his beard has thirteen locks.

The Thirteenth Arcanum is the Ancient of Days. Only by defeating death can we incarnate the Ancient of Days. The funeral ordeals of the Thirteenth Arcanum are more frightful and terrible than the abyss.

We need a supreme death in order to have the right to incarnate the Ancient of Days. Only the one who incarnates him has the right to internally wear the hair and the beard of the venerable elder.

Only after becoming victorious in the funeral ordeals in the presence of the angels of death can we incarnate the Ancient of Days. Whosoever incarnates him becomes another elder in eternity.

The Ancient of Days is the first outstandingly divine emanation of the Abstract Absolute Space.

Coatlicue

Chapter 48

The First Divine Couple

From the Ancient of Days (Kether), who is Christ (Chokmah), emanates the divine couple (Binah); this is the Holy Spirit and his virgin wife.

In each person, the wife of the Holy Spirit resembles an ineffable woman. The Divine Mother wears a white robe and a blue cloak. The blessed goddess, mother of the world, carries a precious lamp (Chesed) in her hand.

The divine male is a complete Christ, and is symbolized by a phallus in erection, by a scepter of power on high, by a tower, by every pointed rock, and by the robe of glory. He is a spring of divine origin.

The divine woman is an ineffable virgin. The Divine Mother is symbolized among the Aztecs by a mysterious virgin. This virgin has a mysterious mouth (cavity) in her throat. This is so because the throat is really the uterus where the word is gestated. The gods create by means of the larynx.

> *"In the beginning was the Word, and the Word was with God, and the Word was God."* —John 1:1

The Holy Spirit is the light maker:

> *"And God said, Let there be light: and there was light."*
> —Genesis 1:3

The esoteric meaning is, "The light became, because he uttered it."

The Aztec virgin has four hands. The esoteric meaning is: she receives life from the Father, and by delivering the Word she bestows life to all things. Thus, she is the mother of the world.

Two strange intertwined serpents in profile form a strange head; those two serpents are the two sympathetic cords (Ida and Pingala) of the spinal medulla. Our sexual energy ascends to the brain through these two canals:

> *"What be these two olive branches which through the two golden pipes empty the golden oil out of themselves..."*
> —Zechariah 4:12

These are the two witnesses,

> *"These are the two olive trees, and the two candlesticks standing before the God of the earth."* —Revelation 11:4

These also represent the two serpents that are intertwined on the caduceus of Mercury.

The two other serpents that form the arms and shoulders of the goddess are the tempting serpent of Eden and the serpent of bronze that healed the Israelites in the wilderness.

The skirt of this Aztec virgin is woven with serpents.

Under her chest she has what represents death. There is the need to die in order to live. There is the need to lose everything in order to gain everything.

In the temple of serpents named the Temple of Quetzalcoatl, the Holy Spirit was worshiped as follows: before sunrise, a priest dressed in a robe and cloak of black, white, and red colors sprinkled a seashell-powder into red fiery embers; the powder was made with white, black, and red seashells. The white represents the pure spirit, the black symbolizes the falling of the spirit into matter, and the red is the fire of the Holy Spirit, through which we return to the whiteness of the pure spirit. In the moments when the smoke offering was rising up to heaven, the priest was praying for life, thus the plants bloomed, because the Holy Spirit is the sexual fire of the universe. This rite was performed in the Temple of Quetzalcoatl before sunrise, because the Holy Spirit is the light maker. The priest vocalized the mantras **IN EN**.

The prophet Jonah also performed the rite of the Holy Spirit, exactly in the same way as the Aztecs, and he used for this purpose the same vestures and the same seashell-powder. He also vocalized the mantra **IN EN** as he sprinkled the incense into the fire.

This rite must be established in all the Gnostic sanctuaries. The seashells are related with the water of the sea, and the water is the habitat of the fire of the Holy Spirit. Therefore, the seashells become the perfect smoke offering to the Holy Spirit.

The mother, or Holy Spirit, grants us power and wisdom. The symbols of the Virgin are the yoni, the chalice, and the tunic of occultation.

When the semen is not ejaculated, the total sexual energy of the divine couple returns towards its origin, opening centers and awakening outstandingly divine igneous powers.

On Mount Horeb, Moses attained the incarnation of the Mother and thus became enlightened. Others had attained the incarnation of the divine couple; very few succeed in incarnating the Ancient of Days.

Father, Son, and Holy Spirit: these are the three aspects of the crown, the trinity within the unity of life.

Before Jesus, many buddhas received the crown of life and they died crucified. After Jesus, a few of us have received it, and in the future many other buddhas will receive the crown of life. The spirit of wisdom (Chokmah) always lives crucifying itself in matter in order to save the world.

The Holy Four, the Tetragrammaton, the יהוה Iod Hei Vav Hei, the divine "I am," is symbolized by the four fangs of the Aztec virgin.

In Kabbalah, Kether is the Father, Chokmah is the Son, and Binah is the Holy Spirit. They form the sephirothic crown, the crown of life. This triad plus the one form the holy four, the holy and mysterious tetragrammaton: יהוה Iod Hei Vav Hei.

The Temple of Karnak

Chapter 49

The Seven Double Columns
of the Temple

The seven columns of the temple of wisdom are double and
are made of burning fire. These are the seven degrees of the
power of fire; these are the seven serpents. After receiving the
crown of life, we have to raise the double of each column; these
are the seven serpents of light of the "I am."

We need to become dwellings of the Lord by means of the
lighting of our candelabra of seven branches. Christ, as the
child of God, as the child of Bethlehem, is born within our
heart.

*"Uselessly Christ in Bethlehem was born
If within our heart his birth is forlorn.*

*"His crucifixion, death and resurrection on the third day
from among the dead were in vain,*

*"Unless his crucifixion, death and resurrection, be set up
within each one of us again."*

The "I am" is born within us as a small child and has to
grow slowly, because nature does not make leaps.

The birth of Christ within us is the nativity of the heart.
Before Jesus, many initiates incarnated Christ. After Jesus, a
few of us have incarnated Christ, and in the future many will
incarnate him. Yes, the spirit of wisdom (Ruach Chokmah-El)
is constantly born in the manger of the world in order to save
humanity.

Thus, Jesus Christ had to patiently lift up each one of his
seven serpents of light. Understand that there are seven serpents of fire and seven serpents of light. The ascension of each
one of the serpents of light is a very arduous and difficult
task; indeed, it is the terror of sanctity, love, and law.

Jesus began by raising the first serpent of light, which is
related with the physical body. Each vertebra demands diffi-

cult virtues and frightful sanctities. Thus, as the first serpent of light reaches each vertebra, we enter into each one of the thirty-three holy chambers of the temple. This serpent makes us kings and queens of the abyss, which is one of the seven unutterable secrets.

The seven serpents of light belong to the mysteries of faith and of nature. These are the seven eternal Calvaries. Thus when the ascension of the first serpent is completed, the first initiation in the mysteries of faith and of nature is attained.

When the initiate awakens the second serpent of light, he can then practice sexual magic only once a week.

Very much later in time, the initiate becomes nonsexual, in other words, one enters to enjoy the delights of love without sexual contact. Here is when we are already omnipotent gods. These are inviolable laws.

Friday is the day for sexual magic. This is how the ethereal body becomes absolutely christified with the second serpent and we return into Eden where Lord Jehovah welcomes us. This is how we become inhabitants of Eden.

The christified ethereal body is the golden body, the wedding garment of the soul. With this garment we can enter into any department of nature and travel within it in order to serve in the Great Work.

The wedding garment of the soul is crystalline like water. This is the Soma Psuchikon. It seems to be made of pure glass, and it grants us continuous cognizance. It is governed by the rays of the moon. It resembles an ineffable maiden.

The third serpent transfigured the astral body of Jesus, and it shone like the sun on the mount of the transfiguration, with the majesty of the "I am."

The fourth serpent of light christifies the mind absolutely. We then have the mind of the Lord, and when he expresses himself through this mind, we are ineffable gods who shine like Christ.

The fifth serpent converts the human will into an ineffable Christ. We then have the will of the Lord.

The sixth serpent of light christifies the consciousness. We then have the consciousness of the Lord.

The seventh serpent of light christifies the Innermost absolutely. We then utter the seventh word; this is, "Father, into thy hands I commend my spirit" [Luke 23:46]. We are then the ineffable, powerful, and divine Christ.

These are the seven terribly divine Golgothas. These heights are achieved by loving, by adoring our spouse. Men and women have the same rights.

These seven serpents of light are the seven seals of Apocalypse (Revelation), which only the Lamb, the "I am," can open. Love is the greatest happiness of the universe. Love transforms us into Christs. Gnostic homes are filled with chastity, love, and beauty.

In the patios of the Aztec temples, many couples of man and woman remained for entire months adoring each other and sexually connecting without ejaculating their semen. This is how men and women attained realization of the Self. This is the doctrine that Christ taught in secrecy to his seventy disciples. This is the holy doctrine of the "I am."

"I am that bread of life."

"I am the living bread."

"Whosoever eateth my flesh, and drinketh my blood, hath eternal life; and I will raise him up at the last day."
—John 6: 48, 51, 54

In order to become as gods, we have to ingest the flesh and blood of the "I Am."

Nevertheless, we know that all of those "super-transcended" people of Spiritualism, Theosophy, Rosicrucianism, etc. are puffed up with such pride that they believe that everything in life is as easy as blowing glass in order to make bottles. Therefore, it will not surprise us if they will profane the revelations of this book by boasting of being "super-transcended" and alleging that they are also receiving the crown of life. Yes, these abusers will now increase in number everywhere, and the "Christs" will appear in bunches, a kind of "super-crowned" harvest.

So, beware,

"For false Christs and false prophets shall rise, and shall show signs and wonders, to seduce, if it were possible, even the elect."

"Take heed lest any man deceive you: For many shall come in my name, saying, I am Christ; and shall deceive many." —Mark 13:22, 5, 6

Moreover, false Christs will appear even within the Gnostic movement.

There will not be a single medium-chaneller from spiritualism without the mania of boasting of having received the crown of life.

We, the inhabitants of the sacred island, give you these warnings in order for you not to be cheated by the Antichrists.

"Then if any man shall say unto you, Lo, here is Christ, or there; believe it not." —Matthew 24:23

With this book we initiate the age of Aquarius, but we know that humanity is not yet prepared to understand this book. Therefore, we warn you of the danger, in order for you to not fall into the abyss of perdition. They will abuse this book worse than they did with the Bible. Therefore, seek your resplendent and luminous "I am." Practice sexual magic and sanctify yourselves totally.

"Heaven and earth shall pass away, but my words shall not pass away." —Matthew 24:35

Right now, because of fornication your two witnesses are dead, but you must resurrect them.

"And their dead bodies shall lie in the street of the great city, which spiritually is called Sodom." —Revelation 11:8

When your two witnesses resurrect with sexual magic and when they stand upon their feet, great fear will fall upon the tenebrous ones.

"And if any man will hurt them, fire proceedeth out of their mouth, and devoureth their enemies."
—Revelation 11:5

Now beware that when your two witnesses are dead, you do not yet possess your Christic powers, and therefore, the tenebrous ones can easily deceive you. Beware of the false Christs, beware of the Spiritualists, namely, Theosophists, Rosicrucians, Aquarianists, etc. since those people state that they follow Christ, nevertheless, indeed, they follow their "divine impostors." They do not even know what the Christ is. Yes, none of those tenebrous ones know what the "I am" is.

The divine Master Jesus said,

"I Am the way, the truth, and the life." —John 14:6

Nonetheless, Spiritualists do not understand this, and instead of seeking their resplendent and luminous "I am" within themselves, they prefer to go around following their sublime impostors—yet they allege that they are following Christ! How cynical they are!

What a muddy hypocrisy, God of mine! They abandon their resplendent "I am" and thereafter they come with the sophism that there are many paths, and that one can reach divinity through any path. How cynical they are! Master Jesus did not talk to us about so many paths. Jesus only said:

"I Am the way, the truth, and the life." —John 14:6

"This beginning of miracles did Jesus
in Cana of Galilee, and manifested
forth his glory; and his disciples
believed on him." —JOHN 2:11

Chapter 50

The Wedding of Cana

The first miracle performed by Jesus was the transmutation of water into wine. Jesus performed this miracle at a wedding. Thus, this is the first miracle that our disciples must perform, because this is how one enters initiation.

Yes, it is certain that by means of sexual contact within marriage we transmute the water into wine. We have to transmute the water (semen) into the wine of the light of the alchemist, and indeed, sexual magic is the way.

So, through his first miracle Jesus publicly taught sexual transmutation, sexual magic, and in this way he began the opening of the path of initiation for all of this suffering humanity!

Jesus Christ represented the entire drama of initiation in the flesh. This drama begins with sexual transmutation, because it is by means of sexual magic that we become as gods.

When spouses upraise themselves to the state of gods, only then can they enjoy the delights of love without sexual contact. This is something that pertains to the gods.

When we study the wedding of Cana within the Akashic archives[121] of nature, we see a great, wonderful party within a great wooden palace. The bride was a young aristocratic female of that old palace. She had a body of medium height, dark features, blunt nose, and a protruding upper lip. She dressed in a white wedding garment and a crown of flowers over her head. The feast was solemn, and Jesus attended it. Yet suddenly, when the wine was consumed, all the guests looked to each other as if saying, "This party is over." However, Jesus crossed the room towards a corner of the luxurious palace where a barrel (a square-shaped container) of pure water was set up; a few olive leaves were floating on the water. So, Jesus Christ extended his right hand over that pure water of life and the water was transmuted into wine. Thereafter, everyone rejoiced and

---

121 The "memories" stored by nature, similar to how our own memories are stored.

continue their feasting celebration. So through this miracle, he publicly taught sexual magic.

We have to transmute the water of life (semen) into the wine of light of the alchemist. This is how the sacred fire awakens. This is how our spinal fires develop.

Let us not forget that the Cosmic Christ dwells within the seed of every plant, animal, and human being.

Chapter 51

The Greatest in the Kingdom of Heaven

> *"In that hour came the disciples unto Jesus, saying, who is the greatest in the kingdom of heaven?*
>
> *"And Jesus called a little child unto him, and set him in the midst of them, and said, Verily I say unto you, except ye be converted, and become as little children, ye shall not enter into the kingdom of heaven.*
>
> *"Whosoever therefore shall humble himself as this little child, the same is greatest in the kingdom of heaven."*
> —Matthew 18:1-4

Nevertheless, in this day and age, those who boast about being Jesus' followers do not want to follow his example; none of them wants to become a child.

Popes, cardinals, archbishops, bishops, and priests from the deviated Church of Rome, puffed up with pride and arrogance, travel in luxurious cars. They do not even remotely want to become children. Instead, they stuff themselves with intellectualisms, high ranking titles, and enormous wealth.

Likewise, the pastors of the different religious sects from this barbarian epoch benefit from their title of pastor and, puffed up with pride and arrogance, feel "peachy" when their ignorant sheep present them greetings and reverence. Yes, they also do not want to be converted, and become as little children.

In this day and age, everybody wants to be a great lord, and they love the chief seats in the synagogues. They all want to be great avatars and great masters, yet no one wants to become as a little child. Nonetheless, all of them know a lot about Jesus' doctrine; yes, they preach his doctrine, "but do not ye after their works: for they say, and do not" [Matthew 23:3]. None of them wants to convert their mind into a little child. This matter about becoming as little child displeases them.

Likewise, the bookworm-devotees of the different schools, orders, lodges, etc., believe that they know a lot, and this matter about becoming as a little child even seems ridiculous to them—nevertheless, just out of pride, they declare themselves to be like children. Instead, they all boast of being famous reincarnations. Yes, none of them wants to be a midget; none of them wants to be the last in line. Sadly, this is how this present humanity is.

Understand that in order to receive the crown of life, one must have a mind like a little child. For this, we have to liberate ourselves from intellectual pride, we have to terminate theosophist fears and theological intellectualisms—in other words, we must liberate ourselves from all spiritual aberrations, cleanse from our understanding all types of intellectualisms and theories, political parties, concepts of country and flag, schools, etc. and we must practice sexual magic, and kill not only desire, but even the very knowledge of desire.

Yes, we must terminate with reasoning in order to have the mind like a little child. A child does not reason, but knows instinctually by intuition. A child does not covet money. A child does not fornicate. A child does not commit adultery, nor is a child an assassin.

In Colombia, South America, during a certain political revolt, the priests hired assassins in order to kill some citizens. Those clergymen cannot even remotely be children; they are assassins, but children? Not at all! Yes, this is a truth! How can someone who kills be a child? How can someone who steals be a child? How can someone who fornicates be a child?

"There are three gates leading to hell — lust, anger, and greed." —Krishna in The Bhagavad Gita 16:21 (Mahabharata)

Chapter 52

The Elixir of Long Life

When the initiate attains the fourth initiation of Major Mysteries, one gains access to Nirvana and enters the world of the gods where unlimited happiness reigns. Thereafter, when the initiate attains the fifth initiation of Major Mysteries, one reaches the mountain of the gods, which has two paths that lead to the summit. One is the spiral path, which going in a spiral around the mountain takes us to the summit. The other is the long, straight, bitter, and difficult path of woe and duty that leads us directly into the Absolute.

Max Heindel speaks about the mountain of men, yet he does not know about the mountain of the gods. The mountain of men also has two paths: the spiral path all of humanity climbs, and the straight, narrow, and difficult path that is tread by the initiates. The summit of this mountain is Nirvana, and in order to reach it, we have to go through nine initiations of Minor Mysteries and five of Major Mysteries.

When the initiate reaches the summit of the mountain of men, one finds oneself before the two paths of the mountain of the gods. Then, before the initiate a remarkable guardian appears, who indicates the spiral nirvanic path, and says, "This is a good labor." The initiate then sees the infinite worlds of space, the suns that journey throughout eternity, where the gods of Nirvana, filled with happiness, blissfully dwell within their paradises.

Thereafter, the guardian shows the initiate the long, straight, bitter, and difficult path of woe and duty that leads us directly into the Absolute, and utters, "This is a superior labor. You must decide right now which of the two paths you will follow." If the initiate tries to think about it, the guardian interrupts and says, "Do not think about it. Give me your answer right now."

This is a remarkable moment, because from it the destiny of many eternities is derived. This is why it is the most remarkable moment of our cosmic evolution.

Know that one who renounces Nirvana for the sake of humanity becomes a bodhisattva and is confirmed as thrice honored, and after many eternities of Nirvanas gained and lost from boundless pity and compassion for the world of deluded mortals, one finally gains the right to enter into the Absolute.

The Pratyekas[122] of the spiral path of Nirvana are different; they have periods of activity and periods of repose within Nirvanic happiness. In other words, they reincarnate in the worlds only after very long intervals, and thereafter they once again submerge for eternities within the infinite happiness of the spheres. Within the music of the stars, they enjoy limitless happiness, because in Nirvana they do not use their four bodies of sin. Thus, throughout limitless eternities, slowly, very slowly, they finally reach the Absolute; this spiral path is extremely long. On February 19, 1919 at 3:40 in the afternoon, Nirvana entered into a period of activity, so presently, Nirvanic hierarchies are struggling for the return of the evolution toward the superior worlds.

Many nirvanis are loaded with karmic debts. They pay these debts during their cycles of manifestation. The great risk for these masters is the fall of their Human Souls (superior manas). Presently in the world, there are thousands of fallen nirvanic souls (superior manas) within whom the masters (Atman-Buddhi) cannot reincarnate. These falls occur because of the fact that their will-soul is not well developed. As long as desire exists within the astral body, the will-soul will not grow. We have to kill desire.

Likewise, a master (Atman-Buddhi, who walks the direct path) can be very resplendent within his "Glorian," yet if his bodhisattva is fallen, then the master cannot serve suffering humanity; this means horrible suffering for the master. The master and his bodhisattva are a mysterious double individuality.

A bodhisattva is the one who renounces Nirvana for the sake of humanity. A bodhisattva has the right to ask for the Elixir

---

122 Literally, "selfish ones." Those concerned only with their own development.

of Long Life, which grants immortality in the physical body during long eternities, as long as one wishes.

Count St. Germain presently lives with the same physical body that he showed in Europe during the seventeenth and eighteenth centuries. Zanoni lived thousands of years with the same physical body. Likewise, Megnour kept himself alive within the same physical body for thousands of years. Sanat Kumara presently lives with his same Lemurian body from 18,000,000 years ago. The great masters of the guardian wall that protect humanity live with the same physical bodies from millions of years ago, namely the Masters Kout Humi, Morya, and many others; they have preserved their bodies since thousands of years ago, thus death has not been able to overcome them.

Therefore, with the Elixir of Long Life we avoid the perils of reincarnations, because bodhisattvas fall when they are exposed to the environment, temptations, heredity, etc. Only those with a will of steel never fall.

ANGEL OF DEATH

Chapter 53

The Bat God

In the Palace of Fine Arts in Mexico City, we find an Aztec sculpture of the bat god. So, let us talk about the bat god, regardless of the tenebrous slander of ignoramuses who will qualify us as black magicians. This sculpture is a precious Aztec symbol that represents one of the principal hierarchs of death. The angels of death work under the influence of Saturn. They divest the souls from their physical existence according to the law of karma. Their symbols are the bat, the owl, and the scythe.

THE BAT GOD

When they take the soul out of the physical body, they cut the silver cord that unites the soul to the body. During normal sleep, the soul can travel anywhere and return into the body, thanks to the silver cord.

When the angels of death officiate, they adopt a skeletal appearance. Yet, after their duty, they assume beautiful appearances, since, indeed, they are angels.

The bat god dwells in the center of Eden. He is an angel of death who has the power to kill and the power to heal.

To invoke the bat god, the Aztecs performed a chain in the shape of a horseshoe. The human links of the chain were loose —no one in the chain touched the hands or bodies of the others. The ends of the opened horseshoe chain ended on the sides of the altar.

During the rite, filled with respect, the attendants remained squatted and curled up. Then the mantra **ISIS** was vocalized by everyone in two syllables. They prolonged the sound of each letter as follows, iiiiiii sssss iiiiiii sssssss; they sustained the sound of each letter as long as possible. The "S" sound is associated with the chirping of the cricket (grasshopper), or with the sound of the rattles of the rattlesnake, which is so sacred among the Aztecs. The "S" sound is the subtle voice that can perform marvels and prodigies. So, the mantra ISIS was vocalized many consecutive times.

Into small braziers, the priest sprinkled an aromatic substance made of seashells that had been reduced to a white powder. Seashells and the sacred fire are internally associated. Thus, small braziers were placed on a table. Two flames, symbols of life and death, burned on the altar. The priest, facing the attendants and after having blessed them with a sharp knife, then summoned the bat god with his heart. Thus, this is how the bat god, the remarkable hierarch of death, attended.

This rite can be practiced in the Gnostic sanctuaries.

The bat god can heal the sick if the law of karma allows it. Any group of people can practice this rite in order to heal gravely sick people. This rite was practiced by the Aztecs in a temple made of solid gold. This temple still exists, yet it is in Jinn state.

The bat god attends the funeral ordeals of the Arcanum Thirteen. When Jesus arrived at the Arcanum Thirteen, he wandered among the sepulchers of the dead. The terrible specters of death besieged him among the terrors of the horrible night. The cadaverous phantoms of death reminded him of horrible things of the past. Jesus had to overcome the supreme council of the angels of death. The struggle was terrible, but he was victorious; he was fearless. Then, the Ancient of Days, like a remarkable breath, entered into Jesus. Thus, this is how the Son and the Father became one. This is performed in the Arcanum Thirteen. The same process occurs within everyone who receives the crown of life. This belongs to the second initiation of the mysteries of faith and Nature.

> *"I thank thee, O Father, Lord of heaven and earth, because thou hast hid these things from the wise and prudent, and hast revealed them unto babes. Even so, Father: for so it seemed good in thy sight. All things are delivered unto me of my Father: and no man knoweth the Son, but the Father; neither knoweth any man the Father, save the Son, and he to whomsoever the Son will reveal him."* —Luke 10:21, 22

Chapter 54
The Supper at Bethany

Indeed, the Elixir of Long Life is a powerful, electropositive and electronegative, immaculate, white gas. When the initiate asks for the Elixir of Long Life, one enters into the temple of Sanat Kumara who reads to the initiate all the conditions and sacred requirements.

Sanat Kumara is the founder of the College of Initiates of the White Lodge. He lives in an oasis in the Gobi desert with other Lemurian initiates. They all continue to use the same physical bodies of more than 18,000,000 years ago. Thus, Sanat Kumara greets the initiate and tells him, "You are another immolated being on the altar of great sacrifice." Thereafter he blesses the initiate.

Subsequently, within the internal worlds, the initiate enters into another temple, on the porch of which there is an inscription that reads, "Gnostic Temple of Those Who Prolong Their Lives." The initiate attends these temples in the astral body. During a ceremony here, one receives the Elixir of Long Life.

That gas remains preserved within the vital body. Thereafter, death has to be overcome in the ordeals of the Arcanum Thirteen, which are indeed terrifying. Very few human beings have enough courage to overcome them with success. The one who becomes victorious is warned that despite victory, one still has to die. Indeed, one dies but does not die, because on the third day after death, the initiate approaches the tomb in the astral body in order to summon the physical body.

The spirit of movement, the angels of death, and other hierarchies help in the resurrection. Thus, the initiate's physical body obeys, and when it rises from the sepulcher, it totally enters the supersensible worlds. Here, holy women massage the physical body with certain secret drugs, and the divine hierarchies infuse life and motion into it.

Subsequently, impelled by supreme powers, the physical body enters into the initiate through the pineal gland. In the astral body, this gland is the one thousand-petalled lotus flower, the crown of the saints, the diamond eye. Thus, this is how the resurrection from the dead is performed.

All the masters who have resurrected live with their physical bodies for millions of years. After having resurrected from among the dead, Zanoni committed the error of taking a wife. This is why he lost his head at the guillotine during the French Revolution.

Only the initiates who have reached these summits can live and direct the current of life of the centuries. Only here the initiate no longer needs a spouse. The initiate's physical body remains in Jinn state; this is the gift of Cupid.

Nevertheless, the initiate can become visible and tangible in this tridimensional world wherever is necessary, and works in the physical world under the commands of the White Lodge. As a resurrected master, the initiate commands the great life; one has power over the fire, air, water, and earth. Yes, all of Nature kneels before one and obeys. One can live among people, and becomes a human-god.

Naturally, it is indispensable to undergo the ordeals of the Arcanum Thirteen in order to reach these summits. The physical body must be embalmed for death.

The supper at Bethany corresponds to this event of the Arcanum Thirteen. Thus, after the body has been embalmed for death, it is submitted to a special evolution for the tomb that develops within the numbers thirty and thirty-five, which when added together give the Arcanum Eleven (the tamed lion); yes, we have to tame nature and overcome it.

Thus, when the body is ready for the sepulcher, the processes of death and resurrection occur. In this case, the angels of death do not cut the silver cord; this is how the initiate dies but does not die. The physical brain of the initiate is submitted to a special transformation: it becomes more subtle, delicate, and radiant.

ARCANUM 11 OF THE ETERNAL TAROT

THE SUPPER AT BETHANY

The supper at Bethany relates with these processes of Jesus Christ.

"Now when Jesus was in Bethany, in the house of Simon the leper, there came unto him a woman having an alabaster box of very precious ointment, and poured it on his head, as he sat at meat. But when his disciples saw it, they had indignation, saying, To what purpose is this waste? For this ointment might have been sold for much, and given to the poor. When Jesus understood it, he said unto them, Why trouble ye the woman? for she hath wrought a good work upon me. For ye have the poor always with you; but me ye have not always; for in that she hath poured this ointment on my body, she did it for my burial. Verily I say unto you, wherever this gospel shall be preached in the whole world, there shall also this, that this woman hath done, be told for a memorial of her." —Matthew, 26: 6-13

The mysteries of death are astounding. Jesus met the beloved goddess of death after having returned from Jordan into the solitude of the wilderness.

The goddess mother death is known among the Aztecs with the name of Mietlancihuati. She is the supreme commander of the angels of death. She is the only one who can liberate us from pain and bitterness.

Through death, she takes us out of this valley of tears millions of times, always filled with immense maternal love, full of charity, adorable, and good.

The three keys of suffering are: the Moon, the fornicating Eve, and the turbid waters. All of these belong to the horrible kingdom of "Santa Maria,"[123] the abyss...

The blessed goddess death is love and charity. The Aztecs represented her with a diadem of nine skulls. Nine is initiation.

Whosoever fulfills the Arcanum Thirteen becomes completely liberated. The blessed goddess death receives and gives; this is why she is represented with four hands.

---

123 The author explains elsewhere that this person is not Mary the mother of Jesus. "The serpent ascending in the medullar canal is the Virgin. The serpent descending from the coccyx downwards towards the atomic infernos of Nature is the Santa Maria of Black Magic and witchcraft. Behold, the two Marys: the white and the black." —The Perfect Matrimony

Chapter 55

Jesus and the Angel Ehecatl, the God of the Wind

Ehecatl intervened in the resurrection of Jesus Christ. Ehecatl is known as the god of the wind among the Aztecs. Ehecatl entered the tomb of Jesus on the third day and uttered with a loud voice, "Jesus, rise from within your tomb, with your body." Then, Ehecatl induced activity and movement within the body of Jesus. Ehecatl is a lovely angel and spirit of movement. The lords of movement regulate all the activities of cosmic movement. The Aztecs worshiped Ehecatl.

> *"Now upon the first day of the week, very early in the morning, the holy women came (in the astral body) unto the sepulcher, bringing the spices which they had prepared, and certain other women with them."*
> —Luke 24:1

Thus, this is how the physical body of Jesus was submerged within the internal worlds and remained in Jinn state. Thus, the tomb remained empty.

> *"Then arose Peter, and ran unto the sepulcher; and stooping down, he beheld the linen clothes laid by themselves, and departed, wondering in himself at that which was come to pass."* —Luke 24:12

The physical body of Jesus was treated with aromatic spices and sacred ointments. Thereafter it entered through the astral pineal gland of the master. This is how the resurrection of the physical body of Jesus was performed, which later in Jinn state became visible and tangible before the disciples of Emmaus.

> *"And it came to pass, as he sat at meat with them, he took bread, and blessed it, and brake, and gave to them. And their eyes were opened, and they knew him; and he vanished out of their sight."* —Luke 24:30, 31

When the eleven apostles gathered together, it seemed impossible to them that Jesus could have resurrected.

> *"And as they thus spoke, Jesus himself stood in the midst of them, and saith unto them, Peace be unto you. But they were terrified and affrighted, and supposed that they had seen a spirit."* —Luke 24:36-37

Logically, they were terrified because it seemed impossible for them for a cadaver to have life.

> *"And he said unto them, why are ye troubled? and why do thoughts arise in your hearts? Behold my hands and my feet, that it is I myself: handle me, and see; for a spirit hath not flesh and bones, as ye see me have."*
> —Luke 24:38-39

And in order to completely prove to them that he had a body of flesh and blood,

> *"...he said unto them, Have ye here any meat? And they gave him a piece of a broiled fish, and of an honeycomb. And he took it, and did eat before them."* —Luke 24:41-43

Later on, Master Jesus left towards the East: to Tibet.

Thus, this is how Jesus taught and demonstrated physically to humanity the doctrine of the resurrection from the dead.

Thus, by practicing sexual magic, by adoring our spouse, by knowing how to love, any human being can climb these very high summits of resurrection.

Chapter 56
Shambhala

Jesus Christ presently lives in Shambhala[124] (a secret country of Tibet) with his same resurrected physical body. Yes, in Shambhala he also has his temple of mysteries. The entire country of Shambhala is in the Jinn state. Here is where the principal monasteries of the White Lodge are.

In Shambhala live many masters whose stream of life of their physical bodies comes from very ancient ages, and who are in the Jinn state.

When Jesus walked upon the waters, he carried his body in the Jinn state. Any disciple can travel in the same manner. The disciple becomes slightly asleep, then filled with faith and preserving the slumber state, one rises from the bed like a somnambulist. Subsequently, one will perform a little jump with the intention of submerging oneself within the supersensible worlds. With the jump, one will float in the atmosphere. This is called the Jinn state. This is how one floats in space and walks upon the waters. Some succeed immediately, while others take months and even years.

In all the corners of the world there are monasteries of the White Lodge in the Jinn state. Our disciples (in the astral body or in Jinn state) can visit Shambhala and converse with Jesus Christ.

A road from the northeast goes from the city of Ghandara until arriving at the Sita and Bhastani rivers. Two sacred columns are found behind these two rivers, and thereafter a lake where an initiated elder guides the traveler to the secret country, Shambhala. Profane people will never find this country, since it is very well hidden.

Jesus Christ will return at the zenith of Aquarius with his same resurrected physical body, which he still preserves in Jinn state. Later on, Master Jesus will come again in the continent of Antarctica in order to illuminate the Koradhi, the sixth root

---

124 See glossary.

race. Much later, he will come back in order to instruct the seventh root race.

Jesus Christ is the savior of the world. Indeed, the only one who can save us is our resplendent and luminous "I am." Jesus Christ brought the doctrine of the I am: this is why he is the savior.

The Roman priests stole the secret doctrine of the Lord. Any mystic in a state of ecstasy can see within many spiritual schools, religions, and sects the Christ tied to the column where they whipped him 5,000 and more times. Yes, all those schools and religions are whipping the Lord daily.

Some Theosophists still believe that above Jesus Christ there are more elevated beings, yet those diverted, wretched souls are mistaken, because Jesus Christ is a paramarthasatya[125] who renounced the Absolute in order to come to this valley of tears.

Jesus Christ is a leader of all souls, an inhabitant of the Absolute.

Many devotees commit the mistake of affiliating themselves with impostors, i.e. like the Aquarianists who affiliated themselves to a perverse French engineer who disguised himself as Jesus Christ. This evildoer, this horrible larva, is already severed from his Innermost. Yes, La Ferriere[126] is a perverse demon of the abyss.

Impostors are monsters who will receive their punishment.

> "For without (the Heavenly Jerusalem) are dogs, and sorcerers, and whoremongers, and murderers, and idolaters, and whosoever loveth and maketh a lie."
> —Revelation 22:15

In any war, traitors are shot in the back. What type of punishment is deserved by the ones who betray the leader of all souls, those who exchange the Christ for an impostor?

> "Father, forgive them for they know not what they do."
> —Luke 23:43

Understand our final statement: whosoever becomes a disciple of a demon will go to the abyss to accompany his beloved demon-guru.

---

125 See glossary.
126 Serge Raynaud de la Ferriere (1916-1962)

THIRD PART

JESUS CHRIST

Chapter 57

The Gnostic Movement

Victoriously, the powerful, universal, revolutionary Gnostic movement advances on all the battlefields. Hence, now, nothing, no one, can stop us on this luminous and triumphant march. Our leader is our Lord Jesus Christ, who dwells in Shambhala (in Tibet) with the same body that resurrected from the dead, and with him dwell many other masters whose physical bodies are children of the resurrection. Yes, we are the initiators of the new Aquarian age.

In the new era, we will establish Gnostic governments on the face of the earth. Then, country borders, customs, wars, hatred, etc. will disappear.

We, the masters of the White Lodge, did not authorize mister "de la Ferrière" or any of his followers to open initiatic colleges. Those tenebrous, sanctimonious evil doers are dangerous impostors, and in the presence of impostors we should keep an eye on our money.

Until 1976, the central headquarters of the Gnostic movement in the western world was in the Summum Supremum Sanctuarium of la Sierra Nevada of Santa Marta, in the republic of Colombia, South America.

All the temples of the White Lodge are subterranean. They are in the forests and mountains all over the entire world. E.g. within the mountains of la Sierra Nevada we have a subterranean temple.

The director of Gnostic movement until 1976 was Julio Medina V, who at that time was the sovereign gnostic commander for Latin America. Now, there are thousands of Gnostics throughout America.

Yet, indeed, the true supreme headquarters of our Gnostic movement is in Shambhala (eastern Tibet).

The Gnostic flag has two bands: the upper one is red and the lower one is white. Between these two horizontal stripes there is a great golden cross. It carries an iron cross at the top of the pole.

We are the followers of the "I am." The *"I am"* is the authentic avatar of Aquarius.

Allow us to affirm that the Gnostic movement is not just another school, but a revolutionary, international, universal movement, opposed to sluggish schools.

Now, allow me, a wretched servant of the Lord, a miserable sinner, to affirm the majesty of my luminous "I am," before whom I kneel, since before him I feel that I am miserable, poor in virtue, and very bountiful in sin.

"I am," the avatar of Aquarius. *"I am,"* the living bread which came down from heaven: if any man eats of this bread, he shall live for ever: and the bread that I will give is my flesh, which I will give for the life of the world." *"I am,"* the initiator of the new era; *"I am,* Alpha and Omega, the beginning and the ending." *"I am,"* the energy that throbs in each atom and in each sun; *"I am,* the light of the world: he that follows me shall not walk in darkness, but shall have the light of life." *"I am,"* the strength of all powers, and all strength is reflected in me. *"I am,"* the one who IS. The greatest force in the entire world is the force of love. *"I am,"* the force of love.

Thus, discriminate all spiritual schools and perverted religions and kneel with humility before the resplendent and luminous *"I Am."* He, He, He, is your only savior.

Chapter 58

Gnostic Tradition

For the crime of having accompanied Jesus Christ in the holy land, and because of having celebrated our rituals within Rome's catacombs, we, the Gnostics, faced the lions in the circus of Rome. Then later in time, we were burnt alive in the flames of the Roman Catholic inquisition. Previously, we were the mystical Essenes of Palestine. So, we are not improvising opportunist doctrines. We were hidden for twenty centuries, but now we are returning once again to the street in order to carry on our shoulders the old, rough, and heavy cross.

Paul of Tarsus took our doctrine to Rome. Yes, he was a Gnostic Nazarene.

Jesus Christ taught our doctrine in secrecy to his seventy disciples.

The Sethians, Peratae, Carpocratians, Nazarenes, and Essenes were Gnostics. The Egyptian and Aztec mysteries, the mysteries of Rome, Troy, Carthage, of Eleusis, India, of the Druids, Pythagoreans, Kambirs, of Mithra and Persia, etc., are in their depth that which we call Gnosis or Gnosticism.

We are now once again opening the ancient Gnostic sanctuaries that were closed with the arrival of the dark age. Thus, we are now opening the authentic initiatic colleges.[127]

---

127 These colleges are not in the physical world. "The authentic schools of mystery are found in the astral plane. This is why it is necessary for the disciple to learn how to "separate" the astral body from the physical body. It is necessary for the student to learn how to enter into those sanctuaries of inner instruction in order to receive direct instruction from the masters... Whosoever wants to learn esoteric science has to travel in the astral body, because esoteric science is studied in the internal worlds, and esoteric science is learned only by personally conversing with the masters." —Samael Aun Weor.

ENOCH TAKEN BY GOD

Chapter 59

Practice, Not Theories

Resolute people are tired of theories. Now, they want to know, see, hear, and touch for themselves, because the new Aquarian age is for practical esotericists. Thus, it is necessary for them to learn how to project themselves at will in their astral body, and to travel with their physical body in Jinn state (to fly with the body of flesh and blood, to enter within the internal worlds and to visit the souls of the dead, to enter into the world of the angels with the physical body). Indeed, all of this is a gigantic victory for the Spirit.

This is how we can travel and visit all the temples of the White Lodge, and thus study at the feet of the great masters. Yes, by knowing the mysteries of life and death we will liberate ourselves from so many theories and so much absurd intellectualism.

We advise our disciples to carefully avoid dealing with the tenebrous devotees of the kingdom of "Saint Mary" (the abyss).

The tenebrous "Aquarianists" will tell you that projecting yourself in your astral body is dangerous, since this is what they learned from their dangerous impostor who disguised himself as Jesus Christ.

Theosophists will stuff you with fear and confusion by means of their very complicated theories.

Spiritualists will try to confuse your mind in order to convince you that their mediumistic sessions are the best of all, ignoring that in all their spiritual centers, repugnant and horrible demons of the abyss usually present themselves as ineffable saints or as Jesus Christ in person. Regrettably, these wretched medium-channelers are victims of repugnant larvae and demons of the abyss, and the gravest of all is that they are convinced that they are in the light. No tenebrous individual believes that he is doing iniquitous acts.

The pseudo-Rosicrucians will tell you that to project yourself in your astral body is dangerous and that it is not yet time.

These ignoramuses are firmly convinced of their superiority over the profane.

All of these people belong to the abyss. They have a terrible and frightful pride, and are puffed up with fear and fornication. Yes, they fornicate, because they spill their semen miserably: this is why they are black magicians. However, they never accept that they are dismal. Rather, they defend their beloved fornication with refined sophisms and subtle philosophies, which they wrap up within with sweet smiles and apparent sweetness.

Understand that every association of fornicators forms a black lodge, and each lodge or school of this kind has its boss or manager who they venerate as a saint or master. Obviously, these managers exploit their school, since their school is just a business that they defend with sweet and hypocritical words.

Logically, for these hypocritical impostors who pass as masters, gurus, avatars, elder brothers, great reformers, and princes from India, etc. it is not convenient that their disciples learn how to travel in the astral body, since they fear that their charade will be exposed to their own disciples. Moreover, since these impostors do not know how to project themselves in their astral body, how are they going to teach this to others? This is why they try to obstruct their wretched followers with their theories, as fearmongers.

Others, through cunningness, or the pretext of organizing the great universal fraternity without any distinction of race, creed, caste, or color, let their beard and hair grow long and try to monopolize all the schools. Naturally, many wretched victims of their infamy end up transforming themselves into an intolerant and harmful stampede, a fanatical flock of goats.

Sadly, this is the reality of these times. This is why we advise our disciples to carefully avoid dealing with those schools of the abyss. Indeed, the way things have become, it is better not to follow anyone, because it is very dangerous.

Thus, let us adore our "I Am."

Chapter 60

Jinn State

The first thing that any disciple needs in order to practice with the Jinn state is a lot of faith. Whosoever has a mind filled with doubts is advised not to enter these studies, because they could become insane.

The second thing that one needs is the tenacity and patience of Saint Job. The lack of tenacity in these exercises causes inevitable failure. Those who begin to practice and become immediately weary and stop are not good for these studies; so do not try: withdraw.

The third thing is to have methodology and order in these Jinn exercises.

The disciple can utilize the energies of the god Harpocrates in order to learn to travel with the physical body in the Jinn state.

HARPOCRATES

Practice

Take a hen egg and warm it in water. Make a small hole on the coned, pointed end; then, by utilizing any pointed instrument, extract its yolk and albumen. The eggshell contains the forces of the god Harpocrates, which are a variant of the Christic energies.

The student will place the cortex or eggshell over the head of one's bed or near the bed. Thereafter, one will enter into a slumber state while invoking the god Harpocrates. One needs just a little bit of sleep and very much faith. Thus, one must fall asleep while praying with much faith the prayer of the god Harpocrates, as follows:

> "I believe in God, I believe in Christ, and I believe in Har-po-crat-ist. Take me with my physical body to the Gnostic Church."

This prayer must be mentally prayed many times, repeatedly, Thus, when in a slumber state, like a somnambulist, one must rise from the bed and take the egg, and then walk, while saying:

"Har-po-crat-ist, help me, because I go with my body."

Before exiting the house, one must jump as far as one can, and mark the exact spot where one lands from the jump. On the following night, one repeats the experiment in the same place, trying to surpass the previously recorded mark. Remember, one needs to keep drowsiness like a treasure, because Jinn powers are based on drowsiness and very intense faith.

One must keep a daily record of the landing marks of the daily jumps. Thus, in this way, by persevering for days, months or years, one finally succeeds. The progressive increase of the distance of the jump is an evident sign of great progress, since this demonstrates that one is entering the Jinn state little by little. Afterwards, the disciple will perform jumps of three, four, or more meters in length. To keep this tenacity is very important, because this is the only way for one to triumph.

Finally, one day, the disciple will truly manage to sustain oneself in space, beyond the normal limit; this is when the physical body will be in the Jinn state. Then, people will not be able to physically see one, because the body will become invisible, since while in Jinn state, the body—without losing its physiological characteristics—submerges itself in the internal worlds and becomes subject to the laws of the supersensible worlds, namely levitation, elasticity, plasticity, porosity, etc. This is a modification of somnambulism; it is voluntary and cognizant somnambulism.

The energies of sleep and faith are remarkable. This is how we can receive the teachings directly in the internal temples.

In India, the sannyasi[128] yogis enter into the Jinn state by practicing a samyama[129] on their physical bodies. The samyama consists of concentration, meditation, and simultaneous, instantaneous ecstasies. We, Gnostics, enter into the Jinn state with the help of Harpocrates. When the sannyasi yogi practices his samyama, he flies, walks upon the water, passes through the fire without getting burned, and enters the rocks and caverns of the earth. Those who reach these heights of meditation are already a sannyasin of thought.

In the Western world, we use Western yoga, which has the exercise of Harpocrates as part of it. The required conditions in order to perform this yoga are faith, tenacity, and silence. Those who go around boasting to others about their victories lose their powers and become scoundrels. The Gnostic movement casts out and discards these types of imbecilic chatterboxes.

We can visit Tibet in flesh and blood (in the Jinn state) and converse with the masters and with Jesus Christ himself. Alexandra David-Neel tells us in her book, *Magic and Mystery in Tibet*, about Tibetan lamas who travel great distances in a somnambulistic state without becoming tired.[130] Let us imitate these ascetics. We, Gnostics, are totally practical. We are not intellectual vagabonds who waste their time in intellectual vagueness. Yes, boldly, this is how we Gnostics speak.

People are weary of so many theories, now they want practical matters. They do not want more theories, or more intellectual vagueness, or more exploitation. So, let us come to practical facts. Let us come to the point.

---

128 Renunciate.

129 "The three [dharana, dhyana, and samadhi] together constitute samyama." —Patanjali, Yoga Sutras 3:4. "The great yogi Patanjali states in his aphorisms that by practicing a samyama on the physical body, it becomes as light as cotton and can float on air. A samyama consists of three tempos: concentration, meditation and ecstasy. First, the yogi concentrates on his physical body. Second, he meditates on his physical body inducing sleep. Third, full of ecstasy, he gets up from his bed with his body in the Jinn state. Then, he penetrates into hyperspace and escaping from the law of gravity, he floats in the air." —Samael Aun Weor, *The Perfect Matrimony*

130

Nevertheless, those who acquire these powers must only utilize them in order to visit the monasteries of the White Lodge, or in order to study the marvels of nature. Woe unto those who will utilize these powers for fornication and wickedness.

After performing each practice of Harpocrates, little by little we accumulate enormous quantities of energy within our internal bodies, which eventually grant us the power of placing the body into the Jinn state. So, we need a lot of patience.

Whosoever misuses these powers shall be "cast out into outer darkness: there shall be heard weeping and gnashing of teeth."[131] It would be better for them that "a millstone be hanged about their neck, and they be cast into the sea."[132]

This is a divine science. Unfortunately, humanity only wants money, fornication, and crime.

Some spiritual devotees are like vipers within bouquets of flower. Yes, they are worse than profaners.

Note: with a great deal of drowsiness, one is projected in the astral body. Yet, in order to travel with the physical body in the Jinn state, one only needs a little drowsiness and an ardent faith. Therefore, what we need is to learn how to modulate our drowsiness.

---

131 Matthew 8:12, 22:13, 25:30
132 Matthew 18:6, Mark 9:42, Luke 17:2

Chapter 61

Imagination, Inspiration, Intuition

Imagination is clairvoyance. To imagine is to see.

The inventor who imagines his invention is indeed clairvoyantly seeing it. Before appearing in this physical world, any invention already exists in the internal worlds. Thus, all inventions previously existed within the internal worlds. The inventor imagines them, and thereafter he makes them concrete in this physical world. If the painter captures the images of the painting that he is going to paint, it is because the painting already exists within the internal worlds.

In order to develop clairvoyance, it is necessary to know how to be silent. Clairvoyants who boast about their visions are worthless. These types of sacrilegious individuals must be cast out of the Gnostic sanctuaries.

When we impel the frontal chakra to spin, then within it, images are reflected full of light, color, and sound; this is trained clairvoyance. Thus, the clairvoyant must know how to suffer, how to abstain, and how to die.

Inspiration

When we learn how to interpret the symbolic images of the internal worlds, we have then attained inspired knowledge. Internal images are interpreted based on the law of philosophical analogies, the law of the analogy of opposites, the law of correspondences, and the law of numerology.

What does an enemy resemble? It resembles a furious bull. What does the rain look like? It looks like tears.

Intuition

When we see a symbolic image within the superior worlds and we instantly know its meaning, it is because we have attained intuitive knowledge; this is to know without any need for reasoning. The intuitive person knows everything without the need for reasoning. The new Aquarian age is the era of intuition.

The mantra **OM** has the power to awaken the frontal and cardiac chakras, namely clairvoyance and intuition. We attain enlightenment by meditating on the mantra OM. Imagination, inspiration, and intuition are the three obligatory paths of initiation.

Warning: those who attain illumination and thereafter go around boasting to others about their esoteric achievements transform themselves into profaners of the temple. Instructors must severely admonish these types of "Gnostics."

Chapter 62

The Apostolate

Those who want powers must sacrifice themselves for humanity, because powers are payments that the governing Logos grants to any human when the Logos owes something to him or her. Thus, nothing is paid to those whom nothing is owed.

The name of the governing Logos of this solar system is Atin. This great being always pays what he owes.

Clairvoyants must not spy on their neighbors' lives, nor judge anyone, because this is wrong. Each person is what that person wants to be, thus the private life of the neighbor is a business that must not concern anyone else. What we must do is to work in the Great Work, thus we will collect our salary. Initiations, degrees, and powers are attained by practicing sexual magic, by terminating our bad habits, and by unselfishly working in the work of the Father.

Those who want initiations and degrees must study this book. Thereafter, they must practice it and teach the doctrine to everybody, everywhere. In this way, Gnostic congregations will be formed everywhere, within any humble home. Become an apostle, a Gnostic leader. In this way, as a grace, you will receive a great deal. In this way, as payment, you will also receive a great deal. So, call your friends, gather people, and teach them this doctrine. Become heralds of the powerful, revolutionary, universal Gnostic movement.

People of genius: teach this doctrine but do not make business with it. Nor should you use clairvoyance in order to spy on the neighbors' lives. We must organize pure sanctuaries, with humble people, simple and sincere laborers. Let us transform the world.

Let us go and battle for the new Aquarian age. Down with all chains! Let us go with this doctrine and battle. Let us wave the Gnostic flag upon the smoky ruins of the Vatican. To the battle, to the battle, to the battle! Yes, let us battle against all of that which in these times is rotten, evil, and perverse.

Often we hear the objections of those "gentlemen" of aristocracy (those who are in fashion), those "gentlemen" with stiff necks: what do they want to declare? The truth is that during these times everything is rotten.

Listen: work in the Great Work of the Father. This is the only way for you to pay your debts and become liberated from the law of karma. Later in time, you will be justified by your faith in Christ, then you will live under grace. Understand that when we are servants of sin, we are subjected to the law of karma. Yet, when finally we become servants of the Lord, then we live under the action of grace and we receive everything through cognizant faith. This is where powers are granted to us as a grace or blessing.

The laborers collect their salary, which is payment from the law. Yet, when they have already Christified themselves, then they receive gifts, powers, glory, and majesty as grace or blessing.

Wherever the law does not exist, sin also does not exist. Therefore, sacrifice yourself for the Great Work of the Father; sanctify yourself.

There are few initiates who comprehend the attributes of the great initiates. This is why Gnostic apostles never lack a Judas who betrays them, a Peter who denies them, a Thomas who mortifies them with his doubts, and a Magdalene who cries for them. Great initiates are very simple, and this is why people underestimate and despise them. Everybody wants these initiates to live according to peoples' routine life, according to peoples' established customs of erroneous criterion.

When judgmental people try to evaluate the daily lives of the great initiates, they always judge mistakenly, since judgmental people do not comprehend the extreme simplicity of the great initiates.

True Gnostic apostles always know how to be silent, how to abstain, and how to die.

Chapter 63

Meetings' Regulations

Meetings must be performed with order and veneration. Instructors must not be called masters, but "friends."

> *"But be not ye called master: for one is your master, even Christ."* —Matthew 23:8

The Gnostic movement is impersonal. It is made up of humble laborers. Therefore, let us reject any personalization. Let us not accept imposing individuals. No one is better than anyone else. Among us, we are laborers, bricklayers, mechanics, farmers, writers, physicians, etc.

The idolatry of the golden calf will be demolished in the Aquarian age; this is why we reject it in the Gnostic movement. A god of fire told us, "In the Aquarian age, capital will be decapitated." This great being dwells in the igneous stratum of the Earth.

Likewise, there will be no intellectuals in the new era, because they are dangerous due to their barbarism and perversity. We advise you to avoid interacting with them.

There will be no wealthy or poor people in the new era, but only worthy and decent laborers of the Great Work, that is all.

We do not worship noble titles, nor resounding titles like "doctor, lawyer, guru, master, elder brother, avatar," etc., because among Gnostics we are all friends, and Aquarius is the house of friends.

Any Gnostic meeting must begin with the study and commentary of any part of this doctrine.

Remember that the only master is Christ (a multiple perfect unity). We humans are more or less imperfect, thus I, the one who writes this book, am not anyone's master, and I beg people to not follow me. I am an imperfect human just like anyone else, and it is an error to follow someone who is imperfect. Let every one follow their "I am."

When a new congregation is formed, information should be given to the directors in command of that Gnostic movement.

Thus, this is how you will receive the necessary support; this way you will receive protection. We always assist anyone who asks for help.

Chapter 64

Selection of Personnel

Presently, the brothers and sisters of the great College of Initiates of the White Lodge are selecting human personnel. They are separating "the sheep from the goats"[133] so that the new era can be initiated. It would be impossible to initiate an age of light with personnel of murderers, prostitutes, and thieves.

We state that those who spill their semen eventually become demons, even if they are Theosophists or Rosicrucians. Yes, just as raging murderers do, mystical thieves also become demons.

Presently, there are millions of souls who are divorced from their Innermosts, thus they have horns on their foreheads. Among these demons we find thousands of Theosophists, Rosicrucians, Aquarianists, etc. Regrettably, many of them are sincere but mistaken souls who, despite their good intentions, have already unconsciously descended to the degree of demons. Nevertheless, they believe themselves to be saints. How naive they are.

Understand that demons are inhabitants of the abyss (infradimensions) and demons will not be reborn physically in Aquarius, which is the millennium mentioned in the Apocalypse (Revelation). The rebirth of demons in the physical plane will be postponed until the age of Capricorn (the age of the Holy Spirit); yes, in Capricorn the last opportunity will be granted unto them.

During the age of Capricorn, Javhe will also have a physical body, and he will be born in Palestine; he will be a warrior.

---

133 "When the Son of man shall come in his glory, and all the holy angels with him, then shall he sit upon the throne of his glory: And before him shall be gathered all nations: and he shall separate them one from another, as a shepherd divideth his sheep from the goats: And he shall set the sheep on his right hand, but the goats on the left. Then shall the King say unto them on his right hand, Come, ye blessed of my Father, inherit the kingdom prepared for you from the foundation of the world..." -Matthew 25

Then, the inhabitants of the abyss, after having experienced the terrors of the abyss, will be called to order, and they will have to define themselves in the flesh for either Christ or Javhe.

The Jews will then present Javhe as their authentic, promised Messiah, and all the definitely perverse personalities will follow Javhe into the abyss. Finally, throughout successive eternities, they will be disintegrated. The Monads, the Innermosts, of those dismal personalities will continue their evolution at the level of those remnants. After eternities, these Monads will build new personalities, and through them, they will inevitably reach their goal.

The present human evolution has failed. Yes, this entire humanity, the Great Babylon, will be destroyed by blood and fire; regrettably, more than one half of the present humanity has horns on their foreheads. These souls will follow a slow, arduous, and frightful devolution.

The Aryan[134] root race is the entire present humanity. This is the great harlot[135] that will be precipitated into the abyss. The gods judged the great harlot, and she was found to be unworthy. To the abyss! To the abyss! To the abyss!

Before the beginning of the Third World War,[136] politicians will search for peace with multiple formulae, but their intellects will totally fail.

---

134 The word Aryan is not a term only for "white people" or an ancient, dead civilization, but instead refers to to the vast majority of the population. All modern races are "Aryan." While formerly it was believed that the ancient Aryans were European (white), most scientists now believe that the ancient people commonly referred to as Aryan were the original inhabitants of India, which Manu called Aryavarta, "Abode of the Aryans."

135 "Come hither; I will shew unto thee the judgment of the great whore that sitteth upon many waters..." -Christian Bible, Revelation 17 and 19

136 Read *The Aquarian Message* by Samael Aun Weor.

Chapter 65
World Karma

Before the initiation of the new Aquarian age begins, all nations will have to pay their great karmic debts. For the good of humanity, there will be war between East and West; this is what Lord Jehovah stated. We know that the East will win the war. There will be combat on land, sea, and air, even in the poles. The East will win.

> *"In the Aquarian age, the capital will be decapitated.*
> *The United States will be punished."*

This is how it is written in the law. The Vatican will be bombarded and destroyed by blood and fire. Soon, it will pay its horrible debts. Spain will be transformed. All of Europe will become totally "sovietized." During the sign of Aquarius, the Americas will form a great confederation.

In the year 2018, even flashlights or portable lamps will be atomic.[137]

Imbecilic people believe that by uniting little schools they are going to initiate the new era; wretched people. Listen, the new era will be initiated upon the smoky ruins of this perverse civilization of vipers.

The beginning (overture) of the Aquarian Age started the 4th of February of 1962, between two and three in the afternoon.

In the year 2500, in the large cities there will be interplanetary stations for cosmic ships.

Regarding cosmic ships, in the superior worlds there was a great meeting of masters in order to deal with the problem of interplanetary navigation. We were sharing our concerns in order to determine if it was convenient or not to provide interplanetary ships to this humanity. Thus, every master expressed their view. Our concern was that the human beings of the Earth will use cosmic ships to go to other planets of the solar system in order to commit the same crimes and wickedness

---

137 There are many such technologies that are unavailable to the public.

that they have already committed here during their historical conquests. It was enough for us to remember the crimes of the Spaniard Hernán Cortés in Mexico, or Pizarro in Peru, in order to comprehend the great responsibility implied by providing interplanetary ships to this humanity.

We made a comparative evaluation of humanities. Namely, the inhabitants of the Earth have failed. The inhabitants of Venus are very much more advanced, since they already know the bad from the good and the good from the bad. And the humans from Mars are somewhat more evolved than the earthlings, etc.

So, the last one who expressed his concept—in his capacity as initiator of the new era—was me, your humble servant, the one who writes this book. Thus I, your servant, filled with pain and comprehending the terrible responsibility of the word, withdrew toward my Innermost and said, "Abba, Father, all things are possible unto thee; take away this cup from me: nevertheless not what I will, but what thou wilt" [Mark 14:36]. Then, my "I am" answered, "Let relations between the worlds be established." Since any advanced humanity has those ships, let those flying spheres be delivered to praiseworthy terrestrials.

We know that some scientists will try to build these cosmic ships but their enterprises will fail; their pride will be mortally wounded. The inhabitants of other worlds will come to teach us how to build these cosmic ships. This is how the science of the "iniquitous ones" will fall mortally wounded, and earthly scientists will have to kneel when in front of the inhabitants of the solar system.

Scientists of this century are launching satellites with the pretext of conquering space. Nonetheless, the truth is that they want to establish cosmic bases in order to advantageously bombard defenseless people and nations.

In the age of Aquarius, many inhabitants of other planets will be established on the Earth; yes, they will be the instructors of Aquarius. Some of them already live in concealment in Tibet. Thus, journeys to other planets of the solar system will become routine. This is an extra help that will be granted to our evolution.

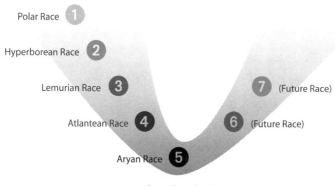

SEVEN ROOT RACES

The abuse of nuclear energy will awaken many volcanoes, thus towards the end of the seventh subrace[138] of this present Aryan root race,[139] there will be huge earthquakes and sea-quakes (tsunamis) that will transform the terrestrial cortex completely. This Aryan root race will perish in these cataclysms.

Later in time, the sixth root race will flourish on the continent of Antarctica.[140] The sixth root race will be smaller in body but greater in soul. Their twelve senses will be totally developed. The avatar of that root race will be Zachariel, the ruler of Jupiter, who, at that time, will incarnate in a body in order to teach the Sixth Truth.

I, Samael, humble servant of the new era, have merely taught you the Fifth Truth. Listen to me, humans! The Fifth Truth is sexual magic.

Gabriel was the avatar of the first root race. Raphael was that of the second root race. Uriel was the avatar of the third root race. Michael was the avatar of the fourth root race. I, Samael Aun Weor, am the avatar of the fifth root race. Zachariel will be the avatar of the sixth root race, and Orifiel will be the avatar of the seventh root race.

These are the seven truths:

---

138 North American culture.
139 Contemporary humanity is the Aryan race, the fifth race on this planet. See graphic.
140 This will be after the shift of the poles, making Antarctica temperate.

1. Knowledge of the pains and miseries of this world

2. Knowledge of human fragility

3. Knowledge of desire and sin

4. Knowledge of the human mind

5. The Tree of Knowledge

6. Human consciousness

7. The Tree of Life

So, there are seven avatars and seven truths; each one teaches a remarkable truth.

Jesus Christ is not an avatar, he is more than that. He is the savior of the world, the leader of all souls. Jesus Christ confirms the teachings of the avatars and improves them. Jesus Christ will come at the zenith of Aquarius and will confirm the teachings that I, Samael, have given you.

Jesus Christ will come successively in the other root races until the restitution of the kingdom of God that he has spoken of through the mouths of all his servants, the prophets.

Each root race ends in a cataclysm. The pit of the abyss is now opened. The smoke that blows out from it brings wars, famine, and misery.

The entire twentieth and twenty-first centuries will be lethal wars so that all the souls who have the mark of the beast on their hands and foreheads will enter into the abyss. Each of the seven angels has blown his trumpet for the great cataclysm.

Woe to those who do not want to accept the Fifth Truth, the Tree of Knowledge!

Study the chapters 8, 9, and 10 of the Book of Revelation (Apocalypse). All the countries will be desolated, destroyed. This great Babylon will sink into the abyss.

Chapter 66

How to Charge Talismans and Cleanse Our Sanctuaries

Pentagrams, crosses, or other sacred items can be charged, or the environment of our sanctuaries can be cleansed, by reciting the Conjuration of the Seven. The talismans must be placed on a table set in order to serve us as an altar. We must light three candles, and filled with faith, we begin to pray as follows:

CONJURATION OF THE SEVEN

In the name of Michael, may Jehovah command thee and drive thee hence, Chavajoth!

In the name of Gabriel, may Adonai command thee, and drive thee hence, Bael!

In the name of Raphael, begone before Elial, Samgabiel!

By Samael Sabaoth, and in the name of Elohim Gibor, get thee hence, Andrameleck!

By Zachariel and Sachiel-Meleck, be obedient unto Elvah, Sanagabril!

By the divine and human name of Shaddai, and by the sign of the Pentagram which I hold in my right hand, in the name of the angel Anael, by the power of Adam and Eve, who are Yod-HaVah, begone Lilith! Let us rest in peace, Nahemah!

By the holy Elohim and by the names of the Genii Cashiel, Sehaltiel, Aphiel and Zarahiel, at the command of Orifiel, depart from us Moloch. We deny thee our children to devour!

Amen. Amen. Amen.

Thereafter, with faith, sprinkle water over the items to be charged or within the area that will be your sanctuary, while reciting:

*In nomine Elohim et per spiritum aquarum viventum, sis mihi,
in signus lucis et sacramentum voluntatis.*

Smoke the items with frankincense and recite:

Per serpentum oeneum sub quo cadut serpentes igneis, sis mihi.

Then blow seven times over the items that are being charged
and recite:

Per firmamentum et spiritum vocis, sis mihi.

Sprinkle salt or earth in a triangular form over the items
and recite:

In sale terrae et per virtutem vitae eternae, sis mihi.

Thus, the sacred or consecrated items are blessed, which
become powerful accumulators of divine cosmic forces. These
items are talismans of light, which irradiate light, force, power,
and glory. For these ritualistic works, every Gnostic must have
an ornamental sword on the altar, which must be consecrated
as a talisman. In the astral, we receive sacred jewels. Any talisman must be consecrated in order to wear it.

The Invocation of Solomon must also be recited aloud or
mentally before our ritualistic works or when falling asleep.
Thus, in this way, during sleep we will be astrally transported
to the most elevated planes of cosmic consciousness. This is
how we will ask for help from the high divine hierarchies.

INVOCATION OF SOLOMON

*Powers of the kingdom, be ye under my left foot and in my right
hand!*

*Glory and eternity, take me by the two shoulders and direct me
in the paths of victory!*

*Mercy and justice, be ye the equilibrium and splendor of my
life!*

Intelligence and wisdom, crown me!

*Spirits of Malkuth, lead me betwixt the two pillars upon which
rests the whole edifice of the temple!*

*Angels of Netzach and Hod, establish me upon the cubic stone of
Yesod!*

Oh Gedulael! Oh Geburael! Oh Tiphereth!

Binael, be thou my love!

Ruach Chokmael, be thou my light!

Be that which thou art and thou shalt be, oh Ketheriel!

Ishim, assist me in the name of Shaddai!

Cherubim, be my strength in the name of Adonai!

Beni-Elohim, be my brethren in the name of the Son, and by the powers of Sabbaoth!

Elohim, do battle for me in the name of Tetragrammaton!

Melachim, protect me in the name of Yod Hei Vau Hei!

Seraphim, cleanse my love in the name of Eloah!

Hasmalim, enlighten me with the splendors of Elohim and Shekinah!

Aralim, act!

Orphanim, revolve and shine!

Hajoth ha Kadosh, cry, speak, roar, bellow!

Kadosh, Kadosh, Kadosh!

Shaddai, Adonai, Yod-Havah,

Eheieh Asher Eheieh!

Hallelu-jah, Hallelu-jah, Hallelu-jah,

Amen. Amen. Amen.

This is better than the spiritual-mediumistic invocations. Mediums end up insane, deranged, because they are always searching for buried treasures. They are always cheated by those tenebrous entities who possess them and pass themselves off as saints, geniuses, etc.

CONSECRATION OF THE TEMPLE

The word magic is derived from the ancient word "mag" that means priest (from magos "one of the members of the learned and priestly class," from O.Pers. magush). Thus, genuine magic is the power of a priest or holy person to help others. Real magic is the work of a priest. A real magician is a priest.

Chapter 67

Ceremonial Procedures of High Magic

Before any ceremony of high magic, the four elements of nature must be exorcised.

Exorcism of the Air

Holding in the hand the feather of a bird (preferably of an eagle), we blow towards each of the four cardinal points while tracing the sign of the cross in the air with the feather. Thus, facing the east, we recite the Prayer of the Sylphs, as follows:

Spiritus Dei ferebatur super aquas, et inspiravit in faciem hominis spiraculum vitae. Sit Michael dux meus, et Sabtabiel servus meus, in luce et per lucem.

Fiat verbum halitus meus; et imperabo Spiritibus, aeris hujus, et refrenabo equos solis voluntate cordis mei, et cogitatione mentis meae et nutu oculi dextri.

Exorciso igitur te, creatura aeris, per Pentagrammaton, et in nomine Tetragrammaton, in quibus sunt voluntas firma et fides recta. Amen. Sela, fiat. So be it. Obey me sylphs and syiphids, by the Christ, by the Christ, by the Christ, Amen.

Exorcism of the Water

Facing the west, one commands the creatures of water by holding a cup of water in the hands, and reciting:

In the name of Christ, by the Christ, by the Christ. Fiat firmamentum in medio aquarum et separet aquas ab aquis, quae superius sicut quae inferius, et quae inferius sicut quae superius, ad perpetranda miracula rei unius. Sol ejus pater est, luna mater et ventus bane gestavit in utero suo, ascendit a terra ad coelum et rursus a chelo in terram descendit.

Exorciso te, creatura aquae, ut sis mihi speculum die rivi in operibus ejus, et fons vitae, et abllutio pecatorum. Amen.

Exorcism of the Earth

Facing the north and holding a rod in the hand, we exorcise the gnomes while reciting the following:

> *By the twelve stones of the holy city, by the hidden talismans, by the pole of loadstone which passes through the center of the world, I conjure thee subterranean toilers of the earth! Obey me in the name of Christ, by the blood of Christ, by the love of Christ. Amen.*

Exorcism of the Fire

Facing the south and holding a sword in the hand, we command the elementals of fire while reciting:

> *Michael, king of the Sun and lightning! Samael, king of volcanoes and earthquakes! Anael, prince of the Astral Light! Assist me in the name of Christ, by the majesty of Christ, by the power of Christ. Amen.*

Then sprinkle frankincense on the burning embers in a small brazier.

Secret in Order to Become Invisible

If a beloved relative dies, do not grieve; transmute those energies of pain into waves of peace, happiness, and joy. You can transmute your grief into a power that will make you invisible at will any time you wish. Jesus attained that power by means of the science of transmutations. "Permute nature, thus you will find what you are looking for." Yes, all powers are attainable by means of the science of transmutations.

"Death is the crown of everyone."

We must not distress the souls of our dead relatives with our mourning and crying. Instead, let us pray for the dead, thus we grant them happiness and peace.

Chapter 68

Invocations

When in accordance with the law of karma we want to resolve any personal problem, the four exorcisms of fire, air, water, and earth must be recited in front of our altar. Thereafter, we must invoke the great master of karma, Anubis, and his forty-two judges of the law, in the following manner:

> *In the name of Christ, in the name of Christ, in the name of Christ, we invoke you Anubis, Anubis, Anubis. Amen.*

Then, facing the altar, we kneel before the altar where we will mentally converse with Anubis and ask for whatever we deem necessary.

Remember that the judges of karma will remedy our needs in accordance with the law. They cannot violate the laws. Therefore, if our petition is not granted, it is because of our lack of merits, thus we must not protest; we must always bow before their verdict.

If what we need is to heal the ill, then we must invoke Raphael, Paracelsus, Aesculapius, etc. If we are ill, then we must kneel before the altar and ask for healing.

Before the altar, we can invoke any of the seven, since each one of them is a specialist in his own domain.

1. Gabriel is related to conception

2. Raphael with medicine

3. Uriel with love, family, children, etc.

4. Michael with high dignitaries

5. Samael with strength

6. Zachariel with authorities

7. Orifiel with land, mines, etc.

We can invoke them by pronouncing their name three times, in the name of Christ, as follows:

In the name of Christ, by the Christ, by the Christ, we call upon thee, glorious (pronounce here the name of the invoked being), in order to beg of thee (the petition here).

This is how we work in white ceremonial magic. Remember that the holy beings always help us according with the law. They do not violate laws. Therefore, we must not impose our mental force on others, because this is black magic. Let us respect the law.

Good sense tells us when to utilize these teachings.

We need to develop intuitive clairvoyance in order to see these things.

Recite the Conjuration of the Seven in order to conjure the demons of the possessed and in order to defend ourselves from the tenebrous ones.

However, in order to defend ourselves from black magicians, the following plant magic is advised.

Plant Magic

On the ground, trace a circle around a lemon tree. Near the tree, dig a small hole and firmly insert nine small wooden sticks (distributed into three groups of three) inside the hole, and thereafter fill it with water, making a small puddle. You must also light a fire (in a portable grill, such as an hibachi). You will then beg the elemental of the lemon tree to serve you (each lemon tree has its soul which has a remarkable power). Using the following procedure, you must throw nine lemons into the fire, one by one: look fixedly at a lemon, then pick it, and repeat until you have three in hand; throw them one by one into the fire; gather three more and repeat, until you have thrown nine lemons in the fire. If a lemon explodes (producing an explosion), it is because the black magicians are performing sorcery on you. So, command the elemental of that lemon tree to defend you. When fallen into the fire, each of the nine lemons will explode in the astral plane like a bomb, destroying the works of sorcery from the black magicians. Thereafter, the elemental will come out of the lemon tree and, shapeshifting itself into the form of a dog, will go and attack the tenebrous ones.

Note: the exorcisms must be learned by memory, since these may be needed unexpectedly. E.g. an ill person may need an exorcised drink of water, or we may need to see clairvoyantly in the water, or we may need to drive away a storm by conjuring the sylphs of space, or we may need to invoke the salamanders in order to command them to stop a fire, or invoke the gnomes, etc.

Pranayama

Chapter 69
Sexual Transmutation for Singles

Pranayama is a system of sexual transmutation for bachelors and bachelorettes. We already know that the two ganglionic cords, entwined along the spinal medulla in the form of an eight, ascend from the male's testicles and from the woman's ovaries towards the brain. These two ganglionic cords are the two witnesses mentioned in the book of Revelation (Apocalypse); likewise, "these are also the two olive branches... and the two anointed ones, that stand by the LORD of the whole earth," mentioned in Zachariah 4:12, 14. These are two hollow nerves, two fine canals through which the sexual energies ascend to the brain.

The student inhales the air through the left nostril and exhales it through the right, and vice-versa. With the thumb and index fingers, one controls the nostrils in an alternating manner. When inhaling through Pingala, the solar nostril, we intensely imagine the radiant and sublime solar atoms rising through the solar cord to the brain; then hold the breath and carry that solar force to the area between the eyebrows, and the throat, successively. When exhaling the air, one focuses (with imagination and willpower) on the energy being placed within the heart. Now, when inhaling through Ida, the lunar nostril, we imagine the lunar atoms, like the pure water of life, rising through the lunar cord and by taking the same route, namely, to the area between the eyebrows and the throat, successively. We then exhale with profound faith and fix this lunar energy within the heart. So, this is how bachelors and bachelorettes can transmute their sexual energies.

Bachelors and bachelorettes must find a spouse if they want to Christify themselves, because the Gnostic esotericists can only perform sexual contact when they are married. The fires cannot be awakened without sexual magic. Yes, without chastity, nothing is achieved in these studies. Kill desire, kill the "I," and its thoughts: this is how you will become a liberated one.

Remember, true marriage has nothing to do with the social or religious formulas of this barbaric humanity. The authentic marriage is performed when a couple unites in spirit, soul, and sex; the true marriage must be pure like a lotus flower.

Chapter 70
Esoteric Vocalization for Singles

The vowel "I" [pronounced ee as in "tree"] awakens the frontal chakra and makes us clairvoyant.

The vowel "E" [pronounced eh as in "red"] awakens the thyroid chakra and makes us clairaudient.

The vowel "O" [pronounced oo as in "no"] awakens the heart chakra and makes us intuitive.

The vowel "U" [pronounced uu as in "you"] awakens the solar plexus and makes us telepathic.

The vowel "A" [pronounced ah as in "tall"] awakens the pulmonary chakra in order to remember past existences.

These vowels are vocalized by sustaining and prolonging the sound of each one of them. By combining mental vocalization with pranayama, one can vocalize in the following order, I... E... O... U... A... One will mentally imitate the sound of the air, hurricane, or breeze. Each letter must be mentally vocalized separately.

By means of these studies and exercises, any human can attain the degree of a Christ.

Women can attain the degree of Virgin. I.e. Litelantes is a powerful Virgin of the Law. The eleven thousand Inca Virgins are divine and ineffable. The Virgin of the Sea, who was Mary, the mother of Jesus, is the Immaculate Conception, because she directs immaculate conceptions. The Virgin of the Stars, etc. These are different female adepts who attained perfection, who attained Nirvana.

When a Virgin of Nirvana wants to incarnate her "I Am," she must then renounce Nirvana and incarnate preferably in the body of a male, i.e. the Virgin of the Sea has now incarnated in a male body in Egypt in order to elevate herself to the degree of a Christ.

Thus, we have finished this book. Unfortunately, we can count with our fingers those who are prepared for Gnosis. Up until now, I have only known two people who are prepared for Gnosis: an illiterate Indian Mama (shaman) and a woman. Yes, those who want to **know** have to kill the great destroyer of reality: the mind.

Final Instruction

Gnostics must greet each other with the mantra "Inverencial peace." Alternatively, they should recognize each other with the hand-sign with which Jesus Christ is usually depicted, namely, extending the thumb, index, and middle fingers of the right hand.

They must address each other with the terms "Mr., Mrs., gentleman, friend," etc. The use of the words "brother" or "sister" is forbidden, since it has been abused. Yes, mutual disrespect, disorder, fornication, adultery, theft, etc., have been hidden behind this word. Humanity is not yet prepared to use such noble words.

Let us preserve mutual respect, decency, and gentlemanliness.

JESUS DEMONSTRATING THE GREETING

Epilogue

Closing Speech at the 1975 Gnostic Congress

At these moments, I address my words to all the brothers and sisters of the universal Christian Gnostic movement who are reunited here at this great banquet.

The hour has arrived in which we have to comprehend that we are in fact one great family, without distinction of races or nations.

Indeed, at any cost we are organizing the army for the salvation of the world.

Terrible moments are approaching for this humanity, since our solar system has finished its voyage around the zodiacal belt. This means that the sidereal year is ending. I want all of you to know in a clear and precise manner that as there is a terrestrial year,[1] likewise there is a sidereal year;[2] that as the Earth travels around the Sun, similarly our solar system travels around the zodiacal belt. Just as the terrestrial year has four seasons, namely spring, summer, autumn, and winter, thus the sidereal [solar system] year has four seasons spring (golden age), summer (silver age), autumn (copper age), winter (iron age).

The present sidereal [solar system] year is approaching its last degrees in the constellation of the water carrier [Aquarius]; this means that it is finishing. Unquestionably, a great cosmic cataclysm always occurs whenever a sidereal [solar system] year concludes. I.e. When the sidereal [solar system] year concluded in ancient Atlantis, then that gigantic continent—which once

1   Terrestrial is from Latin terra, "earth," thus the author is using this term to describe what is commonly called a tropical or solar year of approximately 365 days, 5 hours, 48 minutes and 45 seconds.
2   Sidereal is from Larin sidus "star" and the term sidereal year is used by modern science to describe the time it takes for the Earth to orbit the Sun, which is nearly identical to the tropical or solar year. Samael Aun Weor is using the term to describe a much larger pattern: the circular movement of the entire solar system through space.

magnificently gleamed on the Atlantic Ocean—was submerged in the dreadful waves of that ocean. And when the sidereal year approached its end in the Lemurian epoch, then the Lemurians perished in the fire and earthquakes. Now, in this Aryan race, the sidereal [solar system] year is arriving at its end, and unquestionably this humanity will perish in the fire and earthquakes.

The times of the end have arrived, and we are in them. Everything is already lost. The evil of the world is so great that it already reached unto heaven.[3] Babylon the great, the mother of harlots and abominations of the Earth, will be destroyed, and from the entirety of this perverse civilization of vipers, nothing will remain, not even one stone upon another. This humanity is sufficiently mature for the final punishment.

Therefore, Gnostic brothers and sisters who are reunited here today at this banquet in order to celebrate this true agape[4] of love, this mystical agape, I want you to know in a definitive manner that we work in accordance with the plans of the White Brotherhood. My real, inner, profound Being is the manu[5] of the sixth root race. Therefore, at this moment we are making the human nucleus that will be the basis for the development of the future great root race.

As a first facet, we will have to divulge the doctrine across the entire face of the Earth. Our Gnostic movement has become powerful from North America to Patagonia. It is

---

3   "And he cried mightily with a strong voice, saying, Babylon the great is fallen, is fallen, and is become the habitation of devils, and the hold of every foul spirit, and a cage of every unclean and hateful bird. For all nations have drunk of the wine of the wrath of her fornication, and the kings of the earth have committed fornication with her, and the merchants of the earth are waxed rich through the abundance of her delicacies. And I heard another voice from heaven, saying, Come out of her, my people, that ye be not partakers of her sins, and that ye receive not of her plagues. For her sins have reached unto heaven, and God hath remembered her iniquities." -Revelation 18

4   Greek (ἀγάπη), "love" a Christian term that sometimes relates to a communal meal.

5   "Just as each planetary Round commences with the appearance of a 'Root Manu' (Dhyan Chohan) and closes with a 'Seed-Manu,' so a Root and a Seed Manu appear respectively at the beginning and the termination of the human period on any particular planet." —H.P. Blavatsky

a strong movement. At the present moment, it is the most powerful movement ever founded. Soon, we will have to begin our operations in Europe. Thereafter we will continue in the Middle East. And, according to what is written, finally the Gnostic movement will produce a true spiritual revolution on the Asian continent. When this occurs, I myself—together with some other brothers and sisters—will retire to the central plateau of Asia, to a solitary cavern. It will be necessary to leave for a certain time so that "the leaven will ferment." Then, before the approach of the final cataclysm, we will return in order to reunite all of those who worked in the Great Work of the Father; that is, in order to reunite all of those who dissolved at least and no less than fifty percent of the animal ego. Then, those who for such a reason will deserve it will be taken in a new exodus[6] to a certain secret place in the Pacific Ocean. From thence we will see the catastrophe; from thence we will contemplate the duel of the fire and the water, for several centuries.

The presence of a gigantic planet that travels through space will precipitate the revolution of the axes of the Earth. That planet receives the name of "Hercolubus." It is six times bigger than Jupiter. Hercolubus will pass at an angle through our solar system. Its force of attraction will be powerful: the fire contained inside the Earth will be attracted, thus volcanoes will emerge everywhere. Obviously, with the emergence of volcanoes, frightful earthquakes and terrible tsunamis will be unleashed. Likewise, due to the revolution of the axes of the Earth, the water will change its bases; that is, the seas will move, and the present continents will be submerged in the boisterous waves of the oceans.

All of this humanity will perish, because this humanity is already mature for the final punishment, a shameful humanity that deserves the karma that approaches. This humanity did not want to listen to the voice of the prophets. This humanity did not want to listen to the voice of Jesus Christ. They stoned Stephen. They repeatedly jailed Paul of Tarsus. They poisoned

---

6   A reference to the book of Exodus written by Moses that symbolically describe how initiates are saved.

Gautama, the Buddha Shakyamuni. They poisoned Milarepa. They persecuted the saints of the eternal one. Now, obviously, they will have to "pay the uttermost farthing."[7]

It is good for everyone present here to comprehend that the times of the end have arrived. Yes, it is good for us to understand that Hercolubus, the gigantic planet that is to affect the revolution of the axes of the Earth, is already in view of all the astronomical observatories of the world. It is not a chimera, since no astronomer ignores that there is a very distant solar system traveling towards the Earth. I am talking about the solar system of Tylo. "Hercolubus" rotates, it has its center of gravity, around the sun of that system, and navigates at gigantic velocities towards the orbit of the planet Earth. Therefore, what I am stating will be discussed by million of human beings. I know that many will mock, that many will laugh, but it is written:

> "The one who laughs at what he does not know is an
> ignoramus who walks on the path of idiocy."

In the times of Atlantis,[8] we the initiates also shouted warnings. Yes, we warned humanity that a great catastrophe was coming, and many were those who laughed, many were those who mocked us, many were those who threw the dribble of their criticism against us. Nevertheless, when they saw the catastrophe, when they felt the earthquakes, when the seas moved, then they wanted to follow us; however, it was useless: only the select ones were saved, a world salvation army that was formed at that time similar to the one that we are forming now, at these very moments. Hence, the objective for which we have created a world salvation army is with the purpose of forming a selected people that will serve as a foundation for the sixth root race.

It pleases me to see all of you reunited here. It pleases me to see all of you in this agape. Indeed, when contemplating each of these, your brotherly countenances, we feel that our heart becomes inflamed with love. In the name of the great cosmic

---

7   Matthew 5:26
8   The previous root race, symbolized in all the univeral flood traditions
     from around the world, such as those of Noah, Deucalion, etc.

truth, I only long for that light to illuminate all of you, that it shine in each one present here. I sincerely long that everyone march on the path of the realization of the inner self, until complete triumph. I sincerely long that the inner star that guides each of you finally leads you to the blessings. I sincerely long that this Gnostic people—based on intentional sacrifices, conscious efforts, and voluntary sufferings[9]—finally arrive to real liberation.

May all of you here present never forget the esoteric work. May all sincerely in truth dedicate themselves to work on themselves, here and now.

> "For if any be a hearer of the word, and not a doer, he is like unto a man beholding his true face in a mirror, and as soon as he beholds himself he turns his back and goes away." —James 1:23

Thus, brothers and sisters, it is not enough to be a hearer of the word. It is necessary to be a doer of the word.

Thus, as we fight more and more, we will receive inner help. I want you to know that the inner Christ comes to you when indeed we have worked untiringly, night and day.

I want you to know that Jesus, the great Kabir, gave—he brought to the world 1,975 years ago—the doctrine of the inner Christ. Yes, if the advent of Jesus the great Kabir is something grandiose, it is because indeed he brought to us the doctrine of the inner Christ.

When the apostle Paul of Tarsus speaks about the Christ, he does not exclusively talk about the historical Jesus: he talks about the inner Jesus.

Many are those who wait for the coming of the great master, yet verily I say unto you, my beloved brothers and sisters, that he comes from within, from within the very bottom of our souls.

Thus as we persevere in the esoteric work, as we fight for the elimination our inhuman elements that we carry in our interior, we will approach the inner Christ more and more.

---

9   These are the three factors required in our daily lives. Read *Spiritual Power of Sound* by Samael Aun Weor.

Thus, in this way, the day will arrive in which he will come to save us. That day he will take charge of all of our mental, emotive, sentimental, sexual processes, etc. That day, he will become flesh in us. He will become a man of flesh and bone in each one of us so that he can transform, beautify, and dignify us.

Thus, the hour has arrived to love the lord of martyrdoms. He is the one who indeed is ready to sacrifice himself within us and for us, here and now.

The inner Christ is our savior. Thus, this how I formally declare it here before you, in this agape.

The inner Christ is something sublime: he loves us, thus we must love him. He offers himself as an immolated lamb in order to redeem us. He suffers within us and wants to transform us radically.

Who would not love, for instance, a good friend, who, us being imprisoned, comes to visit us and would even come to secure our freedom?

Who would not love a great friend, who, us being ill and abandoned, will bring us medicines and even manage to heal us?

Who would not love a friend, who, us being in misery, would give us his hand and feed us?

Who would not love his mother, who from childhood guarded us, who fed us with her breasts, who did everything she could for us and who suffered for us, until raising us to the state in which we are?

Well then, my beloved brothers and sisters, the inner Christ does that and more. He comes to us when we have sincerely worked in the Great Work of the Father, when we have truly fought to eliminate our psychological defects, when we have struggled to eliminate all those "I"s that in their conjunction constitute "the myself," "the self-willed..." He comes to us when we really are working for our liberation.

He suffers from within the very bottom of our soul. He comes in order to take possession of our emotions, our thoughts, our desires. He comes in order to fight, within himself, against the "inhuman elements" that we carry within our interior. He becomes a person of flesh and bone, even though people do not recognize him. He comes to live the cosmic drama, here and now, within us, from instant to instant, from moment to moment.

He returns again in order to be betrayed by Judas, the demon of desire, by Pilate, the demon of the mind (who finds excuses for everything), and by Caiaphas, the demon of evil will.

He again returns in order to be humiliated, slapped by all those "I's" that we carry in our interior. He returns in order to endure the crown of thorns. He returns again in order to be whipped, with five thousand and more whips, within us, here and now. And finally, he who becomes the immolated lamb, the lamb that erases our sins, goes up to the Golgotha of supreme sacrifice and exclaims with a loud voice,

> *"Father, into thy hands I commend my spirit."*
> —Luke 23:46

Thereafter, he descends into the sepulcher, and with his death he kills death.

> *"Death is swallowed up in victory. O death, where is thy sting? O grave, where is thy victory?"* —1 Corinthians 15:54

Therefore, brothers and sisters, the hour has arrived to love the inner Christ. These are the teachings that the great Kabir Jesus brought to us...

When within us here and now the Lord of Perfection resuscitates, we then resuscitate within him and he within us, and we become in fact splendid, immortal creatures.

Before the incarnation of the inner Christ, we are truly dead. Only after incarnating within our interior the inner Christ do we have life in abundance.

Gnostic brothers and sisters who tonight are reunited in this mystical agape, I want all of you in a deeper manner to love the inner Christ. I want you to truly work upon yourselves, so that one day he may arise definitively within you in order to definitively transform you.

> *"Uselessly a thousand times Christ in Bethlehem will be born*

If within our heart his birth is forlorn.
His crucifixion, death and resurrection on the third day
from among the dead were in vain,
Unless his crucifixion, death and resurrection
be set up within each one of us again."

Let us love the beloved one, the one who truly sacrifices himself for us, here and now! Let us love him, brothers and sisters, let us love him!

Inverencial peace,
Samael Aun Weor

Glossary

Absolute: Abstract space; that which is without attributes or limitations. Also known as sunyata, void, emptiness, Parabrahman, Adi-buddha, and many other names.

"The Absolute is the Being of all Beings. The Absolute is that which Is, which always has Been, and which always will Be. The Absolute is expressed as Absolute Abstract Movement and Repose. The Absolute is the cause of Spirit and of Matter, but It is neither Spirit nor Matter. The Absolute is beyond the mind; the mind cannot understand It. Therefore, we have to intuitively understand Its nature." —Samael Aun Weor, *Tarot and Kabbalah*

"In the Absolute we go beyond karma and the gods, beyond the law. The mind and the individual consciousness are only good for mortifying our lives. In the Absolute we do not have an individual mind or individual consciousness; there, we are the unconditioned, free and absolutely happy Being. The Absolute is life free in its movement, without conditions, limitless, without the mortifying fear of the law, life beyond spirit and matter, beyond karma and suffering, beyond thought, word and action, beyond silence and sound, beyond forms." —Samael Aun Weor, *The Major Mysteries*

Adultery: Etymologists say that the English word adultery comes from the Old French avoutrie, aoulterie, a noun of condition from avoutre / aoutre, and from the Latin adulterare "to corrupt," meaning, "debauch; falsify, debase." The term adulterate is used correctly when describing a lie or a corruption of something that was pure. Thus, broadly speaking, an act of adultery is an act that makes purity into impurity.

In the scriptures of Judaism and Christianity, the word adultery is usually placed as the translation for נאף na'aph: "To perform voluntary violation of the marriage bed." This word does not mean just adultery in a limited, literal sense, but is far more broad.

Strictly defined, adultery is sexual infidelity: to lust after someone other than one's partner, or to have sex with multiple partners.

"Three evil deeds [that create suffering] depending upon the body are: killing, stealing, and committing adultery." —Buddha, from The Practice of Dhyâna

"Have nought to do with adultery; for it is a foul thing and an evil way." —Mohammed, from Qu'ran, Sura XVII, The Night Journey, Mecca

"The husband receives his wife from the gods; he does not wed her according to his own will; doing what is agreeable to the gods, he must always support her while she is faithful. "Let mutual fidelity continue until death;" this may be considered as a summary of the highest law for husband and wife." —Laws of Manu 9.95, 101

Throughout the world, adultery is commonly defined as "sexual intercourse between a married person and someone else" and while there are many varieties of interpretation on this point, the scriptures are actually quite clear about what adultery is:

"Adultery can be committed with the eyes." —Jewish, Leviticus Rabba 23

"Commit no adultery. This law is broken by even looking at the wife of another with a lustful mind." —Buddha

"Ye have heard that it was said by them of old time, Thou shalt not commit adultery: But I say unto you, That whosoever looketh on a woman to lust after her hath committed adultery with her already in his heart." —Jesus, in Matthew 5

"But I say unto you, That whosoever shall put away his wife, saving for the cause of fornication, causeth her to commit adultery: and whosoever shall marry her that is divorced committeth adultery." —Jesus, in Matthew 5

"Immorality is not confined to action; it is rooted in the very thought. It can be effectively eliminated not by merely restraining the external organs, as the hypocrites do, but by making the mind and heart pure. "Whosoever looketh on a woman to lust after her hath committed adultery with her already in the heart." Sin is in the mind; the body is a mere tool of the mind." —Swami Sivananda, *Life and Teachings of Lord Jesus* (1959)

"Adultery is the cruel result of the lack of love. The woman who is truly in love would prefer death to adultery. The man who commits adultery is not truly in love. [...] There are also many women who, under the pretext of supposed profound Realization of the Self, unite with any male. What all these passionate women really want is to satiate their carnal desires. The world is always the world, and since we have been divulging the Great Arcanum there have appeared, as one might expect, those swine who trample the doctrine and then die poisoned by the bread of wisdom. The cult of Sexual Magic can only be practiced between husband and wife. [...] We must clarify that Sexual Magic can only be practiced between husband and wife. The adulterer and the adulteress inevitably fail. You can only be married when there is love. Love is law, but it must be conscious love." —Samael Aun Weor, *The Perfect Matrimony*

Alchemy: Al (as a connotation of the Arabic word Allah: al-, the + ilah, God) means "The God." Also Al (Hebrew) for "highest" or El "God." Chem or Khem is from kimia (Greek) which means "to fuse or cast a metal." Also from Khem, the ancient name of Egypt. The synthesis is Al-Kimia: "to fuse with the highest" or "to fuse with God."

Ancient of Days: (עתיק יומין Atik Yomin, from Aramaic) A name for God in many traditions.

"I beheld till the thrones were cast down, and the Ancient of days did sit, whose garment [was] white as snow, and the hair of his head like the pure wool: his throne [was like] the fiery flame, [and] his wheels [as] burning fire." —Daniel 7:9

"The First Mystery is [the sephirah] Kether, the Ancient of Days..." —Samael Aun Weor, *The Gnostic Bible: The Pistis Sophia Unveiled*

"...the ineffable Ancient of Days who is the Being of our Being, the Father/ Mother within us." —Samael Aun Weor, *Tarot and Kabbalah*

"The tree [of life] begins with the Ancient of Days, Kether, who is in the most elevated place of the tree." —Samael Aun Weor, *Tarot and Kabbalah*

Aquarius: An era of time under the influence of the zodiacal sign of Aquarius that will last for approximately 2,140 years. The new Aquarian era began with the celestial conjunction of February 4-5, 1962. On February 4-5, 1962, exactly when there was a new moon AND a full solar eclipse, there was also an extraordinary celestial conjunction of the seven primary planets with the Earth. The Sun, the Moon, Mercury, Venus, Mars, Jupiter, and Saturn were all visibly grouped close together, and their orbits were aligned with the Earth. This event signaled a change of era, similar to how the hands of a clock move into a new day. The Earth had completed an era of approximately 2,140 years under the influence of Pisces, and then entered an era influenced by Aquarius.

When the age of Aquarius arrived, humanity entered into a very new situation. With the new celestial influence we saw the arrival of a huge shift in society: mass rebellion against the old ways, sexual experimentation, giant social earthquakes shaking up all the old traditions. We also saw the arrival in the West of a strong spiritual longing, and deep thirst for true, authentic spiritual experience. These two elements: 1) rebellion to tradition and 2) thirst for spiritual knowledge are a direct effect of the influence of Aquarius, the most revolutionary sign of the zodiac. Aquarius is the Water Carrier, whose occult significance is knowledge, the bringer of knowledge. With the new age came a sudden revealing of all the hidden knowledge. The doors to the mysteries were thrown open so that humanity can save itself from itself. Of course, the Black Lodge, ever-eager to mislead humanity, has produced so much false spirituality and so many false schools that it is very difficult to find the real and genuine path.

"The majority of the tenebrous brothers and sisters of Aquarius are wicked people who are going around teaching black magic." —Samael Aun Weor, *The Major Mysteries*

"The age of sex, the new Aquarian Age, is at hand. The sexual glands are controlled by the planet Uranus which is the ruling planet of the constellation of Aquarius. Thus, sexual alchemy is in fact the science of the new Aquarian Age. Sexual Magic will be officially accepted in the universities of the new Aquarian Age. Those who presume to be messengers of the new Aquarian Age, but nevertheless hate the Arcanum A.Z.F., provide more than enough evidence that they are truly impostors, this is because the new Aquarian Age is governed by the regent of sex. This regent is the planet Uranus. Sexual energy is the finest energy of the infinite cosmos. Sexual energy can convert us into angels or demons. The image of truth is found deposited in sexual energy. The cosmic design of Adam Christ is found deposited in sexual energy." —Samael Aun Weor, *The Perfect Matrimony* To learn more about the Aquarian era, read *Christ and the Virgin* by Samael Aun Weor.

Arcanum: (Latin. plural: arcana). A secret or mystery known only to the specially educated. The root of the term "ark" as in the Ark of Noah and the Ark of the Covenent.

Arcanum A.Z.F.: The practice of sexual transmutation as couple (male-female), a technique known in Tantra and Alchemy. Arcanum refers to a hidden truth or law. A.Z.F. stands for A (agua, water), Z (azufre, sulfur), F (fuego, fire), and is thus: water + fire = consciousness.. Also, A (azoth = chemical element that refers to fire). A & Z are the first and last letters of the alphabet thus referring to the Alpha & Omega (beginning & end).

Astral: This term is dervied from "pertaining to or proceeding from the stars," but in the esoteric knowledge it refers to the emotional aspect of the fifth dimension, which in Hebrew is called Hod.

Astral Body: What is commonly called the astral body is not the true astral body, it is rather the lunar protoplasmatic body, also known as the kama rupa (Sanskrit, "body of desires") or "dream body" (Tibetan rmi-lam-gyi lus). The true astral body is solar (being superior to lunar nature) and must be created, as the Master Jesus indicated in the Gospel of John 3:5-6, "Except a man be born of water and of the Spirit, he cannot enter into the kingdom of God. That which is born of the flesh is flesh; and that which is born of the Spirit is spirit." The solar astral body is created as a result of the Third Initiation of Major Mysteries (Serpents of Fire), and is perfected in the Third Serpent of Light. In Tibetan Buddhism, the solar astral body is known as the illusory body (sgyu-lus). This body is related to the emotional center and to the sephirah Hod.

"Really, only those who have worked with the Maithuna (White Tantra) for many years can possess the astral body." —Samael Aun Weor, *The Elimination of Satan's Tail*

Atman: (Sanskrit, literally "self") An ancient and important word that is grossly misinterpreted in much of Hinduism and Buddhism. Many have misunderstood this word as referring to a permanently existing self or soul. Yet the true meaning is otherwise.

"Brahman, Self, Purusha, Chaitanya, Consciousness, God, Atman, Immortality, Freedom, Perfection, Bliss, Bhuma or the unconditioned are synonymous terms." —Swami Sivananva

Thus, Atman as "self" refers to a state of being "unconditioned," which is related to the Absolute, the Ain Soph, or the Shunyata (Emptiness). Thus, Atman refers to the Innermost, the Spirit, the Son of God, who longs to return to that which is beyond words.

"Atman, in Himself, is the ineffable Being, the one who is beyond time and eternity, without end of days. He does not die, neither reincarnates (the ego is what returns), but Atman is absolutely perfect." —Samael Aun Weor In general use, the term Atman can also refer to the spirit or sephirah Chesed.

"The Being Himself is Atman, the Ineffable. If we commit the error of giving the Being the qualifications of superior "I," alter ego, subliminal "I," or divine ego, etc., we commit blasphemy, because That which is Divine, the Reality, can never fall into the heresy of separability. Superior and inferior are two sections of the same thing. Superior "I" or inferior "I" are two sections of the same pluralized ego (Satan). The Being is the Being, and the reason for the Being to be is to be the same Being. The Being transcends the personality, the "I," and individuality." —Samael Aun Weor

"Bliss is the essential nature of man. The central fact of man's being is his inherent divinity. Man's essential nature is divine, the awareness of which he has lost because of his animal propensities and the veil of ignorance. Man, in his ignorance, identifies himself with the body, mind, Prana and the senses. Transcending these, he becomes one with Brahman or the Absolute who is pure bliss. Brahman or the Absolute is the fullest reality, the completest consciousness. That beyond which there is nothing, that which is the innermost Self of all is Atman or Brahman. The Atman is the common consciousness in all beings. A thief, a prostitute, a scavenger, a king, a rogue, a saint, a dog, a cat, a rat-all have the same common Atman. There is apparent, fictitious difference in bodies and minds only. There are differences in colours and opinions. But, the Atman is the same in all. If you are very rich, you can have a steamer, a train, an airship of your own for your own selfish interests. But, you cannot have an Atman of your own. The Atman is common to all. It is not an individual's sole registered property. The Atman is the one amidst the many. It is constant amidst the forms which come and go. It is the pure, absolute, essential consciousness of all the conscious beings. The source of all life, the source of all knowledge is the Atman, thy innermost Self. This Atman or Supreme Soul is transcendent, inexpressible, uninferable, unthinkable, indescribable, the ever-peaceful, all-blissful. There is no difference between the Atman and bliss. The Atman is bliss itself. God, perfection, peace, immortality, bliss are one. The goal of life is to attain perfection, immortality or God. The nearer one approaches the Truth, the happier one becomes. For, the essential nature of Truth is positive, absolute bliss. There is no bliss in the finite. Bliss is only in the Infinite. Eternal bliss can be had only from the eternal Self. To know the Self is to enjoy eternal bliss and everlasting peace. Self-realisation bestows eternal existence, absolute knowledge, and perennial bliss. None can be saved without Self-realisation. The quest for the Absolute should be undertaken even sacrificing the dearest object, even life, even courting all pain. Study philosophical books as much as you like, deliver lectures and lectures throughout your global tour, remain in a Himalayan cave for one hundred years, practise Pranayama for fifty years, you cannot attain emancipation without the realisation of the oneness of the Self." —Swami Sivananda

Bodhisattva: (Sanskrit) Literally, the Sanskrit term bodhi means "enlightened, wisdom, perfect knowledge," while sattva means "essence, goodness." Therefore, the term bodhisattva literally means "essence of wisdom."

A bodhisattva is a human soul (consciousness) who is on the direct path. A bodhisattva is the messenger or servant of their inner Being / Buddha. The inner Being or Buddha resides in the superior worlds, and sends the bodhisattva into the lower worlds to work for others.

"The bodhisattva is the human soul of a master. The master is the internal God [Atman, the Innermost Buddha]." —Samael Aun Weor, *The Aquarian Message*

One becomes a bodhisattva upon:

• creating the solar bodies (astral, mental, causal) through sexual transmutation

• choosing to enter the direct path to the absolute rather than the slower spiral path

• having developed sufficient Bodhichitta (love for others in combination with comprehension of the absolute)

The word bodhisattva is a title or honorific that describes a level of consciousness earned through internal initiation, not physical. A bodhisattva is a person who through dedication to compassionate service to humanity has some degree of Bodhichitta — a psychological quality uniting deep compassion with profound insight into the nature of reality, the Absolute — and has also created the solar bodies, which correspond to the first five serpents of kundalini (candali).

In Tibetan Buddhism the term bodhisattva is sometimes publicly used in a more "generous" way to include those who aspire to become bodhisattvas.

The Tibetan translation of bodhisattva is jangchub sempa. Jangchub (Sanskrit bodhi) means "enlightenment," and sempa (Sanskrit sattva) means "hero" or a being, therefore meaning "enlightened hero." The word jangchub is from jang, "the overcoming and elimination of all obstructive forces," and chub, "realization of full knowledge." Sempa is a reference to great compassion.

"...bodhisattvas are beings who, out of intense compassion, never shift their attention away from sentient beings; they are perpetually concerned for the welfare of all beings, and they dedicate themselves entirely to securing that welfare. Thus the very name bodhisattva indicates a being who, through wisdom, heroically focuses on the attainment of enlightenment out of compassionate concern for all beings. The word itself conveys the key qualities of such an infinitely altruistic being." —The 14th Dalai Lama

"We, the bodhisattvas of compassion who love humanity immensely, state: as long as there is a single tear in any human eye, as long as there is even one suffering heart, we refuse to accept the happiness of Nirvana... We must seek the means to become more and more useful to this wretched, suffering humanity." —Samael Aun Weor, *The Major Mysteries*

Strictly speaking, the term bodhisattva addresses not a physical person but the human soul of someone walking the Direct Path. The bodhisttva is the human soul (Tipereth, the causal body), which is the servant or messenger of the inner Being (Chesed). The human soul earns the title bodhisattva by —because of love for humanity — choosing to advance spiritually by entering the terrifying Direct Path instead of the easier Spiral Path, a choice that is made only after finishing the Fifth Initiation of Fire (Tiphereth, causal body). By means of this sacrifice, this individual incarnates the Christ (Chenresig, Kuan Yin, Avalokitesvara), thereby embodying the supreme source of wisdom and compassion. That human soul is then a mixture of the divine and human, and by carrying that light within becomes a messenger or active exponent of the light. The Direct Path demands rapid and complete liberation from the ego, a route that only very few take, due to the fact that one must pay the entirety of one's karma imminently. Those who have taken this road have been the most remarkable figures in human history: Jesus, Buddha, Mohamed, Krishna, Moses, Padmasambhava, Milarepa, Joan of Arc, Fu-Xi, and many others whose names are not remembered or known.

Even among bodhisattvas there are many levels of Being: to be a bodhisattva does not mean that one is enlightened. In fact, there are many fallen bodhisattvas: human souls who resumed poor behavior and are thus cut off from their inner Being.

"Let no one seek his own good, but the good of his neighbor." —1 Corinthians 10.24

"The truly humble Bodhisattva never praises himself. The humble Bodhisattva says, 'I am just a miserable slug from the mud of the earth, I am a nobody. My person has no value. The work is what is worthy.' The Bodhisattva is the human soul of a Master. The Master is the internal God." — Samael Aun Weor, *The Aquarian Message*

"Let it be understood that a Bodhisattva is a seed, a germ, with the possibility of transcendental, divine development by means of pressure coming from the Height." —Samael Aun Weor, *The Gnostic Bible: The Pistis Sophia Unveiled*

Interestingly, the Christ in Hebrew is called Chokmah, which means "wisdom," and in Sanskrit the same is Vishnu, the root of the word "wisdom." It is Vishnu who sent his Avatars into the world in order to aid humanity. These avatars were Krishna, Buddha, Rama, and the Avatar of this age: the Avatar Kalki.

Bons: (or Bhons) The oldest religion in Tibet. It was largely overshadowed (some say persecuted) by the arrival of Buddhism. Samael Aun Weor had accepted the statements of earlier investigators which described the Bon religion as essentially Black; but upon further investigation he discovered that they are not necessarily Black, just extreme in some practices.

Buddha: (Sanskrit) n. "awakened one, enlightened, sage, knowledge, wise one." adj. "awake, conscious, wise, intelligent, expanded."

Commonly used to refer simply to the Buddha Shakyamuni (the "founder" of Buddhism), the term Buddha is actually a title. There are a vast number of Buddhas, each at different levels of attainment. At the ultimate level, a Buddha is a being who has become totally free of suffering. The Inner Being (Hebrew: Chesed; Sanskrit: Atman) first becomes a Buddha when the Human Soul completes the work of the Fourth Initiation of Fire (related to Netzach, the mental body).

One of the Three Jewels (Tri-ratna), which are Buddha (the awakened one, our own inner Being), Dharma (the teaching he gives to perfect us), Sangha (the community of awakened masters who can help us awaken).

The historical Buddha Shakyamuni is a very great master who continues to aid humanity. Nevertheless, he is not the only Buddha.

"Much has been said of the Buddhas. There is no doubt that there are Contemplation Buddhas and Manifestation Buddhas. Manifestation Buddhas are creatures who dominated the mind, who destroyed the ego, who did not let negative emotions enter their hearts, who did not create mental effigies in their own mind nor in the minds of others. Let us remember Tsong Khapa who reincarnated in Tibet; he was the Buddha Gautama previously. The Buddha of Buddha Amitabha is another thing, his true divine prototype. Amitabha is the Contemplation Buddha, and Gautama, we could say, is the Manifestation Buddha, the worldly Buddha or Bodhisattva. We cannot deny that Amitabha expressed himself brilliantly through Gautama. We cannot deny that later Amitabha sent Gautama (the Bodhisattva or worldly Buddha) directly to a new reincarnation. Then he expressed himself as Tsong Khapa. These are Contemplation Buddhas, they are masters of their mind, creatures who liberated themselves from the mind. The Lords worship the Great Buddha that we also know as the Logos and they pray to him." —Samael Aun Weor from the lecture entitled Mental Representations

"The Buddha appears in the world so that sentient beings may obtain the gnosis that he himself obtained. Thus, the Buddha's demonstrations of the path are strictly means to lead sentient beings to buddhahood." —The Fourteenth Dalai Lama

Buddhi: (Sanskrit, literally "intelligence") An aspect of mind, psyche.

"Buddhi is pure [superior] reason. The seat of Buddhi is just below the crown of the head in the Pineal Gland of the brain. Buddhi is manifested only in those persons who have developed right intuitive discrimination or Viveka. The ordinary reason of the worldly people is termed practical reason, which is dense and has limitations... Sankhya Buddhi or Buddhi in the light of Sankhya philosophy is will and intellect combined. Mind is microcosm. Mind is Maya. Mind occupies an intermediate state between Prakriti and Purusha, matter and Spirit." —Swami Sivananda, *Yoga in Daily Life*

"When the diverse, confining sheaths of the Atma have been dissolved by Sadhana, when the different Vrittis of the mind have been controlled by mental drill or gymnastic, when the conscious mind is not active, you enter the realm of spirit life, the super-conscious mind where Buddhi and pure reason and intuition, the faculty of direct cognition of Truth, manifest. You pass into the kingdom of peace where there is none to speak, you will hear the voice of God which is very clear and pure and has an upward tendency. Listen to the voice with attention and interest. It will guide you. It is the voice of God." —Swami Sivananda, *Essence of Yoga*

In Kabbalah: The feminine Spiritual Soul, related to the sephirah Geburah. Symbolized throughout world literature, notably as Helen of Troy, Beatrice in *The Divine Comedy,* and Beth-sheba (Hebrew, literally "daughter of seven") in the Old Testament. The Divine or Spiritual Soul is the feminine soul of the Innermost (Atman), or his "daughter."

All the strength, all the power of the gods and goddesses resides in Buddhi / Geburah, Cosmic Consciousness, as within a glass of alabaster where the flame of the Inner Being (Gedulah, Atman the Ineffable) is always burning.

Centers, Seven: The human being has seven centers of psychological activity. The first five are the Intellectual, Emotional, Motor, Instinctive, and Sexual Centers. However, through inner development one learns how to utilize the Superior Emotional and Superior Intellectual Centers. Most people do not use these two at all.

Chakra: (Sanskrit) Literally, "wheel." The chakras are subtle centers of energetic transformation. There are hundreds of chakras in our hidden physiology, but seven primary ones related to the awakening of consciousness.

"The chakras are points of connection through which the divine energy circulates from one to another vehicle of the human being." —Samael Aun Weor, *Aztec Christic Magic*

Chastity: Although modern usage has rendered the term chastity virtually meaningless to most people, its original meaning and usage clearly indicate "moral purity" upon the basis of "sexual purity." Contemporary usage implies "repression" or "abstinence," which have nothing to do with real chastity. True chastity is a rejection of impure sexuality. True chastity is pure sexuality, or the activity of sex in harmony with our true nature, as explained in the secret doctrine. Properly used, the word chastity refers to sexual fidelity or honor.

"The generative energy, which, when we are loose, dissipates and makes us unclean, when we are continent invigorates and inspires us. Chastity is the flowering of man; and what are called Genius, Heroism, Holiness, and the like, are but various fruits which succeed it." —Henry David Thoreau, *Walden*

Christ: Derived from the Greek Christos, "the Anointed One," and Krestos, whose esoteric meaning is "fire." The word Christ is a title, not a personal name.

"I [John] indeed baptize you with water unto repentance: but he [Christ] that cometh after me is mightier than I, whose shoes I am not worthy to bear: he [Christ] shall baptize you with the Holy Ghost, and [with] fire: Whose fan [is] in his hand, and he will throughly purge his floor, and gather his wheat into the garner; but he will burn up the chaff with unquenchable fire." —Matthew3:12, Luke 3:16

"I [Christ] am come to send fire on the earth..."—Luke 12:49

10) Jesus [Christ] said, "I [Christ] have cast fire upon the world, and see, I am guarding it until it blazes." —Gospel of Thomas

82) Jesus [Christ] said, "He who is near Me [Christ] is near the fire, and he who is far from Me is far from the Kingdom." —Gospel of Thomas

"If someone is near me [Christ], he will burn. I [Christ] am the fire that blazes. Whoever is near me is near fire; whoever is far from me is far from life." —Gospel of the Savior

"Now therefore if any one hath received the mysteries of Baptism, those mysteries become a great fire, exceeding strong, and wise, so as to burn up all the sins: and the Fire [Christ] entereth into the soul secretly, so that it may consume within it all the sins which the counterfeit of the spirit hath printed there." —Pistis Sophia

"Indeed, Christ is a Sephirothic Crown (Kether, Chokmah and Binah) of incommensurable wisdom, whose purest atoms shine within Chokmah, the world of the Ophanim. Christ is not the Monad, Christ is not the Theosophical Septenary; Christ is not the Jivan-Atman. Christ is the Central Sun. Christ is the ray that unites us to the Absolute." —Samael Aun Weor, *Tarot and Kabbalah*

"The Gnostic Church adores the Saviour of the World, Jesus. The Gnostic Church knows that Jesus incarnated Christ, and that is why they adore him. Christ is not a human nor a divine individual. Christ is a title given to all fully self-realised Masters. Christ is the Army of the Voice. Christ is the Verb. The Verb is far beyond the body, the soul and the Spirit. Everyone who is able to incarnate the Verb receives in fact the title of Christ. Christ is the Verb itself. It is necessary for everyone of us to incarnate the Verb (Word). When the Verb becomes flesh in us we speak with the verb of light. In actuality, several Masters have incarnated the Christ. In secret India, the Christ Yogi Babaji has lived for millions of years; Babaji is immortal. The Great Master of Wisdom Kout Humi also incarnated the Christ. Sanat Kumara, the founder of the Great College of Initiates of the White Lodge, is another living Christ. In the past, many incarnated the Christ. In the present, some have incarnated the Christ. In the future many will incarnate the Christ. John the Baptist also incarnated the Christ. John the Baptist is a living Christ. The difference between Jesus and the other Masters that also incarnated the Christ has to do with Hierarchy. Jesus is the highest Solar Initiate of the Cosmos..." —Samael Aun Weor, *The Perfect Matrimony*

Consciousness: "Wherever there is life, there exists the consciousness. Consciousness is inherent to life as humidity is inherent to water." —Samael Aun Weor, *Fundamental Notions of Endocrinology and Criminology*

From various dictionaries: 1. The state of being conscious; knowledge of one's own existence, condition, sensations, mental operations, acts, etc. 2. Immediate knowledge or perception of the presence of any object, state, or sensation. 3. An alert cognitive state in which you are aware of yourself and your situation. In Universal Gnosticism, the range of potential consciousness is allegorized in the Ladder of Jacob, upon which the angels ascend and descend. Thus there are higher and lower levels of consciousness, from the level of demons at the bottom, to highly realized angels in the heights.

"It is vital to understand and develop the conviction that consciousness has the potential to increase to an infinite degree." —The 14th Dalai Lama

"Light and consciousness are two phenomena of the same thing; to a lesser degree of consciousness, corresponds a lesser degree of light; to a greater degree of consciousness, a greater degree of light." —Samael Aun Weor, *The Esoteric Treatise of Hermetic Astrology*

Divine Mother: The Divine Mother is the eternal, feminine principle, which is formless, and further unfolds into many levels, aspects, and manifestations.

"Devi or Sakti is the Mother of Nature. She is Nature Itself. The whole world is Her body. Mountains are Her bones. Rivers are Her veins. Ocean is Her bladder. Sun, moon are Her eyes. Wind is Her breath. Agni is Her mouth. She runs this world show. Sakti is symbolically female; but It is, in reality, neither male nor female. It is only a Force which manifests Itself in various forms. The five elements and their combinations are the external manifestations of the Mother. Intelligence, discrimination, psychic power, and will are Her internal manifestations." —Swami Sivananda

"Among the Aztecs, she was known as Tonantzin, among the Greeks as chaste Diana. In Egypt she was Isis, the Divine Mother, whose veil no mortal has lifted. There is no doubt at all that esoteric Christianity has never forsaken the worship of the Divine Mother Kundalini. Obviously she is Marah, or better said, RAM-IO, MARY. What orthodox religions did not specify, at least with regard to the exoteric or public circle, is the aspect of Isis in her individual human form. Clearly, it was taught only in secret to the Initiates that this Divine Mother exists individually within each human being. It cannot be emphasized enough that Mother-God, Rhea, Cybele, Adonia, or whatever we wish to call her, is a variant of our own individual Being in the here and now. Stated explicitly, each of us has our own particular, individual Divine Mother." —Samael Aun Weor, *The Great Rebellion*

"Devi Kundalini, the Consecrated Queen of Shiva, our personal Divine Cosmic Individual Mother, assumes five transcendental mystic aspects in every creature, which we must enumerate:

1. The unmanifested Prakriti

2. The chaste Diana, Isis, Tonantzin, Maria or better said Ram-Io

3. The terrible Hecate, Persephone, Coatlicue, queen of the infemos and death; terror of love and law

4. The special individual Mother Nature, creator and architect of our physical organism

5. The Elemental Enchantress to whom we owe every vital impulse, every instinct." —Samael Aun Weor, *The Secret of the Golden Flower*

Drukpa: (Also known variously as Druk-pa, Dugpa, Brugpa, Dag dugpa or Dad dugpa) The term Drukpa comes from from Dzongkha and Tibetan 'brug yul, which means "country of Bhutan," and is composed of Druk, "dragon," and pa, "person." In Asia, the word refers to the people of Bhutan, a country between India and Tibet.

Drukpa can also refer to a large sect of Buddhism which broke from the Kagyug-pa "the Ones of the Oral Tradition." They considered themselves as the heirs of the indian Gurus: their teaching, which goes back to Vajradhara, was conveyed through Dakini, from Naropa to Marpa and then to the ascetic and mystic poet Milarepa. Later on, Milarepa's disciples founded new monasteries, and new threads appeared, among which are the Karmapa and the Drukpa. All those schools form the Kagyug-pa order, in spite of episodic internal quarrels and extreme differences in practice. The Drukpa sect is recognized by their ceremonial large red hats, but it should be known that they are not the only "Red Hat" group (the Nyingmas, founded by Padmasambhava, also use red hats). The Drukpas have established a particular worship of the Dorje (Vajra, or thunderbolt, a symbol of the phallus).

Samael Aun Weor wrote repeatedly in many books that the "Drukpas" practice and teach Black Tantra, by means of the expelling of the sexual energy. If we analyze the word, it is clear that he is referring to "Black Dragons," or people who practice Black Tantra. He was not referring to all the people of Bhutan, or all members of the Buddhist Drukpa sect. Such a broad condemnation would be as ridiculous as the one made by all those who condemn all Jews for the crucifixion of Jesus.

"In 1387, with just reason, the Tibetan reformer Tsong Khapa cast every book of Necromancy that he found into flames. As a result, some discontent Lamas formed an alliance with the aboriginal Bhons, and today they form a powerful sect of black magic in the regions of Sikkim, Bhutan, and Nepal, submitting themselves to the most abominable black rites." —Samael Aun Weor, *The Revolution of Beelzebub*

Eden: (Hebrew) Eden means "bliss, pleasure, delight." In the book of Genesis written by Moses [Moshe], Eden is a symbol with many levels of meaning.

Of primary importance, in the book of Genesis / Bereshit, the primeval state of humanity is depicted in the Garden of Eden. This story symbolizes that when the man and the woman are performing the sexual act, they are in that moment in the Garden of Eden, enjoying that bliss, delight, or voluptuousness, and it is in that state when the serpent (Lucifer) appears in order to tempt them.

"Eden is the Ethereal World. Eden is sex itself. The Ethereal World is the abode of the sexual forces. The Ethereal World is Eden. We were driven out of Eden through the doors of sex, thus we can return to Eden only through the doors of sex. We cannot enter into Eden through false doors; we must enter into Eden through the doors out of which we were driven. The governor of Eden is the Lord Jehovah." —Samael Aun Weor, *The Major Mysteries*

In Kabbalah, there are two Edens.

"...there is a Garden of Eden above and another below." —Zohar

The Upper Eden is the sephirah Daath. The Lower Eden is the sephirah Yesod. Both are related to sex.

Ego: The multiplicity of contradictory psychological elements that we have inside are in their sum the "ego." Each one is also called "an ego" or an "I." Every ego is a psychological defect which produces suffering. The ego is three (related to our Three Brains or three centers of psychological processing), seven (capital sins), and legion (in their infinite variations).

"The ego is the root of ignorance and pain." —Samael Aun Weor, *The Esoteric Treatise of Hermetic Astrology*

"The Being and the ego are incompatible. The Being and the ego are like water and oil. They can never be mixed... The annihilation of the psychic aggregates (egos) can be made possible only by radically comprehending our errors through meditation and by the evident Self-reflection of the Being." —Samael Aun Weor, *The Gnostic Bible: The Pistis Sophia Unveiled*

Elohim: [אלהים] An Hebrew term with a wide variety of meanings. In Christian translations of scripture, it is one of many words translated to the generic word "God," but whose actual meaning depends upon the context. For example:

1. In Kabbalah, אלהים is a name of God the relates to many levels of the Tree of Life. In the world of Atziluth, the word is related to divnities of the sephiroth Binah (Jehovah Elohim, mentioned especially in Genesis), Geburah, and Hod. In the world of Briah, i t is related beings of Netzach and Hod.

2. El [אל] is "god," Eloah [אלה] is "goddess," therefore the plural Elohim refers to "gods and goddesses," and is commonly used to refer to Cosmocreators or Dhyan-Choans.

3. אלה Elah or Eloah is "goddess." Yam [ים] is "sea" or "ocean." Therefore אלהים Elohim can be אלה-ים "the sea goddess" [i.e. Aphrodite, Stella Maris, etc.]

There are many more meanings of "Elohim." In general, Elohim refers to high aspects of divinity.

"Each one of us has his own Interior Elohim. The Interior Elohim is the Being of our Being. The Interior Elohim is our Father-Mother. The Interior Elohim is the ray that emanates from Aelohim." —Samael Aun Weor, *The Gnostic Bible: The Pistis Sophia Unveiled*

Ens Seminis: (Latin) Literally, "the entity of semen." A term used by Paracelsus.

Essence: From the Chinese 體 ti, which literally means "substance, body" and is often translated as "essence," to indicate that which is always there throughout transformations. In gnosis, the term essence refers to our consciousness, which remains fundamentally the same, in spite of the many transformations it suffers, especially life, death, and being trapped in psychological defects. A common example given in Buddhism is a glass of water: even if filled with dirt and impurities, the water is still there; its original pure essence is latent and ultimately unchanged by the presence of filth. However, one would not want to drink it that way. Just so with the Essence (the consciousness): our Essence is trapped in impurities; to use it properly, it must be cleaned first.

"Singularly radiating is the wondrous Light;
Free is it from the bondage of matter and the senses.
Not binding by words and letters.
The Essence [體] is nakedly exposed in its pure eternity.
Never defiled is the Mind-nature;
It exists in perfection from the very beginning.
By merely casting away your delusions
The Suchness of Buddhahood is realized." —Shen Tsan

"Zen, however, is interested not in these different "fields" but only in penetrating to 體 the Essence, or the innermost core of the mind for it holds that once this core is grasped, all else will become relatively insignificant, and crystal clear... only by transcending [attachment] may one come to the innermost core of Mind—the perfectly free and thoroughly nonsubstantial illuminating-Voidness. This illuminating-Void character, empty yet dynamic, is the Essence (Chinese: 體 ti) of the mind... The Essence of mind is the Illuminating-Void Suchness." —G.C.Chang, The Practice of Zen (1959)

"Without question the Essence, or consciousness, which is the same thing, sleeps deeply... The Essence in itself is very beautiful. It came from above, from the stars. Lamentably, it is smothered deep within all these "I's" we carry inside. By contrast, the Essence can retrace its steps, return to the point of origin, go back to the stars, but first it must liberate itself from its evil companions, who have trapped it within the slums of perdition. Human beings have three percent free Essence, and the other ninety-seven percent is imprisoned within the "I's"." —Samael Aun Weor, *The Great Rebellion*

"A percentage of psychic Essence is liberated when a defect is disintegrated. Thus, the psychic Essence which is bottled up within our defects will be completely liberated when we disintegrate each and every one of our false values, in other words, our defects. Thus, the radical transformation of ourselves will occur when the totality of our Essence is liberated. Then, in that precise moment, the eternal values of the Being will express themselves through us. Unquestionably, this would be marvelous not only for us, but also for all of humanity." —Samael Aun Weor, *The Revolution of the Dialectic*

Fornication: Originally, the term fornication was derived from the Indo-European word *gwher*, whose meanings relate to heat and burning. Fornication means to make the heat (solar fire) of the seed (sexual power) leave the body through voluntary orgasm. Any voluntary orgasm is fornication, whether between a married man and woman, or an unmarried man and woman, or through masturbation, or in any other case; this is explained by Moses: "A man from whom there is a discharge of semen, shall immerse all his flesh in water, and he shall remain unclean until evening. And any garment or any leather [object] which has semen on it, shall be immersed in water, and shall remain unclean until evening. A woman with whom a man cohabits, whereby there was [a discharge of] semen, they shall immerse in water, and they shall remain unclean until evening." —Leviticus 15:16-18

To fornicate is to spill the sexual energy through the orgasm. Those who "deny themselves" restrain the sexual energy, and "walk in the midst of the fire" without being burned. Those who restrain the sexual energy, who renounce the orgasm, remember God in themselves, and do not defile themselves with animal passion, "for the temple of God is holy, which temple ye are."

"Whosoever is born of God doth not commit sin; for his seed remaineth in him: and he cannot sin, because he is born of God." —1 John 3:9

This is why neophytes always took a vow of sexual abstention, so that they could prepare themselves for marriage, in which they would have sexual relations but not release the sexual energy through the orgasm. This is why Paul advised:

"...they that have wives be as though they had none..." —I Corinthians 7:29

"A fornicator is an individual who has intensely accustomed his genital organs to copulate (with orgasm). Yet, if the same individual changes his custom of copulation to the custom of no copulation, then he transforms himself into a chaste person. We have as an example the astonishing case of Mary Magdalene, who was a famous prostitute. Mary Magdalene became the famous Saint Mary Magdalene, the repented prostitute. Mary Magdalene became the chaste disciple [and wife] of Christ." —Samael Aun Weor, *The Revolution of Beelzebub*

Gnosis: (Greek) Knowledge.

1. The word Gnosis refers to the knowledge we acquire through our own experience, as opposed to knowledge that we are told or believe in. Gnosis —by whatever name in history or culture —is conscious, experiential knowledge, not merely intellectual or conceptual knowledge, belief, or theory. This term is synonymous with the Hebrew "daath" and the Sanskrit "jna."

2. The tradition that embodies the core wisdom or knowledge of humanity.

"Gnosis is the flame from which all religions sprouted, because in its depth Gnosis is religion. The word "religion" comes from the Latin word "religare," which implies "to link the Soul to God"; so Gnosis is the very pure flame from where all religions sprout, because Gnosis is Knowledge, Gnosis is Wisdom." —Samael Aun Weor, *The Esoteric Path*

"The secret science of the Sufis and of the Whirling Dervishes is within Gnosis. The secret doctrine of Buddhism and of Taoism is within Gnosis. The sacred magic of the Nordics is within Gnosis. The wisdom of Hermes, Buddha, Confucius, Mohammed and Quetzalcoatl, etc., etc., is within Gnosis. Gnosis is the Doctrine of Christ." —Samael Aun Weor, *The Revolution of Beelzebub*

Harpocrates: Greek Ἁρποκράτης derived from Egyptian Har-pa-khered, "Horus the child." An Egyptian symbol appropriated and modified by the Greeks and Romans.

"The God Harpocrates governs the energy of the Astral Light. He was the living symbol of the Sun when it was rising at the beginning of spring. Child of Isis and Osiris, he was born after the death of his father, during the shortest day of the year and during the blossoming of the lotus flower. Traditions represented him as a delicate being who did not reach his maturity save when he transformed himself into Horus, in other words, when he transformed himself into the Sun with all of its splendors. His cult was introduced in Greece and Rome with some alterations; there, he appears as the god of silence, and they represented him with the index finger over his lips." —Samael Aun Weor, *Aztec Christic Magic*

"The disciple can utilize the energies of the god Harpocrates in order to learn to travel with the physical body in the Jinn state." —Samael Aun Weor, *The Major Mysteries*

Hermes Trismegistus: (Greek: Ἑρμῆς ὁ Τρισμέγιστος, "thrice-great Hermes"; Latin: Mercurius ter Maximus).

"Hermes Trismegistus (who was the author of the divine Pymander and some other books) lived some time before Moses. He received the name of Trismegistus, or Mercurius ter Maximus, i. e. thrice greatest Intelligencer, because he was the first intelligencer who communicated celestial and divine knowledge to mankind by writing.

"He was reported to have been king of Egypt; without doubt he was an Egyptian; nay, if you believe the Jews, even their Moses; and for the justification of this they urge, 1st, His being well skilled in chemistry; nay, the first who communicated that art to the sons of men; 2dly, They urge the philosophic work, viz. of rendering gold medicinal, or, finally, of the art of making aurum potabile; and, thirdly, of teaching the Cabala, which they say was shewn him by God on Mount Sinai: for all this is confessed to be originally written in Hebrew, which he would not have done had he not been an Hebrew, but rather in his vernacular tongue. But whether he was Moses or not, it is certain he was an Egyptian, even as Moses himself also was; and therefore for the age he lived in, we shall not fall short of the time if we conclude he flourished much about the time of Moses; and if he really was not the identical Moses, affirmed to be so by many, it is more than probable that he was king of Egypt; for being chief philosopher, he was, according to the Egyptian custom, initiated into the mysteries of priesthood, and from thence to the chief governor or king. He was called Ter Maximus, as having a perfect knowledge of all things contained in the world (as his Aureus, or Golden Tractate, and his Divine Pymander shews) which things he divided into three kingdoms, viz. animal, vegetable, and mineral; in the knowledge and comprehension of which three he excelled and transmitted to posterity, in enigmas and symbols, the profound secrets of nature; likewise a true description of the Philosopher's Quintessence, or Universal Elixir, which he made as the receptacle of all celestial and terrestrial virtues. The Great Secret of the philosophers he discoursed on, which was found engraven upon a Smaragdine table, in the valley of Ebron." —Quoted from *The Magus* by Francis Barrett (London, 1801)

Human Being: Although the words human or human being are used generally to refer to the people of this planet, the real meaning of the word human is far more demanding. Human is derived from Latin humanus "of man, human," also "humane, philanthropic, kind, gentle, polite; learned, refined, civilized." In classical philosophy, we are not yet human beings, but have the potential to become so. A famous illustration of this is the story of Diogenes wandering around crowded Athens during this day with an illuminated lantern, searching for "anthropos" (a real human being), yet failing to find even one.

In general, there are three types of human beings:

- The ordinary person (called human being out of respect), more accurately called the "intellectual animal."

- The true human being or man (from Sanskrit manas, mind; this does not indicate gender): someone who has created the soul (the solar bodies), symbolized as the chariot of Ezekiel or Krishna, the Wedding Garment of Jesus, the sacred weapons of the heroes of mythology, etc. Such persons are saints, masters, or buddhas of various levels.

- The superhuman: a true human being who has also incarnated the Cosmic Christ, thus going beyond mere sainthood or buddhahood, and into the highest reaches of liberation. These are the founders of religions, the destroyers of dogmas and traditions, the great rebels of spiritual light.

According to Gnostic anthropology, a true human being is an individual who has conquered the animal nature within and has thus created the soul , the Mercabah of the Kabbalists, the Sahu of the Egyptians, the To Soma Heliakon of the Greeks: this is "the Body of Gold of the Solar Man." A true human being is one with the Monad, the Inner Spirit. It can be said that the true human being or man is the inner Spirit (in Kabbalah, Chesed. In Hinduism, Atman).

"Every spirit is called man, which means that only the aspect of the light of the spirit that is enclothed within the body is called man. So the body of the spirit of the holy side is only a covering; in other words, the spirit is the actual essence of man and the body is only its covering. But on the other side, the opposite applies. This is why it is written: "you have clothed me with skin and flesh..." (Iyov 10:11). The flesh of man is only a garment covering the essence of man, which is the spirit. Everywhere it is written the flesh of man, it hints that the essence of man is inside. The flesh is only a vestment for man, a body for him, but the essence of man is the aspect of his spirit." —Zohar 1A:10:120

A true human being has reconquered the innocence and perfection of Eden, and has become what Adam was intended to be: a king or queen of nature, having power over nature. The intellectual animal, however, is controlled by nature, and thus is not a true human being. Examples of true human beings are all those great saints of all ages and cultures: Jesus, Moses, Mohammed, Krishna, and many others whose names were never known by the public.

Human Soul: "The Being, the Innermost of each one of us, has Twin Souls: the Spiritual and the Human Souls. In the ordinary intellectual animal, the Being, the Innermost, is not born, does not die, is not reincarnated, but it does send the Essence to each new personality. The Essence is a fraction of the Human Soul, the Buddhata... We can and must affirm, beyond all doubt, that only a fraction of the Human Soul lives within the lunar bodies. This fraction is the Essence, the psychic material that creates a soul, develops the Human Soul, and thereby the Spiritual Soul. The Monad, the Being, creates, fabricates, develops his two Souls, and these Souls must serve and obey him. We must distinguish between Monads and Souls. A Monad, in other words, a Spirit, is. A Soul is acquired." —Samael Aun Weor, *Practical Astrology*

"The Innermost [Atman] is the Sephirah Chesed, and Buddhi [Buddhi] is the Sephirah Geburah. The Innermost and Buddhi express themselves through the Human Soul. The Human Soul [Manas] is Tiphereth, will-power, beauty." —Samael Aun Weor, *Tarot and Kabbalah*

"Atman unfolds Himself into the Spiritual Soul. The Spiritual Soul unfolds into the Human Soul who is the Superior Manas; the Human Soul unfolds into the Essence, or Buddhata." —Samael Aun Weor, *Tarot and Kabbalah*

"Every elemental Essence can convert itself into a human soul, at its time and hour, and according to the law." —Samael Aun Weor, *The Gnostic Bible: The Pistis Sophia Unveiled*

From the Human Soul descends the percentage of free consciousness that enters into manifestation in a physical body. That Essence is only a fraction of the Human Soul. The Human Soul is incarnated in the Human Being when the initiate enters into the world of Tiphereth in the Fifth Initiation of Major Mysteries.

Initiation: The process whereby the Innermost (the Inner Father) receives recognition, empowerment and greater responsibilities in the Internal Worlds, and little by little approaches His goal: complete Self-realization, or in other words, the return into the Absolute. Initiation NEVER applies to the "I" or our terrestrial personality.

"Nine Initiations of Minor Mysteries and seven great Initiations of Major Mysteries exist. The INNERMOST is the one who receives all of these Initiations. The Testament of Wisdom says: "Before the dawning of the false aurora upon the earth, the ones who survived the hurricane and the tempest were praising the INNERMOST, and the heralds of the aurora appeared unto them." The psychological "I" does not receives Initiations. The human personality does not receive anything. Nonetheless, the "I" of some Initiates becomes filled with pride when saying 'I am a Master, I have such Initiations.' Thus, this is how the "I" believes itself to be an Initiate and keeps reincarnating in order to "perfect itself", but, the "I" never ever perfects itself. The "I" only reincarnates in order to satisfy desires. That is all." —Samael Aun Weor, *The Aquarian Message*

Initiations of Major Mysteries: The qualifications of the consciousness as it ascends into greater degrees of wisdom. The first five Initiations of Major Mysteries correspond to the creation of the real Human Being. Learn more by studying these books by Samael Aun Weor: *The Perfect Matrimony, The Three Mountains,* and *The Revolution of Beelzebub.*

"High initiation is the fusion of two principles: Atman-Buddhi, through the five principal Initiations of Major Mysteries. With the first we achieve the fusion of Atman-Buddhi, and with the fifth, we add the Manas to this fusion, and so the septenary is reduced to a trinity: "Atman-Buddhi Manas." There are a total of Nine Initiations of Major Mysteries." —Samael Aun Weor, *The Zodiacal Course*

"We fulfill our human evolution with the five Initiations of Major Mysteries. The remaining three Initiations and the degree of "Lord of the World" are of a "Super-Human" nature." —Samael Aun Weor, *Esoteric Medicine and Practical Magic*

Initiations of Minor Mysteries: The probationary steps required of all who wish to enter into the path of Self-realization. These nine tests are given to all disciples who begin to perform the Gnostic work in themselves. Only those who complete these tests can receive the right to enter into the Major Mysteries. For more information, read *The Perfect Matrimony.*

"Remember that each one of the nine Initiations of Lesser Mysteries has a musical note and an instrument which produces it." —Samael Aun Weor, *The Revolution of Beelzebub*

"To want to rapidly become fused with the Innermost without having passed through the nine initiations of Lesser Mysteries is akin to wanting to receive a doctor's degree in medicine without having studied all the required years at university, or like wanting to be a general without having passed through all the military ranks." —Samael Aun Weor, *The Zodiacal Course*

"Throughout the Initiations of Lesser Mysteries, the disciple has to pass through the entire tragedy of Golgotha..." —Samael Aun Weor, *The Zodiacal Course*

Innermost: "Our real Being is of a universal nature. Our real Being is neither a kind of superior nor inferior "I." Our real Being is impersonal, universal, divine. He transcends every concept of "I," me, myself, ego, etc., etc." —Samael Aun Weor, *The Perfect Matrimony*

Also known as Atman, the Spirit, Chesed, our own individual interior divine Father.

"The Innermost is the ardent flame of Horeb. In accordance with Moses, the Innermost is the Ruach Elohim (the Spirit of God) who sowed the waters in the beginning of the world. He is the Sun King, our Divine Monad, the Alter-Ego of Cicerone." —Samael Aun Weor, *The Revolution of Beelzebub*

Intellectual Animal: The current state of humanity: animals with intellect. When our inner Being (Atman, Chesed, spirit) sends its spark of consciousness into Nature, that spark (the anima, Latin for soul) enters into manifestation as a simple mineral. Gradually, over millions of years, the anima gathers experience and evolves up the chain of life until it perfects itself in the level of the mineral kingdom. It then graduates into the plant kingdom, and subsequently into the animal kingdom. With each ascension the spark receives new capacities and higher grades of complexity. In the animal kingdom it learns procreation by ejaculation. When that animal intelligence enters into the human kingdom, it receives a new capacity: reasoning, the intellect; it is now an anima with intellect: an intellectual animal. That spark must then perfect itself in the human kingdom in order to become a complete and perfect human being, an entity that has conquered and transcended everything that belongs to the lower kingdoms. Unfortunately, very few intellectual animals perfect themselves; most remain enslaved by their animal nature, and thus are reabsorbed by Nature, a process belonging to the devolving side of life and called by all the great religions "Hell" or the Second Death.

"The present manlike being is not yet human; he is merely an intellectual animal. It is a very grave error to call the legion of the "I" the " soul ." In fact, what the manlike being has is the psychic material, the material for the soul within his Essence, but indeed, he does not have a Soul yet." — Samael Aun Weor, *The Revolution of the Dialectic*

"Whosoever possesses the physical, astral, mental, and causal bodies receives the animistic and spiritual principles, and becomes a true human being. Before having them, one is an intellectual animal falsely called a human being. Regarding the face and shape of the physical body of any intellectual animal, they look like the physical characteristics of a human being, however, if their psychological processes are observed and compared with the psychological processes of a human being, then we find that they are completely different, totally distinct." —Samael Aun Weor, *Kabbalah of the Mayan Mysteries*

"I died as a mineral and became a plant,
I died as plant and rose to animal,
I died as animal and I was Man.
Why should I fear? When was I less by dying?
Yet once more I shall die as Man, to soar
With angels blest; but even from angelhood
I must pass on: all except God doth perish.
When I have sacrificed my angel —soul,
I shall become what no mind e'er conceived.
Oh, let me not exist! for Non-existence
Proclaims in organ tones, To Him we shall return."
—Jalal al-Din Muhammad Rumi (1207 - 1273) founder of the Mevlevi order of Sufism

Internal Worlds: The many dimensions beyond the physical world. These dimensions are both subjective and objective. To know the objective internal worlds (the Astral Plane, or Nirvana, or the Klipoth) one must first know one's own personal, subjective internal worlds, because the two are intimately associated.

"Whosoever truly wants to know the internal worlds of the planet Earth or of the solar system or of the galaxy in which we live, must previously know his intimate world, his individual, internal life, his own internal worlds. Man, know thyself, and thou wilt know the Universe and its Gods. The more we explore this internal world called "myself," the more we will comprehend that we simultaneously live in two worlds, in two realities, in two confines: the external and the internal. In the same way that it is indispensable for one to learn how to walk in the external world so as not to fall down into a precipice, or not get lost in the streets of the city, or to select one's friends, or not associate with the perverse ones, or not eat poison, etc.; likewise, through the psychological work upon oneself we learn how to walk in the internal world, which is explorable only through Self-observation." —Samael Aun Weor, *Treatise of Revolutionary Psychology*

Through the work in Self-observation, we develop the capacity to awaken where previously we were asleep: including in the objective internal worlds.

Jinn State: The condition that results from moving the physical body into the fourth dimension. "A body while in the "Jinn" state can float in the air (Laghima) or be submerged within the waters (Prakamya), or pass through fire without being burned, or be reduced to the size of an atom (Anima), or be enlarged to the point of touching the sun or the moon with the hand (Mahima). A body submerged within the supra-sensible worlds is submitted to the laws of those worlds. Then, this body is plastic and elastic, so it can change form, decrease its weight (Laghima), or increase its weight (Garima) willingly... When Jesus was walking upon the waters of the Sea of Galilee, he had his body in the state of "Jinn." Peter was able to liberate himself from the chains and to leave the prison, thanks to the assistance of an Angel who helped him place his body in the state of "Jinn."" —Samael Aun Weor, *The Aquarian Message*

Kabbalah: (Hebrew) Alternatively spelled Cabala, Qabalah (etc., ad nauseam) from the Hebrew KBLH or QBL, "to receive." An ancient esoteric teaching hidden from the uninitiated, whose branches and many forms have reached throughout the world. The true Kabbalah is the science and language of the Superior Worlds and is thus Objective, complete and without flaw; it is said that "All Enlightened Beings Agree," and their natural agreement is a function of the Awakened Consciousness. The Kabbalah is the language of that Consciousness, thus disagreement regarding it's meaning and interpretation is always due to the Subjective elements in the psyche.

"The objective of studying the Kabbalah is to be skilled for work in the Internal Worlds... One that does not comprehend remains confused in the Internal Worlds. Kabbalah is the basis in order to understand the language of these worlds." —Samael Aun Weor, *Tarot and Kabbalah*

Kundabuffer: The negatively polarized sexual energy.

"The Lord sent against the people the fiery snakes, and they bit the people, and many people of Israel died. The people came to Moses and said, "We have sinned, for we have spoken against the Lord and against you. Pray to the Lord that He remove the snakes from us." So Moses prayed on behalf of the people." —Numbers 21:6

"It is necessary to know that the Kundabuffer organ is the negative development of the fire. This is the descending serpent, which precipitates itself from the coccyx downwards, towards the atomic infernos of the human being. The Kundabuffer organ is the horrifying tail of Satan, which is shown in the "body of desires" of the Intellectual Animal, who in the present times is falsely called man." —Samael Aun Weor, *The Elimination of Satan's Tail*

"The diabolic type whose seduction is here, there, and everywhere under the pretext of working in the Ninth Sphere, who abandons his wife because he thinks she will not be useful to him for the work in the fiery forge of Vulcan, instead of awakening Kundalini, will awaken the abominable Kundabuffer organ. A certain initiate, whose name will not be mentioned in this treatise, commits the error of attributing to the Kundalini all the sinister qualities of the Kundabuffer organ... When the fire is cast downwards from the chakra of the coccyx, the tail of Satan appears; the abominable Kundabuffer organ. The hypnotic power of the organ of Witches' Sabbath holds the human multitude asleep and depraved. Those who commit the crime of practicing Black Tantra (Sexual Magic with seminal ejaculation) clearly awaken and develop the organ of all fatalities. Those who betray their Guru or Master, even if practicing White Tantra (without seminal ejaculation), will obviously activate the organ of all evils. Such sinister power opens the seven doorways of the lower abdomen (the seven infernal chakras) and converts us into terribly perverse demons." —Samael Aun Weor, *The Mystery of the Golden Flower*

Kundalini: "Kundalini, the serpent power or mystic fire, is the primordial energy or Sakti that lies dormant or sleeping in the Muladhara Chakra, the centre of the body. It is called the serpentine or annular power on account of serpentine form. It is an electric fiery occult power, the great pristine force which underlies all organic and inorganic matter. Kundalini is the cosmic power in individual bodies. It is not a material force like electricity, magnetism, centripetal or centrifugal force. It is a spiritual potential Sakti or cosmic power. In reality it has no form. [...] O Divine Mother Kundalini, the Divine Cosmic Energy that is hidden in men! Thou art Kali, Durga, Adisakti, Rajarajeswari, Tripurasundari, Maha-Lakshmi, Maha-Sarasvati! Thou hast put on all these names and forms. Thou hast manifested as Prana, electricity, force, magnetism, cohesion, gravitation in this universe. This whole universe rests in Thy bosom. Crores of salutations unto thee. O Mother of this world! Lead me on to open the Sushumna Nadi and take Thee along the Chakras to Sahasrara Chakra and to merge myself in Thee and Thy consort, Lord Siva. Kundalini Yoga is that Yoga which treats of Kundalini Sakti, the six centres of spiritual energy (Shat Chakras), the arousing of the sleeping Kundalini Sakti and its union with Lord Siva in Sahasrara Chakra, at the crown of the head. This is an exact science. This is also known as Laya Yoga. The six centres are pierced (Chakra Bheda) by the passing of Kundalini Sakti to the top of the head. 'Kundala' means 'coiled'. Her form is like a coiled serpent. Hence the name Kundalini." — Swami Sivananda, *Kundalini Yoga*

Logos: (Greek) means Verb or Word. In Greek and Hebrew metaphysics, the unifying principle of the world. The Logos is the manifested deity of every nation and people; the outward expression or the effect of the cause which is ever concealed. (Speech is the "logos" of thought). The Logos has three aspects, known universally as the Trinity or Trimurti. The First Logos is the Father, Brahma. The Second Logos is the Son, Vishnu. The Third Logos is the Holy Spirit, Shiva. One who incarnates the Logos becomes a Logos.

"The Logos is not an individual. The Logos is an army of ineffable beings." —Samael Aun Weor, *Sexology, the Basis of Endocrinology and Criminology*

Lunar: From Latin lunaris "of the moon," from luna luna, the Moon. The Romans called the moon goddess Luna, which in Greek is Selene.

In esotericism, the term lunar is generally used in concert with its solar companion, and this duality can have many implications. In Western esotericism and the writings of Samael Aun Weor, the lunar aspect is seen as feminine, cold, and polarized as negative (not "bad," just the opposite polarity of solar, which is positive). In Asian mysticism, the symbolic genders are often reversed, with the lunar current seen as masculine and related to Chandra, the masculine moon god.

Some example uses of the term lunar:

1. In general "lunar" can indicate something that proceeds mechanically, automatically, — like the movements of the Moon, tides, seasons, etc. —

according to the fundamental natural laws. While this is perfectly normal, it is inferior to the solar attributes, which are not bound by mechanical movements, but instead have liberty, freedom of movement, etc.

2. In another context, for example within the body, there are lunar and solar currents. Within us, the lunar current is fallen into disgrace and must be restored, while the solar current remains intact.

3. There are solar and lunar religions: a lunar religion faces backwards, looking only at the past, and remains attached to traditions, habits, mechanical rules. A lunar mind is similar.

4. The lunar bodies are the vehicles we receive from nature automatically: the physical body, vital body, and astral-mental body. Since they were made by nature, they must be returned to nature, thus they are not immortal, eternal, thereby illustrating the need to create solar bodies, which transcend the mechanical, lunar laws of nature.

Magic: The word magic is derived from the ancient word "mag" that means priest. Real magic is the work of a priest. A real magician is a priest.

"Magic, according to Novalis, is the art of influencing the inner world consciously." —Samael Aun Weor, *The Mystery of the Golden Flower*

"When magic is explained as it really is, it seems to make no sense to fanatical people. They prefer to follow their world of illusions." —Samael Aun Weor, *The Revolution of Beelzebub*

Mahamanvantara: (Sanskrit महमन्वन्तर) "The Great Day." A manvatara is a period of activity, thus adding maha —"great" to the beginning means an even greater or longer period of activity, as opposed to a Mahapralaya, a cosmic night or period of rest. Manvataras and mahamanvantaras are relative, not fixed periods or times. Everything has periods of activity and periods of rest, and those times are relative: our own periods of activity and sleep vary widely; moreover, we also have "great" times of activity (such as when engaged in a project) and "great" times of repose (like retirement, long vacations, illnesses, etc). The same is true of atoms, cells, planets, solar systems, universes....

"Truthfully, the quantities of years assigned to a cosmic day are symbolic. The cosmic night arrives when the ingathering of the perfect souls is complete, which means, when the cosmic day is absolutely perfected." —Samael Aun Weor, *The Gnostic Bible: The Pistis Sophia Unveiled*

"I was absorbed within the Absolute at the end of that Lunar mahamanvantara, which endured 311,040,000,000,000 years, or, in other words, an age of Brahma." —Samael Aun Weor, *The Revolution of Beelzebub*

Manas: (Sanskrit मनस्) In general use, "mind." However, in Sanskrit the word manas can mean "imagination, intellect, inclination, will, excogitation, temper, understanding, intention, mind, spirit or spiritual principle, mood, perception, opinion, intelligence, breath or living soul which escapes from the body at death, desire, sense, reflection, thought, affection, conscience, invention, spirit." Manas is derived from the root मन् man, "to think." Manas is the root of the English term "man."

In Hinduism, the word manas is used with great flexibility and range, and thus can be applied in a variety of ways in the understanding of our psyche. In most cases it refers to the undisciplined mind of the common person, that is ruled by desires and ignorant of the true nature of the self (Atman). Manas is understood as the capacity for thought, which is one aspect of the antahkarana, the "inner organ."

The Vedas posit two forms of manas:

• buddhi manas

• kama manas

The Upanishads also present two forms of manas:

"Manas (mind) is said to be of two kinds, the pure and the impure. That which is associated with the thought of desire is the impure, while that which is without desire is the pure. To men, their mind alone is the cause of bondage or emancipation. That mind which is attracted by objects of sense tends to bondage, while that which is not so attracted tends to emancipation." —Amritabindu Upanishad

"Suddha Manas or Sattvic mind (pure mind) and Asuddha (impure) Manas or the instinctive mind or desire-mind as it is called are the two kinds of mind according to Upanishadic teaching. There is the lower mind filled with passion. There is the higher mind filled with Sattva (purity). There are two minds. You will have to make it into one —Sattvic mind only —if you want to meditate. It is through the higher or Sattvic mind that you will have to control the lower or instinctive mind of passions and emotions." —Swami Sivananda

In Buddhism, manas is used to refer to "mind" or "intelligence," in terms of mental function and activity.

Samael Aun Weor uses the term manas primarily in two ways:

• Superior Manas: the Human Soul, the causal body, the sephirah Tiphereth

• Inferior Manas: the intellect, the mental body (whether solar or lunar), the sephirah Netzach

Mantra: (Sanskrit, literally "mind protection") A sacred word or sound. The use of sacred words and sounds is universal throughout all religions and mystical traditions, because the root of all creation is in the Great Breath or the Word, the Logos. "In the beginning was the Word..."

Master: Like many terms related to spirituality, this one is grossly misunderstood. Samael Aun Weor wrote while describing the Germanic *Edda*, "In this Genesis of creation we discover Sexual Alchemy. The Fire fecundated the cold waters of chaos. The masculine principle Alfadur fecundated the feminine principle Niffleheim, dominated by Surtur (the Darkness), to bring forth life. That is how Ymir is born, the father of the giants, the

Internal God of every human being, the Master." Therefore, the Master is the Innermost, Atman, the Father.

"The only one who is truly great is the Spirit, the Innermost. We, the intellectual animals, are leaves that the wind tosses about... No student of occultism is a Master. True Masters are only those who have reached the Fifth Initiation of Major Mysteries. Before the Fifth Initiation nobody is a Master." —Samael Aun Weor, *The Perfect Matrimony*

Meditation: "When the esoterist submerges himself into meditation, what he seeks is information." —Samael Aun Weor

"It is urgent to know how to meditate in order to comprehend any psychic aggregate, or in other words, any psychological defect. It is indispensable to know how to work with all our heart and with all our soul, if we want the elimination to occur." —Samael Aun Weor, *The Pistis Sophia Unveiled*

"1. The Gnostic must first attain the ability to stop the course of his thoughts, the capacity to not think. Indeed, only the one who achieves that capacity will hear the Voice of the Silence.

"2. When the Gnostic disciple attains the capacity to not think, then he must learn to concentrate his thoughts on only one thing.

"3. The third step is correct meditation. This brings the first flashes of the new consciousness into the mind.

"4. The fourth step is contemplation, ecstasy or Samadhi. This is the state of Turiya (perfect clairvoyance). —Samael Aun Weor, *The Perfect Matrimony*

Medium: In the 1840s in upstate New York arose a belief that it is possible to communicate with the spirits of the dead. Sessions (séances) were held by "mediums" (intermediaries) who would convey information back and forth. The primary influences and methods of this system were derived from Mesmer and hypnotism, a technique that manipulates the sleeping consciousness, which is black magic. Mediumism is a technique of black magic that is more commonly known now as channelling. Channellers are either cunning hoaxes or outright states of possession by demons. No genuine spiritual master needs to communicate through the body of another person.

"We have frequently heard of so many unbalanced individuals who state that they "channel" entities from beyond! Usually, those "channelers" are mediums." —Samael Aun Weor, *The Divine Science*

"Any Master of Samadhi can clearly verify when in the state of ecstasy the following: that which is manifested through the mediums of Spiritism are not the souls or the spirits of the dead, but the devil-"I's" of the dead, which are the psychic aggregates that continue beyond the burial chamber. It has been said to us with much emphasis that during the postmortem (after death) states the mediums continue to convert themselves into beings who are possessed by a demon or demons. It is unquestionable that after a certain time the mediums conclude by divorcing themselves from their own divine Being. Then they enter into the submerged devolution of the infernal worlds." —Samael Aun Weor, *The Three Mountains*

"Remember that spiritualist mediums often serve as vehicles for black entities. These entities pose as saints and advise against the perfect marriage. Usually, they declare themselves Jesus Christ or Buddha, etc., to cheat the fools." —Samael Aun Weor, *The Perfect Matrimony*

Melchizedek: (Hebrew קדצי-כלמ. Alternatively, Malkhi-tzedek, Malki Tzedek, or Melchisedek, which means "king of justice / virtue") See Gen. 14:18-20, Ps. 110:4, and Epistle to the Hebrews, ch. 7.

"Malkhi-tzedek king of Salem brought forth bread and wine. He was a priest to God, the Most High. He blessed [Abram], and said, 'Blessed be Abram to God Most High, Possessor of heaven and earth. And blessed be God Most High, who delivered your enemies into your hand.' [Abram then] gave him a tenth of everything." —*Genesis / Bereshit 14:18-20*

"[Jesus] Who in the days of his flesh, when he had offered up prayers and supplications with strong crying and tears unto him that was able to save him from death, and was heard in that he feared; Though he were a Son, yet learned he obedience by the things which he suffered; And being made perfect, he became the author of eternal salvation unto all them that obey him; Called of God an high priest after the order of Melchisedec. Of whom we have many things to say, and hard to be uttered, seeing ye are dull of hearing." —*Hebrews 5*

"And Melchisedec, the Receiver of the Light; purifieth those powers and carrieth their light into the Treasury of the Light, while the servitors of all the rulers gather together all matter from them all; and the servitors of all the rulers of the Fate and the servitors of the sphere which is below the æons, take it and fashion it into souls of men and cattle and reptiles and wild-beasts and birds, and send them down into the world of mankind." —*The Pistis Sophia*

"Melchisedec is the planetary Genie of the Earth, of whom Jesus, the great Kabir, gave testimony. Melchisedec is the Great Receiver of the Cosmic Light. Melchisedec has a physical body. He is a Man, or better if we say, he is a Super-Man. The Kingdom of Agharti is found in the subterranean caverns of the Earth. The Earth is hollow and the network of caverns constitute Agharti. The Genie of the Earth lives in Agharti with a group of survivors from Lemuria and Atlantis. The Goros, powerful Lords of life and death, work with Melchisedec. The whole ancient wisdom of the centuries has been recorded on Stone, within the Kingdom of Agharti." — Samael Aun Weor, *The Gnostic Bible: The Pistis Sophia Unveiled*

"If Jesus was God incarnate, as the solemn councils of the church discovered, why is He referred to in the New Testament as "called of God an high priest after the order of Melchizedek"? The words "after the order" make Jesus one of a line or order of which there must have been others of equal or even superior dignity. If the "Melchizedeks" were the divine or priestly rulers of the nations of the earth before the inauguration of the system of temporal rulers, then the statements attributed to St. Paul would indicate that Jesus either was one of these "philosophic elect" or was attempting to reestablish their system of government. It will be remembered that Melchizedek also performed the same ceremony of the drinking of wine and the breaking of bread as did Jesus at the Last Supper." —Manly P. Hall, *The Secret Teachings of All Ages*

Monad: From Latin monas, "unity; a unit" and Greek monas "unit," from monos "alone." The Monad is the Being, the Innermost, our own inner Spirit. In Kabbalah, the Monad is represented by the sephiroth Chesed, Geburah, and Tiphereth. In Sanskrit, this corresponds to Atman-Buddhi-Manas.

"We must distinguish between Monads and Souls. A Monad, in other words, a Spirit, is; a Soul is acquired. Distinguish between the Monad of a world and the Soul of a world; between the Monad of a human and the Soul of a human; between the Monad of an ant and the Soul of an ant. The human organism, in final synthesis, is constituted by billions and trillions of infinitesimal Monads. There are several types and orders of primary elements of all existence, of every organism, in the manner of germs of all the phenomena of nature; we can call the latter Monads, employing the term of Leibnitz, in the absence of a more descriptive term to indicate the simplicity of the simplest existence. An atom, as a vehicle of action, corresponds to each of these genii or Monads. The Monads attract each other, combine, transform themselves, giving form to every organism, world, micro-organism, etc. Hierarchies exist among the Monads; the Inferior Monads must obey the Superior ones that is the Law. Inferior Monads belong to the Superior ones. All the trillions of Monads that animate the human organism have to obey the owner, the chief, the Principal Monad. The regulating Monad, the Primordial Monad permits the activity of all of its subordinates inside the human organism, until the time indicated by the Law of Karma." —Samael Aun Weor, *The Esoteric Treatise of Hermetic Astrology*

"(The number) one is the Monad, the Unity, Iod-Heve or Jehovah, the Father who is in secret. It is the Divine Triad that is not incarnated within a Master who has not killed the ego. He is Osiris, the same God, the Word." —Samael Aun Weor, *Tarot and Kabbalah*

"When spoken of, the Monad is referred to as Osiris. He is the one that has to Self-realize Himself... Our own particular Monad needs us and we need it. Once, while speaking with my Monad, my Monad told me, 'I am self-realizing Thee; what I am doing, I am doing for Thee.' Otherwise, why are we living? The Monad wants to Self-realize and that is why we are here. This is our objective." —Samael Aun Weor, *Tarot and Kabbalah*

"The Monads or Vital Genii are not exclusive to the physical organism; within the atoms of the Internal Bodies there are found imprisoned many orders and categories of living Monads. The existence of any physical or suprasensible, Angelic or Diabolical, Solar or Lunar body, has billions and trillions of Monads as their foundation." —Samael Aun Weor, *The Esoteric Treatise of Hermetic Astrology*

Nirvana: (Sanskrit निर्वाण, "extinction" or "cessation"; Tibetan: nyangde, literally "the state beyond sorrow") In general use, the word nirvana refers to the permanent cessation of suffering and its causes, and therefore refers to a state of consciousness rather than a place. Yet, the term can also apply to heavenly realms, whose vibration is related to the cessation of suffering. In other words, if your mind-stream has liberated itself from the causes of suffering, it will naturally vibrate at the level of Nirvana (heaven).

"When the Soul fuses with the Inner Master, then it becomes free from Nature and enters into the supreme happiness of absolute existence. This state of happiness is called Nirvana. Nirvana can be attained through millions of births and deaths, but it can also be attained by means of a shorter path; this is the path of "initiation." The Initiate can reach Nirvana in one single life if he so wants it." —Samael Aun Weor, *The Zodiacal Course*

"Nirvana is a region of Nature where the ineffable happiness of the fire reigns. The Nirvanic plane has seven sub-planes. A resplendent hall exists in each one of these seven sub-planes of Nirvanic matter where the Nirmanakayas study their mysteries. This is why they call their sub-planes "halls" and not merely "sub-planes" as the Theosophists do. The Nirvanis say: "We are in the first hall of Nirvana or in the second hall of Nirvana, or in the third, or in the fourth, or fifth, or sixth, or in the seventh hall of Nirvana." To describe the ineffable joy of Nirvana is impossible. There, the music of the spheres reigns and the soul is enchanted within a state of bliss, which is impossible to describe with words." —Samael Aun Weor, *The Revolution of Beelzebub*

Paramarthasatya: (Sanskrit) Para, "absolute, supreme." Parama, "that which knows, or the consciousness. " Artha, "that which is known." Satya, "existence, Truth." In synthesis, "The supreme knowledge of all that exists: TRUTH."

1) A being of very high development; an inhabitant of the Absolute.

2) The ultimate truth, as opposed to conventional truth (samvriti-satya) or relative truth of the manifested world.

Personality: (Latin personae: mask) There are two fundamental types of personality:

1. Solar: the personality of the inner Being. This type is only revealed through the liberation of the mind from samsara.

2. Lunar: the terrestrial, perishable personality. We create a new lunar personality in the first seven years of each new physical body, in accordance with three influences: genotype, phenotype and paratype. Genotype is the influence of the genes, or in other words, karma, our inheritance from past actions. Phenotype is the education we receive from our family, friends, teachers, etc. Paratype is related to the circumstances of life.

"The personality is time. The personality lives in its own time and does not reincarnate. After death, the personality also goes to the grave. For the personality there is no tomorrow. The personality lives in the cemetery, wanders about the cemetery or goes down into its grave. It is neither the astral body nor the ethereal double. It is not the soul. It is time. It is energetic and it disintegrates very slowly. The personality can never reincarnate. It does not ever reincarnate. There is no tomorrow for the human personality." —Samael Aun Weor, *The Perfect Matrimony*

"Our personality has to become more and more passive..." —Samael Aun Weor, from the lecture "Knowing How to Listen"

"The human personality is only a marionette controlled by invisible strings... Evidently, each one of these I's puts in our minds what we must think, in our mouths what we must say, and in our hearts what we must feel, etc. Under such conditions the human personality is no more than a robot governed by different people, each disputing its superiority and aspiring to supreme control of the major centers of the organic machine... First of all, it is necessary, urgent and imperative that the magnetic center, which is abnormally established in our false personality, be transferred to the Essence. In this way, the complete human can initiate his journey from the personality up to the stars, ascending in a progressive, didactic way, step by step up the Mountain of the Being. As long as the magnetic center continues to be established in our illusory personality we will live in the most abominable psychological dens of iniquity, although appearing to be splendid citizens in everyday life... These values which serve as a basis for the law of recurrence are always found within our human personality." — Samael Aun Weor, *The Great Rebellion*

"The personality must not be confused with the "I." In fact, the personality is formed during the first seven years of childhood. The "I" is something different. It is the error which is perpetuated from century to century; it fortifies itself each time, more and more through the mechanics of recurrence. The personality is energetic. It is born during infancy through habits, customs, ideas, etc., and it is fortified with the experiences of life. Therefore, both the personality as well as the "I" must be disintegrated. These psychological teachings are more revolutionary than those of Gurdjieff and Ouspensky. The "I" utilizes the personality as an instrument of action. Thus, personalism is a mixture of ego and personality. Personality worship was invented by the "I." In fact, personalism engenders egoism, hatred, violence, etc. All of this is rejected by A-himsa. Personality totally ruins esoteric organizations. Personality produces anarchy and confusion. Personalism can totally destroy any organization... The personality is multiple and has many hidden depths. The karma of previous existences is deposited into the personality. It is karma in the process of fulfillment or crystallization. The impressions which are not digested become new psychic aggregates, and what is more serious, they become new personalities. The personality is not homogenous but rather heterogeneous and plural. One must select impressions in the same manner that one chooses the things of life. If one forgets oneself at a given instant, in a new event, new "I's" are formed, and if they are very strong they become new personalities within the personality. Therein lies the cause of many traumas, complexes and psychological conflicts. An impression which one does not digest may form into a personality within the personality, and if one does not accept it, it becomes a source of frightening conflicts. Not all the personalities (which one carries within the personality) are accepted; the latter giving origin to many traumas, complexes, phobias, etc. Before all else, it is necessary to comprehend the multiplicity of the personality. The personality is multiple in itself. Therefore, there could be someone who may have disintegrated the psychic aggregates, but if he does not disintegrate the personality, he will not be able to attain authentic enlightenment and the joy of living." —Samael Aun Weor, *The Revolution of the Dialectic*

"The personality is energetic. The personality takes form during the first seven years of childhood and is strengthened with time and experiences... The mental body, the body of desires, the ethereal body, and the physical body integrate the personality... We must finish with the personality and with the "I" in order for the Being to be born within ourselves." —Samael Aun Weor, *Tarot and Kabbalah*

Philosophical Stone: An Alchemical symbol of the Intimate Christ dressed with bodies of Gold. When acquired, this stone gives powers over nature. It is lost when thrown in water (through fornication). When the stone is dissolved in (sexual) water, then the metallic Spirit is melted, and interior Magnes escapes. It is said when this happens, one dissolves the stone in water on Saturday (Saturn = death). The Philosophical Stone is passes through phases of development: black, red & white. It is also the Cubic stone of Yesod (Parsifal Unveiled), the stone that Jacob anointed with oil and "a Stone of stumbling, a rock of offense."

Nicolas Valois: "It is a Stone of great virtue, and is called a Stone and is not a stone."

Samadhi: (Sanskrit) Literally means "union" or "combination" and its Tibetan equivilent means "adhering to that which is profound and definitive," or ting nge dzin, meaning "To hold unwaveringly, so there is no movement." Related terms include satori, ecstasy, manteia, etc. Samadhi is a state of consciousness. In the west, the term is used to describe an ecstatic state of consciousness in which the Essence escapes the painful limitations of the mind (the "I") and therefore experiences what is real: the Being, the Great Reality. There are many levels of Samadhi. In the sutras and tantras the term Samadhi has a much broader application whose precise interpretation depends upon which school and teaching is using it. In Yoga, Samadhi is the pinnacle of the steps of yoga. In the state of Samadhi, one is free of the limitations of the terrestrial bonds and can commune directly with the spiritual archetypes.

"Ecstasy is not a nebulous state, but a transcendental state of wonderment, which is associated with perfect mental clarity." —Samael Aun Weor, *The Elimination of Satan's Tail*

Samael: (Hebrew סמאל) A great archangel who has been assisting humanity for ages. He has been known by many names throughout our history, but he is perhaps best known as Ares, Mars, the god of war. His war is always a spiritual one, the war against the corruption of the human mind. Knowing this helps the reader understand why the writings and teachings of Samael Aun Weor are so direct and so potent. Samael (Ares) is the great cosmic intelligence which is responsible for the spiritual development of this current humanity, which has long been known as the "Aryan" (from Ares) race. (Unfortunately, this term "Aryan race" has been corrupted by many ignorant people.) Therefore, he needed his terrestrial part to work here in the physical world on behalf of humanity. His son, the bodhisattva Samael Aun Weor, fell into disgrace for many centuries, and committed many mistakes. Due to this, the esotericists of past ages knew him as a great demon. Subsequently, the bodhisattva was brought to realize his mistakes, and he worked very hard to rectify them. Now, Samael, the inner Being, has his son standing upright once more, and he was able to deliver his teachings to humanity.

"I ended up transforming myself into a fallen angel. Many egos resurged within my mind and I became transformed into a true devil. Now, in this present existence, I comprehend the necessity of eliminating my egos, the necessity of performing the Great Work of the Father. Therefore, this is why today I am here speaking to you all, with my hand placed on my heart. Samael Aun Weor is my true name as a bodhisattva. Samael is the name of my Monad!" —Samael Aun Weor

Satan: (Hebrew, opposer, or adversary) Is the fallen Lucifer, who is born within the psyche of every human being by means of the sexual impulse that culminates in the orgasm or sexual spasm of the fornicators. Satan, the fallen Lucifer directs the lustful animal currents towards the atomic infernos of the human being, thus it becomes the profoundly evil adversary of our Innermost (God) and human values within our own psyche. This is why it is often identified with the leader of the fallen angels or fallen human values (parts) of our consciousness trapped within the animal mind (legions of egos, defects, vices of the mind) in other words, Satan is the Devil or "evil" adversary of God "Good" that every body carries within their own psychological interior.

Self-observation: An exercise of attention, in which one learns to become an indifferent observer of one's own psychological process. True Self-observation is an active work of directed attention, without the interference of thought.

"We need attention intentionally directed towards the interior of our own selves. This is not a passive attention. Indeed, dynamic attention proceeds from the side of the observer, while thoughts and emotions belong to the side which is observed." —Samael Aun Weor, *Treatise of Revolutionary Psychology*

Self-realization: The achievement of perfect knowledge. This phrase is better stated as, "The realization of the Innermost Self," or "The realization of the true nature of self." At the ultimate level, this is the experiential, conscious knowledge of the Absolute, which is synonymous with Emptiness, Shunyata, or Non-being.

Self-remembering: A state of active consciousness, controlled by will, that begins with awareness of being here and now. This state has many levels (see: Consciousness). True Self-remembering occurs without thought or mental processing: it is a state of conscious perception and includes the remembrance of the inner Being.

Semen: The sexual energy of any creature or entity. In Gnosis, "semen" is a term used for the sexual energy of both masculine and feminine bodies. English semen originally meant 'seed of male animals' in the 14th century, and it was not applied to human males until the 18th century. It came from Latin semen, "seed of plants," from serere `to sow.' The Latin goes back to the Indo-European root *se-, source of seed, disseminate, season, seminar, and seminal. The word seminary (used for religious schools) is derived from semen and originally meant 'seedbed.'

That the semen is the source of all virtue is known from the word "seminal," derived from the Latin "semen," and which is defined as "highly original and influencing the development of future events: a seminal artist; seminal ideas."

In the esoteric tradition of pure sexuality, the word semen refers to the sexual energy of the organism, whether male or female. This is because male and female both carry the "seed" within: in order to create, the two "seeds" must be combined.

Sephirah: (Hebrew) plural: Sephiroth. literally, "jewel." A symbol used in Kabbalah to represent levels of manifestation ranging from the very subtle to the very dense, and which apply to everything that exists, from the grandest scale to the most minute. Generally, these levels are represented in a structure of ten sephiroth called "the Tree of Life." This ten-sphered structure is a simplified arrangement of more complex renderings.

1. An emanation of Deity.

"The Ten Sephiroth of universal vibration emerge from the Ain Soph, which is the Microcosmic Star that guides our interior. This Star is the Real Being of our Being. Ten Sephiroth are spoken of, but in reality there are Twelve; the Ain Soph is the eleventh, and its tenebrous antithesis is in the Abyss, which is the twelfth Sephirah. These are twelve spheres or universal regions which mutually penetrate and co-penetrate without confusion." —Samael Aun Weor, *Tarot and Kabbalah*

2. A name of the Divine Mother.

Sexual Magic: The word magic is dervied from the ancient word magos "one of the members of the learned and priestly class," from O.Pers. magush, possibly from PIE *magh—"to be able, to have power." [Quoted from On-line Etymology Dictionary].

"All of us possess some electrical and magnetic forces within, and, just like a magnet, we exert a force of attraction and repulsion... Between lovers that magnetic force is particularly powerful and its action has a far-reaching effect. —Samael Aun Weor, *The Mystery of the Golden Flower*

Sexual magic refers to an ancient science that has been known and protected by the purest, most spiritually advanced human beings, whose purpose and goal is the harnessing and perfection of our sexual forces. A more accurate translation of sexual magic would be "sexual priesthood."

In ancient times, the priest was always accompanied by a priestess, for they represent the divine forces at the base of all creation: the masculine and feminine, the Yab-Yum, Ying-Yang, Father-Mother: the Elohim.

Unfortunately, the term "sexual magic" has been grossly misinterpreted by mistaken persons such as Aleister Crowley, who advocated a host of degenerated practices, all of which belong solely to the lowest and most perverse mentality. This website and the teachings presented here reject all such philosophies, theories, and practices, for they lead only to the enslavement of the consciousness, the worship of lust and desire, and the decay of humanity.

True, upright, heavenly sexual magic is the natural harnessing of our latent forces, making them active and harmonious with nature and the divine.

"People are filled with horror when they hear about sexual magic; however, they are not filled with horror when they give themselves to all kinds of sexual perversion and to all kinds of carnal passion." —Samael Aun Weor, *The Perfect Matrimony*

Shambhala: From Sanskrit: शम्भल "source or origin of happiness." A kingdom considered mythological by modern humanity. It exists in the fourth dimension (called Jinn state), which is why no one can find it in the physical world.

"The entire country of Shambhala is in the Jinn state; here is where the principal monasteries of the White Lodge exist." —Samael Aun Weor, *The Major Mysteries*

"The secret country of Shamballa is in the Orient, in Tibet. The Master Jesus has a temple there. Other masters live with him who have also resurrected and who have kept their bodies over the many ages of time." —Samael Aun Weor, *The Aquarian Message*

Siddhi: (Sanskrit सद्धि) Literally, "success; any unusual skill, faculty or capability." Nowadays this term usually indicates "spiritual powers." Many of the powers (siddhis) of yoga are related to the "Jinn state," the condition that results from moving physical matter into the fourth dimension.

"The yogi acquires multiple powers (siddhis) in accordance with the awakening of superlative consciousness. .. Powers [siddhis] are flowers of the soul that sprout when we have sanctified ourselves. For each step that we walk in the development of the chakras, we must also walk a thousand steps in sanctity." —Samael Aun Weor, *Kabbalah of the Mayan Mysteries*

"If there is Shuddhi (purification), Siddhi (perfection) will come by itself. Siddhi is not possible without Shuddhi." —Swami Sivananda, *Kundalini Yoga*

"Siddhi is produced by sadhana [practice, effort]. The former term, which literally means "success," includes accomplishment, achievement, success, and fruition of all kinds. A person may thus gain siddhi in speech, siddhi in mantra, etc. A person is siddha also who has perfected his spiritual development. The various powers attainable – namely, anima, mahima, laghima, garima, prapti, prakamya, ishitva, vashitva, the powers of becoming small, great, light, heavy, attaining what one wills, and the like – are known as the eight siddhi. The thirty-ninth chapter of the Brahmavaivarta Purana mentions eighteen kinds, but there are many others, including such minor accomplishments as nakhadarpana siddhi or "nail-gazing." The great siddhi is spiritual perfection. Even the mighty powers of the "eight siddhi" are known as the "lesser siddhi," since the greatest of all siddhi is full liberation (mahanirvana) from the bonds of phenomenal life and union with the Paramatma, which is the supreme object (paramartha) to be attained through human birth." —Arthur Avalon, *Mahanirvana Tantra, Tantra of the Great Liberation* [1931]

"An accomplished Purnayogi in the path of Kundalini Yoga is in possession of eight major Siddhis, viz., Anima, Mahima, Laghima, Garima, Prapti, Prakamya, Vasitvam and Ishitvam.

1. Anima: The Yogi can become as minute as he pleases.

2. Mahima: This is the opposite of Anima. He can become as big as he likes. He can make his body assume a very large size. He can fill up the whole universe. He can assume a Virat Svarupa.

3. Laghima: He can make his body as light as cotton or feather. Vayustambhanam is done through this Siddhi. In Jalastambhanam also the power is exercised to a very small degree. The body is rendered light by Plavini Pranayama. The Yogi produces a diminution of his specific gravity by swallowing large draughts of air. The Yogi travels in the sky with the help of this Siddhi. He can travel thousands of miles in a minute.

4. Garima: This is the opposite of Laghima. In this the Yogi acquires an increase of specific gravity. He can make the body as heavy as a mountain by swallowing draughts of air.

5. Prapti: The Yogi standing on the earth can touch the highest things. He can touch the sun or the moon or the sky. Through this Siddhi the Yogi attains his desired objects and supernatural powers. He acquires the power of predicting future events, the power of clairvoyance, clairaudience, telepathy, thought-reading, etc. He can understand the languages of the beasts and birds. He can understand unknown languages also. He can cure all diseases.

6. Prakamya: He can dive into the water and can come out at any time he likes. The late Trilinga Swami of Benares used to live for six months underneath the Ganges. It is the process by which a Yogi makes himself invisible sometimes. By some writers it is defined to be the power of entering body of another (Parakaya Pravesh). Sri Sankara entered the body of Raja Amaruka of Benares. Tirumular in Southern India entered the body of a shepherd. Raja Vikramaditya also did this. It is also the power of keeping a youth-like appearance for any length of time. Raja Yayati had this power.

7. Vashitvam: This is the power of taming wild animals and bringing them under control. It is the power of mesmerising persons by the exercise of will and of making them obedient to one's own wishes and orders. It is the restraint of passions and emotions. It is the power to bring men, women and the elements under subjection.

8. Ishitvam: It is the attainment of divine power. The Yogi becomes the Lord of the universe. The Yogi who has this power can restore life to the dead. Kabir, Tulsidas, Akalkot Swami and others had this power of bringing back life to the dead." —Swami Sivananda, *Kundalini Yoga*

"Many people are attracted to the practice of Pranayama and other Yogic exercises, as it is through Yoga that psychic healing, telepathy, thought-transference, and other great Siddhis are obtained. If they attain success, they should not remain there alone. The Goal of life is not 'healing' and 'Siddhis'. They should utilise their energy in attaining the Highest.. A Yogi on the appearance of certain Siddhis thinks that he has achieved the highest goal. He may give up his further Sadhana through false contentment. The Yogi who is bent upon getting the highest Samadhi, must reject Siddhis whenever they come. Siddhis are invitations from Devatas. Only by rejecting these Siddhis, one can attain success in Yoga. He who craves for Siddhis is a worldly-minded man. He is a very big householder. Those who crave for Siddhis will never get them. If a Yogic student is tempted to attain Siddhis, his further progress is seriously retarded. He has lost the way." —Swami Sivananda, *Kundalini Yoga*

"If the [Jinn] practice has been performed well, then your body will enter the "Jinn" state, meaning that it will submerge within the supra-sensible worlds. A body in the "Jinn" state can float in the air (Laghima) or be submerged within the waters (Prakamya), or pass through fire without being burned, or be reduced to the size of an atom (Anima), or be enlarged to the point of touching the sun or the moon with the hand (Mahima). A body submerged within the supra-sensible worlds is submitted to the laws of those worlds. Then, this body is plastic and elastic, so it can change form, decrease its weight (Laghima), or increase its weight (Garima) willingly... The holy eight is the sign of infinity. The two witnesses of the Apocalypse are entwined around the spinal medulla, thus they form the holy eight. All of the mystical powers of the heavenly Jerusalem emanate from this holy eight. Now the devotees can better comprehend why we speak of eight mystical, ineffable powers." —Samael Aun Weor, *The Aquarian Message*

Solar Bodies: The physical, vital, astral, mental, and casual bodies that are created through the beginning stages of Alchemy/Tantra and that provide a basis for existence in their corresponding levels of nature, just as the physical body does in the physical world. These bodies or vehicles are superior due to being created out of Solar (Christic) Energy, as opposed to the inferior, lunar bodies we receive from nature. Also known as the Wedding Garment (Christianity), the Merkabah (Kabbalah), To Soma Heliakon (Greek), and Sahu (Egyptian).

"All the Masters of the White Lodge, the Angels, Archangels, Thrones, Seraphim, Virtues, etc., etc., etc. are garbed with the Solar Bodies. Only those who have Solar Bodies have the Being incarnated. Only someone who possesses the Being is an authentic Human Being." —Samael Aun Weor, *The Esoteric Treatise of Hermetic Astrology*

Tantra: Sanskrit for "continuum" or "unbroken stream." This refers first (1) to the continuum of vital energy that sustains all existence, and second (2) to the class of knowledge and practices that harnesses that vital energy, thereby transforming the practitioner. There are many schools of Tantrism, but they can be classified in three types: White, Grey and Black. Tantra has long been known in the West as Alchemy.

"In the view of Tantra, the body's vital energies are the vehicles of the mind. When the vital energies are pure and subtle, one's state of mind will be accordingly affected. By transforming these bodily energies we transform the state of consciousness." —The 14th Dalai Lama

Tarot: "Through the Gypsies the Tarot cards may be traced back to the religious symbolism of the ancient Egyptians. [...] Court de Gébelin believed the word Tarot itself to be derived from two Egyptian words, Tar, meaning "road," and Ro, meaning "royal." Thus the Tarot constitutes the royal road to wisdom. (See Le Monde Primitif.) [...] The Tarot is undoubtedly a vital element in Rosicrucian symbolism, possibly the very book of universal knowledge which the members of the order claimed to possess. The Rota Mundi is a term frequently occurring in the early manifestoes of the Fraternity of the Rose Cross. The word Rota by a rearrangement of its letters becomes Taro, the ancient name of these mysterious cards. [...] The Pythagorean numerologist will also find an important relationship to exist between the numbers on the cards and the designs accompanying the numbers. The Qabbalist will be immediately impressed by the significant sequence of the cards, and the alchemist will discover certain emblems meaningless save to one versed in the divine chemistry of transmutation and regeneration.' As the Greeks placed the letters of their alphabet--with their corresponding numbers--upon the various parts of the body of their humanly represented Logos, so the Tarot cards have an analogy not only in the parts and members of the universe but also in the divisions of the human body.. They are in fact the key to the magical constitution of man. [...] The Tarot cards must be considered (1) as separate and complete hieroglyphs, each representing a distinct principle, law, power, or element in Nature; (2) in relation to each other as the effect of one agent operating upon another; and (3) as vowels and consonants of a philosophic alphabet. The laws governing all phenomena are represented by the symbols upon the Tarot cards, whose numerical values are equal to the numerical equivalents of the phenomena. As every structure consists of certain elemental parts, so the Tarot cards represent the components of the structure of philosophy. Irrespective of the science or philosophy with which the student is working, the Tarot cards can be identified with the essential constituents of his subject, each card thus being related to a specific part according to mathematical and philosophical laws. "An imprisoned person," writes Eliphas Levi, "with no other book than the Tarot, if he knew how to use it, could in a few years acquire universal knowledge, and would be able to speak on all subjects with unequalled learning and inexhaustible eloquence." —Manly P. Hall, *The Secret Teachings of All Ages* (1928)

Tree of Knowledge: (Hebrew עץ הדעת טוב ורע) "And out of the ground made the LORD God to grow every tree that is pleasant to the sight, and good for food; the tree of life also in the midst of the garden, and the tree of knowledge of good and evil." —Genesis 2:9

From the Hebrew: עץ for tree. דעת (Daath) means knowledge. טוב means "goodness." רע means "pollution" or "impurity."

One of two trees in the Garden of Eden, the Tree of Knowledge in Hebrew is Daath, which is related to the sexual organs and the study of sexuality, known also as Alchemy / Tantra.

Tree of Life: (Hebrew עץ החיים) Although the Hebrew term is plural ("Tree of Lives") it is usually rendered singular.

"And out of the ground made the LORD God to grow every tree that is pleasant to the sight, and good for food; the tree of life [עץ החיים] also in the midst of the garden, and the tree of knowledge of good and evil." —Genesis 2:9

This tree represents the structure of the soul (microcosm) and of the universe (macrocosm).

"The Tree of Life is the spinal medulla. This tree of wisdom is also the ten sephiroth, the twenty-two creative Major Arcana, letters, sounds, and numbers with which the Logos (God) created the universe." —from Alcione, a lecture by Samael Aun Weor

Venustic Initiation: "The Venustic Initiation is only for true human beings, never for intellectual animals. Let "true human beings" be understood as those who already created the solar bodies. Let "intellectual animals" be understood as all of humanity, all the people who only have lunar bodies. The Venustic Initiation is the true nativity of the tranquil heart. The Venustic Initiation is for the few; it is a grace from the Solar Logos. In Nirvana, there are many Buddhas who—in spite of their great perfections— have never reached the Venustic Initiation." —Samael Aun Weor, *Light from Darkness*

The Venustic Initiations are the seven serpents of light of the first mountain plus one more related with the sephirah Binah. Read *The Three Mountains*.

"...the Venustic Initiation that has eight grades. The first Venustic Initiation is just the superior octave of the first initiation of fire. The second Venustic Initiation is the superior octave of the second initiation of fire. The third Venustic Initiation is the superior octave of the third initiation of fire. The fourth Venustic Initiation is the fourth superior octave of the fourth initiation of fire. The fifth Venustic Initiation is the fifth superior octave of the fifth initiation of fire; after this come the three initiations (the total is eight) that are related with the First Mountain (that is the First Mountain). In the Second Mountain one has to begin the work with the Moon, with Mercury, with Venus, with the Sun, Mars, Jupiter, Saturn, Uranus and Neptune, to then achieve Perfection in Mastery (it is the Mountain of the Resurrection), and the Third Mountain is the Ascension, to finally crystallize (in oneself) the Second and First Logos, and to receive the Inner Atomic Star." —Samael Aun Weor, lecture entitled The Master Key

Vital Body: (Also called Ethereal Body) The superior aspect of the physical body, composed of the energy or vital force that provides life to the physical body.

"It is written that the vital body or the foundation of organic life within each one of us has four ethers. The chemical ether and the ether of life are related with chemical processes and sexual reproduction. The chemical ether is a specific foundation for the organic chemical phenomena. The ether of life is the foundation of the reproductive and transformative sexual processes of the race. The two superior ethers, luminous and reflective, have more elevated functions. The luminous ether is related with the caloric, luminous, perceptive, etc., phenomena. The reflective ether serves as a medium of expression for willpower and imagination." —Samael Aun Weor, *The Gnostic Bible: The Pistis Sophia Unveiled*

In Tibetan Buddhism, the vital body is known as the subtle body (lus phramo).

White Brotherhood or Lodge: That ancient collection of pure souls who maintain the highest and most sacred of sciences: White Magic or White Tantra. It is called White due to its purity and cleanliness. This "Brotherhood" or "Lodge" includes human beings of the highest order from every race, culture, creed and religion, and of both sexes.

Yoga: (Sanskrit) "union." Similar to the Latin "religare," the root of the word "religion." In Tibetan, it is "rnal-'byor" which means "union with the fundamental nature of reality."

"The word YOGA comes from the root Yuj which means to join, and in its spiritual sense, it is that process by which the human spirit is brought into near and conscious communion with, or is merged in, the Divine Spirit, according as the nature of the human spirit is held to be separate from

(Dvaita, Visishtadvaita) or one with (Advaita) the Divine Spirit." —Swami Sivananda, *Kundalini Yoga*

"Patanjali defines Yoga as the suspension of all the functions of the mind. As such, any book on Yoga, which does not deal with these three aspects of the subject, viz., mind, its functions and the method of suspending them, can he safely laid aside as unreliable and incomplete." —Swami Sivananda, *Practical Lessons In Yoga*

"The word yoga means in general to join one's mind with an actual fact..." —The 14th Dalai Lama

"The soul aspires for the union with his Innermost, and the Innermost aspires for the union with his Glorian." —Samael Aun Weor, *The Revolution of Beelzebub*

"All of the seven schools of Yoga are within Gnosis, yet they are in a synthesized and absolutely practical way. There is Tantric Hatha Yoga in the practices of the Maithuna (Sexual Magic). There is practical Raja Yoga in the work with the chakras. There is Gnana Yoga in our practices and mental disciplines which we have cultivated in secrecy for millions of years. We have Bhakti Yoga in our prayers and Rituals. We have Laya Yoga in our meditation and respiratory exercises. Samadhi exists in our practices with the Maithuna and during our deep meditations. We live the path of Karma Yoga in our upright actions, in our upright thoughts, in our upright feelings, etc." —Samael Aun Weor, *The Revolution of Beelzebub*

"The Yoga that we require today is actually ancient Gnostic Christian Yoga, which absolutely rejects the idea of Hatha Yoga. We do not recommend Hatha Yoga simply because, spiritually speaking, the acrobatics of this discipline are fruitless; they should be left to the acrobats of the circus." — Samael Aun Weor, *The Yellow Book*

"Yoga has been taught very badly in the Western World. Multitudes of pseudo-sapient Yogis have spread the false belief that the true Yogi must be an infrasexual (an enemy of sex). Some of these false yogis have never even visited India; they are infrasexual pseudo-yogis. These ignoramuses believe that they are going to achieve in-depth realization only with the yogic exercises, such as asanas, pranayamas, etc. Not only do they have such false beliefs, but what is worse is that they propagate them; thus, they misguide many people away from the difficult, straight, and narrow door that leads unto the light. No authentically Initiated Yogi from India would ever think that he could achieve his inner self-realization with pranayamas or asanas, etc. Any legitimate Yogi from India knows very well that such yogic exercises are only co-assistants that are very useful for their health and for the development of their powers, etc. Only the Westerners and pseudo-yogis have within their minds the belief that they can achieve Self-realization with such exercises.Sexual Magic is practiced very secretly within the Ashrams of India. Any True Yogi Initiate from India works with the Arcanum A.Z.F. This is taught by the Great Yogis from India that have visited the Western world, and if it has not been taught by these great,

Initiated Hindustani Yogis, if it has not been published in their books of Yoga, it was in order to avoid scandals. You can be absolutely sure that the Yogis who do not practice Sexual Magic will never achieve birth in the Superior Worlds. Thus, whosoever affirms the contrary is a liar, an impostor."
—Samael Aun Weor, *Alchemy and Kabbalah in the Tarot*

Index

About the Author

His name is Hebrew סמאל און ואור, and is pronounced "sam-ayel on vay-or." You may not have heard of him, but Samael Aun Weor changed the world.

In 1950, in his first two books, he became the first person to reveal the esoteric secret hidden in all the world's great religions, and for that, accused of "healing the ill," he was put in prison. Nevertheless, he did not stop. Between 1950 and 1977 – merely twenty-seven years – not only did Samael Aun Weor write over sixty books on the most difficult subjects in the world, such as consciousness, kabbalah, physics, tantra, meditation, etc., in which he deftly exposed the singular root of all knowledge — which he called Gnosis — he simultaneously inspired millions of people across the entire span of Latin America: stretching across twenty countries and an area of more than 21,000,000 kilometers, founding schools everywhere, even in places without electricity or post offices.

During those twenty-seven years, he experienced all the extremes that humanity could give him, from adoration to death threats, and in spite of the enormous popularity of his books and lectures, he renounced an income, refused recognitions, walked away from accolades, and consistently turned away those who would worship him. He held as friends both presidents and peasants, and yet remained a mystery to all.

When one reflects on the effort and will it requires to perform even day to day tasks, it is astonishing to consider the herculean efforts required to accomplish what he did in such a short time. But, there is a reason: he was a man who knew who he was, and what he had to do. A true example of compassion and selfless service, Samael Aun Weor dedicated the whole of his life to freely helping anyone and everyone find the path out of suffering. His mission was to show all of humanity the universal source of all spiritual traditions, which he did not only through his writings and lectures, but also through his actions. He said,

"I do not want to receive visitors. Unquestionably, I am nothing more than a postman, a courier, a man that delivers a message... It would be the breaking point of silliness for you to come from your country to the capital city of Mexico with the only purpose of visiting a vulgar postman, an employee that delivered you a letter in the past... Why would you waste your money for that? Why would you visit a simple courier, a miserable postman? It is better for you to study the message, the written teachings delivered in the books...

"I have not come to form any sect, or one more belief, nor am I interested in the schools of today, or the particular beliefs of anyone! ...

"We are not interested in anyone's money, nor are we interested in monthly fees, or temples made out of brick, cement or clay, because we are conscious visitors in the cathedral of the soul and we know that wisdom is of the soul.

"Flattery tires us, praise should only belong to our Father (who is in secret and watches over us minutely).

"We are not in search of followers; all we want is for each person to follow his or her self—their own internal master, their sacred Innermost—because he is the only one who can save and glorify us.

"I do not follow anyone, therefore no one should follow me...

"We do not want any more comedies, pretenses, false mysticism, or false schools. What we want now are living realities; we want to prepare ourselves to see, hear, and touch the reality of those truths..." —Samael Aun Weor

Your book reviews matter.

Glorian Publishing is a very small non-profit organization, thus we have no money to spend on marketing and advertising. Fortunately, there is a proven way to gain the attention of readers: book reviews. Mainstream book reviewers won't review these books, but you can.

The path of liberation requires the daily balance of three active factors:

- birth of virtue
- death of vice
- sacrifice for others

Writing book reviews is a powerful way to sacrifice for others. By writing book reviews on popular websites, you help to make the books more visible to humanity, and you might help save a soul from suffering. Will you do your part to help us show these wonderful teachings to others? Take a moment today to write a review.

Donate

Glorian Publishing is a non-profit publisher dedicated to spreading the sacred universal doctrine to suffering humanity. All of our works are made possible by the kindness and generosity of sponsors. If you would like to make a tax-deductible donation, you may send it to the address below, or visit our website for other alternatives. If you would like to sponsor the publication of a book, please contact us at (844) 945-6742 or help@gnostic-teachings.org.

Glorian Publishing
PO Box 209
Clinton, CT 06413 US
Phone: (844) 945-6742
VISIT US ONLINE AT glorian.org